U0960633

华南理工大学建筑设计研究院有限公司
ARCHITECTURAL DESIGN & RESEARCH INSTITUTE OF SCUT CO., LTD

校 园 设 计 作 品 选

SELECTED WORKS OF CAMPUS DESIGN

CAMPUS PLANNING ARCHITECTURE

校园规划建筑

主 编　丘建发　包 莹

华南理工大学出版社
SOUTH CHINA UNIVERSITY OF TECHNOLOGY PRESS
·广州·

图书在版编目（CIP）数据

校园规划建筑 / 丘建发，包莹主编. — 广州 ：华南理工大学出版社，2021.6
ISBN 978-7-5623-6031-5

Ⅰ. ①校… Ⅱ. ①丘… ②包… Ⅲ. ①校园规划 ②教育建筑-建筑设计
Ⅳ. ①G48 ②TU244

中国版本图书馆 CIP 数据核字(2019)第 123216 号

校园规划建筑
丘建发　包莹　主编

出 版 人：卢家明
出版发行：华南理工大学出版社
（广州五山华南理工大学 17 号楼，邮编 510640）
http:// hg.cb.scut.edu.cn　E-mail: scutc13@scut.edu.cn
营销部电话：020-87113487　87111048（传真）
策划编辑：赖淑华
责任编辑：黄丽谊　骆　婷
责任校对：林嘉欣　梁晓艾
印 刷 者：广州市新怡印务股份有限公司
开　　本：889mm×1194mm　1/12　**印张**:24.5　**字数**: 778 千
版　　次：2021 年 6 月第 1 版　2021 年 6 月第 1 次印刷
定　　价：298.00 元

版权所有　盗版必究　　印装差错　负责调换

编 写 组：刘 骁 / 黄沛宁 / 曾宪策 / 曹韫烨 / 廖育琪 / 陆 歆 / 童敬勇
封面设计：曾宪策 / 廖育琪
版式设计：天下标局设计工作室
内容翻译：广州市玲之翻译有限公司

Editors: Liu Xiao / Huang Peining / Zeng Xiance / Cao Yunye / Liao Yuqi / Lu Xin / Tong Jingyong
Cover designer: Zeng Xiance / Liao Yuqi
Format designer: Tianxia Biaoju Design Studio
Translator: Guangzhou Ling Translation Co., Ltd.

Foreword

As important bases for talent cultivation, universities not only take on the fundamental mission of education and scientific research, but also play a vital role of transforming knowledge into productivity. Since the 1990s, China has entered a new development stage of promoting and expanding undergraduate education in a massive scale, which is characterized by extensive mergers and restructuring of universities, expansion of enrolment, and aspirant construction of first-class universities. Particularly the number of in-school university and college undergraduates has increased almost five-fold since the end of 1999, and that of in-school postgraduates has also grown nearly seven-fold in the past ten years, which has driven a tremendous surge in construction of new campuses. Against such a backdrop, university-affiliated design institutes partook in a slew of practical and scientific research projects and made dazzling achievements in campus planning and design by virtue of their academic strength and profound understanding of the university campus.

In the wave of university campus construction in the past 10 years, the Architectural Design Research Institute of SCUT (hereinafter referred to as "the Institute") has placed a high premium on campus planning and design, given full play to its uniquely advantageous position in integrating the architectural design with teaching and researches, and actively participated in the creative practice of campus planning and architectural design. From the 1990s to 2019, we completed over 400 university campus planning and architectural design projects and won 300-odd design awards, including nearly 100 national awards and over 200 provincial awards. The new campus projects designed by us, such as Zhejiang University, University of Macau, Wuhan University, Yantai University, Zhengzhou University, China University of Mining and Technology, Jiangnan University, Nanjing University of Posts & Telecommunications, Chongqing University, Nanjing Audit University, Chongqing University of Technology, South China University of Technology ("SCUT"), Shanghai University, etc., have been well recognized by society and our peers. In the design practices, we put special emphasis on research and summarization of relevant theories. In terms of research results, SCUT is one of the institutions and universities that published most papers relating to university campus (of which more than 300 papers were published in professional periodicals with the key word "campus" from 2000 through 2019). In the meantime, we have presided over the work of the National Commission for Architectural Education and Academic Research and the compilation of the chapters on colleges and universities of the ***Collection of Architectural Design Materials***, organized and participated in various academic activities, and engaged in extensive academic exchanges to establish our brand for campus planning and design, which is known as the "SCUT Phenomenon" among our peers.

In retrospect of the achievements over the years, the Institute has benefited from the guidance of its core design philosophy of **"Two Concepts and Three Features"** (Holistic and Sustainable Concepts; Features of Place, Culture and Time) in addition to the ample supply of talented professionals from SCUT and the great support from different sectors of the society. University campus is the cradle of professionals, the palace of knowledge and the homeland of humanistic spirit. Design for modern campus should not only satisfy the basic functional requirements, but also accommodate new developments in education and scientific research, ramp up the cultural atmosphere, and bring out and elevate the special temperament of the university, which demands dogged exploration of the regional features, geographic context and prospective development of the campus. Following the design philosophy of Two Concepts and Three Features, the Institute, while further improving the quality of campus design for universities and colleges, has also conducted design explorations and practices for primary schools, middle schools, nine-year compulsory schools and other campuses that cater for the needs of new education development.

In the past 20-odd years of campus planning and architectural design practices, the Institute has brought forward the following design strategies:

First, holistic design strategy. This strategy emphasizes the holistic campus design and advocates that the whole campus is studied to work out the planning mode that best serves the purpose of cultivating talents of the new century. Holistic design encourages integration of different disciplines like planning, landscape and architecture, and emphasizes the penetration and interaction with other disciplines including sociology, architecture, ecology, anthropology, politics, economics, etc.

Second, ecological design strategy. Nowadays, harmony between men and nature, as well as sustainability, have become the mainstream of architecture and planning. Campus planning should follow the principle of prioritizing natural ecology and well integrate with landscape and gardening. By doing so, it can not only highlight the characteristic of green campus, but also bring in the traditional elegance and enchantment of classic Chinese garden and embody the educational concept of campus development in a new era, i.e. putting people in the first place and cultivating talents in an inspiring environment.

Third, place-specific design strategy. The goal is to incorporate the local geographical and cultural features and create unique campus spaces and cultural atmosphere with distinct local features. The campus planning and design should give full consideration to the natural environment, the climatic characteristics and cultural context of the site, and provide layout and spatial solutions accordingly.

Fourth, humanistic design strategy. With reference to impressive classic campus spaces in China and beyond, humanistic design is to center around people. The campus planning should take into full account the material and spiritual needs of the users and the conservation of historical heritage and pedagogical style, so as to create spaces and places that not only meet the academic requirements of the faculty and students but also inspire cultural creativity.

Fifth, comprehensive design strategy. Modern education attaches great importance to the cross-disciplinary learning and constantly pushes the research frontiers. In response to the development trend of modern science towards an ever-increasing complexity and the structural evolution of research organizations towards interdisciplinary modularization and team collaboration, the campus planning is driven to move towards higher comprehensiveness and complexity. The study on modern innovative activities shows that both contact and communication make for innovations, which requires creation of multi-level social network and community atmosphere in the campus spaces.

Nowadays when we have stepped into an era of knowledge economy, the technological innovation will become the core element and driving force for economic and social development. So topics about the planning, renewal and integration for campuses, the important carriers of knowledge, will be further explored. In this context, we will, as always, adhere to the philosophy of "excellence, team work, management, branding and development" and the development path of integrating professional practice, teaching and researches. Under the guidance of Two Concepts and Three Features, we will further study and summarize the evolution of the modern education in concept, connotation and operation mode, and constantly improve and innovate the practice and theory of campus planning and architectural design,so as to create more attractive and timeless campus spaces, and continue to contribute to the education development, talent cultivation, prosperity and stability of China.

序 言

大学，作为国家培养人才的重要基地，不仅承担着教学、科研的基本任务，而且承担着将知识转化为生产力的重要任务。从 20 世纪 90 年代开始，中国经历了大学本科教育的大众化进程，并开始了大规模扩张的发展新阶段，这一阶段以高校合并重组、扩招和建设一流大学为特征。1999 年后至今，在校大学本专科生人数增长了近 5 倍；而近 10 年来，在校研究生的数量也增长了近 7 倍。随之而来的是大学新校园的建设高潮，在这样的形势下，各高校设计院凭借自身学术实力以及对大学校园的深刻理解，在校园规划和设计领域参与了大量的实践和科研工作，取得了令人瞩目的成就。

在近 10 年的大学校园建设高潮中，华南理工大学建筑设计研究院非常重视校园规划与设计创作，充分发挥高校“产学研”一体化的优势，积极参与校园规划及建筑设计的创作实践。通过长期探索和不懈努力，我们从 20 世纪 90 年代至 2019 年，共完成四百多项高校规划及建筑设计项目，荣获设计奖项三百多项，其中包括近一百项国家级奖和两百多项省部级奖。设计建成例如浙江大学、澳门大学、武汉大学、烟台大学、郑州大学、中国矿业大学、江南大学、南京邮电大学、重庆大学、华南理工大学、上海大学等一大批高校新校区，获得社会及同行的一致认同。在设计实践过程中，我们也非常重视相关的理论研究和总结。华南理工大学是发表大学校园规划与设计相关论文最多的科研机构之一（其中 2000—2019 年以“校园”为关键词发表期刊论文三百多篇），同时主持全国教育建筑学术委员会工作，主持编写《建筑设计资料集》中高等院校等章节，积极组织和参与各种学术活动，树立了校园规划设计的品牌并开展广泛的学术交流，被同行称为“华工现象”。

回顾多年来的成果，除了依托高校的人才优势及社会各方的大力支持以外，我院还得益于核心设计理念——“两观三性”（即整体观和可持续发展观；地域性、文化性和时代性）的指导。大学校园是培养人才的摇篮，是知识的殿堂，是人文精神的家园，新时代的校园创作不但应满足使用功能的基本要求，更应该符合新型教育科研发展要求，强调营造校园的文化氛围，体现和弘扬校园独特的气质。这需要从校园的地域特点、文脉和时代发展等方面入手去不断挖掘。基于“两观三性”设计理念，我院在进一步优化、提升大学校园设计水准的同时，也在中小学、九年一贯制学校及其他满足新型教育发展需求的校园设计上进行了探索与实践。

我院在 20 多年的校园规划及建筑设计实践中提出了以下设计策略：

第一，整体化设计策略。强调校园的整体设计，提倡从整体校园范畴研究最适宜培养新世纪人才的规划模式。整体设计既强调规划、景观、建筑各专业的整合，也强调多学科（社会学、建筑学、生态学、人类学、政治学、经济学等）的交叉渗透与相互促进。

第二，生态化设计策略。注重人与自然的和谐，强调生态可持续发展是当今建筑与规划设计发展的大方向。校园规划应以自然生态为优先原则，结合营造园林景观，不但能够充分体现绿色校园的特点，而且能够与中国古典园林优雅的传统神韵很好地结合在一起，体现了新时代校园建设中以人为本、环境育人的教育理念。

第三，地域化设计策略。综合当地地域及校园文化的特点，营造出具有当地特色的独特的校园空间与文化氛围。规划设计中应充分考虑基地内部及周边的自然环境条件、气候特征和文化背景，针对其特点进行结构布局和空间营造。

第四，人文化设计策略。国内外经典校园空间给人留下深刻的印记，人文化就是要以人为本。在校园规划中充分考虑使用者的物质和精神需求，传承历史文脉和办学特色，营造出既能满足师生学习要求，又能激发文化创作的空间和场所。

第五，复合化设计策略。现代教育注重学科的交叉，拓展各自学科的研究范围。而无论是现代科学发展复杂化趋势，还是研究组织结构学科交叉模式化、团队化的倾向，均要求校园规划往综合化、复合化的方向发展。现代创新行为的研究，指出交往交流对创新行为的促进作用，这又要求校园空间更加注重多层次交往网络、社区氛围的营造。

当今世界已步入知识经济时代，科技创新将成为经济与社会发展的核心因素和推动力量。校园作为知识的重要载体，其规划、更新、整合的课题将不断地延续。我院将一如既往地坚持扬优秀、重团队、抓管理、创品牌、促发展，坚持“产学研”相结合的发展道路，在“两观三性”的核心创作理念指导下，对现代教育理念、内涵和教育办学模式的转变进行研究和总结，不断完善和创新校园规划及建筑设计的实践和理论，为社会创造出更多的优美经典的校园空间，为中国的教育发展、人才培养、繁荣稳定、创新建设不断奉献自己的力量。

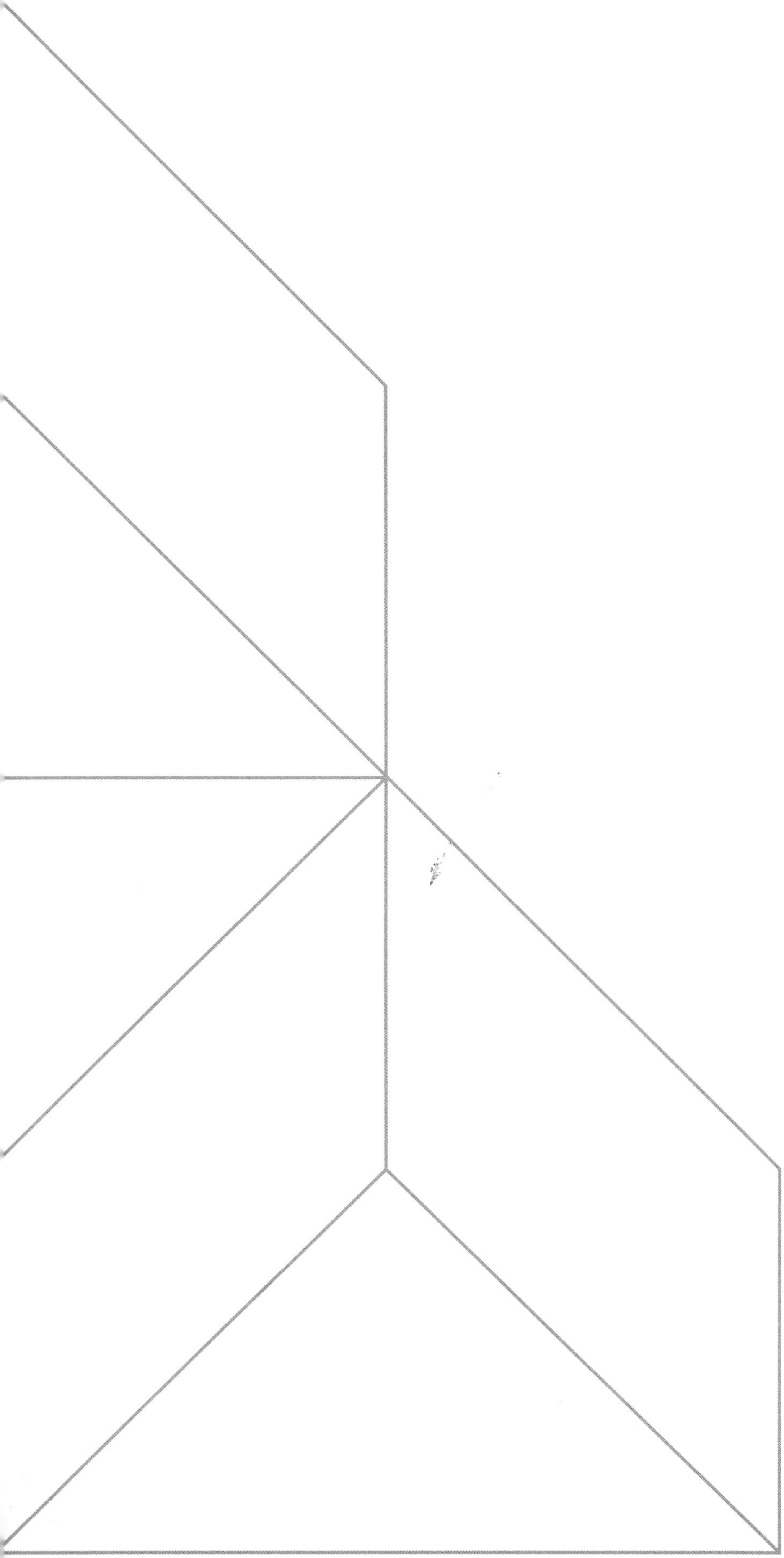

目录

CONTENTS

校园整体设计
HOLISTIC CAMPUS DESIGN

澳门大学横琴岛新校区
HENGQIN ISLAND NEW CAMPUS OF UNIVERSITY OF MACAU

项目地点：广东省珠海市
设计时间：2009 年
竣工时间：2012 年
用地面积：1,090,000 m^2
建筑面积：816,000 m^2

Location: Zhuhai, Guangdong
Design: 2009
Completion: 2012
Site Area: 1,090,000 m^2
GFA: 816,000 m^2

澳门大学横琴岛新校区
HENGQIN ISLAND NEW CAMPUS OF UNIVERSITY OF MACAU

澳门大学立足于用地的山海环境资源和自然条件，融合南欧和华南地区的建筑风格，突显澳门作为中西文化交流平台之角色，打造富有独特魅力和风格的国际化校园和多层次多中心的立体化、书院式发展的生态、人文校园。

围绕校园中心区形成多个组团相互围合的关系，形成大功能组团围绕生态湖泊和园林的公共开敞空间总体形态。各建筑组团形成书院式的发展格局，各书院形成各自的立体化中心与多层次步行系统，形成独立高效的运作系统。以舒适的步行尺度 300 m 为依据控制组团的大小，通过步行轴线联系各组团，形成完善的步行系统。

Based on mountain and ocean resources as well as the natural conditions, University of Macau integrates architectural styles of South Europe and South China, highlighting Macau's role as a platform of Chinese and western cultural exchange and creating an international campus with unique charm and style.

As planned, buildings clusters are placed around the campus center to mutually enclose with each other, thus form a general layout of the public open spaces where the large functional clusters embrace the eco-lake and gardens. Each building cluster is organized into a pattern that resembles the traditional Chinese academy architecture, while each academy forms a multi-leveled center and walking system of its own, and establishes independent and effective operation system as well. The building clusters are sized based on 300 meters, which is the comfortable walking distance. In this way, a complete walking system is created to connect the clusters via walking axes.

澳门大学横琴岛新校区
HENGQIN ISLAND NEW CAMPUS OF UNIVERSITY OF MACAU

横琴岛澳门大学新校区的规划设计

摘要：横琴岛澳门大学新校区的总体规划设计立足于山海环境资源和生态自然条件，采用强调组团式生长的建筑布局模式，融合南欧和华南地区的建筑风格，目的是创造富有独特魅力和风格的国际化校园。以书院式的发展格局作为组团的核心模式，既是对现代校园可持续发展规划理念的呼应，也是对澳门大学人文精神传统的尊重。群体设计融合了岭南建筑与南欧建筑的特色，提炼了廊、骑楼、古典风格、园林环境、灰空间等几大空间组织元素，用现代的设计手法予以灵活搭配使用，创造出与规划理念共生的建筑群体环境。

关键词：建筑规划；中西融汇；生态；集约；人文校园；书院

横琴岛澳门大学新校区选址于广东省珠海市横琴岛东部，在自然地理条件上，依山傍海、环境优美、毗邻港澳，处于“一国两制”的交汇点和“内外辐射”的结合部。澳门大学横琴岛校园占地面积约 109 hm^2，学生规模约 1 万人，总建筑面积约 100 hm^2。作为粤澳合作重点项目，将澳门大学打造成为一所教学与科研并重的国际性大学。因此，总体规划设计立足于山海环境资源和生态自然条件，采用强调组团式生长的建筑布局模式，融合南欧和华南地区的建筑风格，突显澳门作为中西文化交流平台之角色，打造富有独特魅力和风格的国际化校园。

一、规划设计理念

创作理念为依托山海格局，重塑生态环境；融汇中西文化，突显人文关怀；承接传统肌理，弘扬时代精神。规划设计从布局模式、空间格局、人文精神、绿色校园 4 个主要方面入手，结合澳门地域性的中西文化底蕴、横琴岛的山海格局和生态特色以及岭南城市和建筑文化的内涵，创建多层次多中心的立体化、书院式发展的生态、人文校园。

1. 教学与生活并置的多中心布局模式

近年来，国内众多新校区在规划设计中都倾向于明确的功能分区，使教学区和生活区之间存在清晰的空间界面并保持一定的空间距离。这种设计手法在校园的空间形象、功能划分以及校园管理等方面有一定的好处，但是，对于港澳地区的大学来说，相对混合使用的功能区域更能满足他们对于人文交往层面的需求。因此，设计中必须充分考虑这两方面特色的融合，力图做到既保持功能区域的整体性，符合互不干扰的设计原则；又能有效缩短教学区和生活区的空间距离，达到便于相互交流的人性化设计目标。在具体的规划设计中，根据用地形状较为狭长的特点，将教学组团和生活组团成组团布置，形成三大书院区，各书院与校园其余功能组团围绕生态湖泊和园林的南北景观轴线形成总体布局。生活组团与教学组团依据各自功能的相互联系互为依托、紧密相连，如细胞般各自既能够形成独立的运作系统，相互间又组合成更加大的整体网络。

2. 立体化书院式发展的空间格局

书院是港澳地区大学普遍采用的学生生活建筑的布局方式，它是崇尚交往、共生与和谐的思想在建筑理念上的综合体现，传达着深厚的学术和人文精神。因此以书院式的发展格局作为组团的核心模式，既是对现代校园可持续发展规划理念的呼应，也是对澳门大学人文精神传统的尊重。各建筑组团形成书院式的发展格局，除了强调功能的完整性与综合性之外，还着意于空间的多样性和氛围的人性化。各组团拥有各自的立体化中心与多层次的步行系统，形成独立高效的运作系统。达到功能空间高度整合，园林空间层次分明，且组合丰富等多方面的效果。在有效控制校园空间尺度，形成多层次、多中心的立体化校园空间的同时，为组团的生长奠定物质和空间的基础，预留足够的发展余地。

3. 以舒适步行尺度为依据的人性化空间尺度

系统化的步行空间是当代校园规划设计的重要环节，一方面体现了深层次的人性化关怀，另一方面也符合当今世界规划和建筑发展所倡导的节能、减排和环保的主题。因此，规划设计通过车行主环路的设计模式，构建了各自有效运行且互不干扰的人车分流交通系统，为全方位的校园立体化步行空间体系做了很好的铺垫。作为中等大小尺度的校园空间，完全可实现以步行为主的人性化校园交通系统。以舒适的步行尺度 300m 为依据控制组团的大小和相邻组团间的距离，防止出现大而不当的空间，满足通过步行轴线联系各组团，形成完善而且舒适的步行系统的要求。

4. 生态和人文并重的现代化绿色校园

在“教学与生活并置的多中心布局”“立体化书院式发展的格局”和“以舒适步行尺度为依据的人性化空间尺度”这三大规划设计特点的基础上，可以通过多层次的环境和空间设计，最终形成生态和人文并重的现代化校园。生态型循环水体的引入是规划设计的重要亮点，通过溪流、湖泊、湿地、岛屿的多重组合形成多层次的生态环境系统。既能够呼应澳门特区和横琴岛的地域性环境特点，又符合岭南地区特有的水乡情怀，可谓一举两得。同时充分发挥水体资源的空间纽带作用，利用南北方向的轴线组织、书院组团围合界面控制、融入自然的景观设计等手法，全力营造理性与浪漫相结合的整体环境氛围，创造具备优美自然的生态环境，兼有浓郁人文气息的现代化校园总体环境空间。

二、建筑设计概念

1. 因借自然的地域化岭南建筑

建筑群体布局中，以与环境相互融合、相互依托为原则，采用自由灵活的庭院式布局来创造校园的书院气息。例如，中央教学楼的设计遵从校园总体规划布局，与图书馆共同围合形成校园的标志性广场，并向生态湖面打开，同时与校史展览厅相映成趣，形成学校的景观核心区域。各个建筑功能组团结合溪流与岛屿的景观规划特色，通过形成不同的庭院以及架空平台创造出丰富的交往空间以利于学生课间及课余的生活交往。建筑采用平坡结合的造型设计，现代坡屋顶与环境两者之间取得更好的协调，组合错落有致，构成稳重、典雅的建筑组团，与自然环境和谐相融。

2. 注重场所交流空间的建筑

建筑设计概念配合规划理念的人文主义精神，特别强调交流空间的引入。以现代教学理念为核心，注重课堂学习空间与课外交流空间的结合。通过立体生态化交流空间的创造，形成了明确又具有丰富变化的建筑空间。在各建筑系统内部以及建筑组团之间，都有开放的步行廊道和庭院，能够为教学之余的自由交流提供最舒适的场所。这是现代教学中的另一种极为重要的学习和锻炼思维的方式，知识与智慧在师生之间、同学之间的思辨交锋之中得到升华。

3. 经济节能的绿色环保建筑

呼应规划设计倡导的绿色环保主题，结合建筑组团所围合出的积极内向型空间，巧妙地与校园内外景观融为一体，在垂直交通节点、楼层顶端等地方设置绿化平台、挑台、凹入式遮阳绿化空间以及屋顶花园等构成多层次的绿化系统，创造丰富的立体生态绿化空间。同时，吸收岭南及南欧城市建筑适应地域性要求的特点和对通风环境的需求，利用建筑物的首层架空及空中穿透部分，引入自然风，使得内庭院形成对流，增加建筑物通风换气性能。为使用者创造良好的空间生活环境，并将此观念延伸到建筑内部，做到有效改善局部微气候，缓解南方炎热气候的不适感。建筑布局配合规划理念和气候环境，以南北朝向为主，均考虑自然通风采光，采用节能措施，追求生态环保型绿色建筑。

4. 富有地域特色的岭南与南欧结合的建筑造型

设计方案均融合岭南建筑与南欧建筑的特色，提炼廊、骑楼、古典风格、园林环境、灰空间等几大空间组织元素，用现代的设计手法予以灵活搭配使用，创造出与规划理念共生的建筑群体环境。建筑概念构思以典雅的传统风格为基调，融入地域性、文化性和时代性的先进设计思想，重点突出澳门大学校园建筑的文化底蕴与内涵，同时在细部与色彩上又不失简洁明快的现代风格，传统中彰显着时代精神。

三、结语

澳门大学横琴岛新校区的规划设计集近 10 年来我国教学建筑研究的大量经验，结合港澳地区的教育特色和办学模式，创造性地提出中西文化合璧的校园规划理念，融合岭南建筑与南欧建筑的风格特点，建设一个具有独特魅力的多层次多中心的立体化、书院式发展的生态、人文校园。

文章出处：《华南理工大学学报（自然科学版）》2010 年第七期第 38 卷 P151—154

The Planning for Hengqin Island New Campus of University of Macau

Abstract: The master planning for the newly developed Hengqin Island Campus of University of Macau is based on the environmental assets like the mountains and ocean, as well as the various ecological/natural conditions. With an architectural layout that emphasizes the clustered growth, it integrates architectural styles of South Europe and South China to create an international campus of unique charm and style. The traditional Chinese academy for classic learning is referenced and employed as the core development mode of the cluster. This not only echoes to the sustainable development planning concept, but also pays tribute to the humanistic tradition of University of Macau. The complex design incorporates the features of buildings in Lingnan Area and South Europe, and employs the modern approach to flexibly combine such exquisitely selected major spatial elements as corridor, arcade, classic style, garden environment and grey spaces to create the building complex environment in coexistence with the planning concept.

Keywords: building planning; integration of the Chinese and western cultures; ecological; intensive; humanistic campus; Chinese academy for classic learning

Hengqin Island Campus of University of Macau is located in the east of Hengqin Island, Zhuhai City, Guangdong Province. It embraces a picturesque environment against mountains and by the sea and neighbors Hong Kong and Macau, hence a confluence spot of One Country and Two Systems and a junction of Internal and External Influence. Hengqin Island Campus of University of Macau occupies a land area of over 1,090,000 m^2, with a GFA of about 1,000,000 m^2 to accommodate 10,000 students. Macau and Guangdong governments will endeavor to build University of Macau as a key cooperation project and make it an international university focusing on both teaching and scientific research. As a result, the master planning will, based on mountain and ocean resources as well as the ecological natural conditions, adopts the architectural layout mode emphasizing the cluster growth and integrates architectural styles of South Europe and South China to create an international campus with unique charm and style.

Ⅰ .Planning Concept

The planning is conceived to recreate the ecological environment relying on mountains and the sea, integrate the Chinese and western cultures, highlight the humanistic care, carry on the traditional fabrics and advocate the spirit of times. Starting with the four aspects, i.e. layout mode, spatial pattern, humanistic spirit, and green campus in view of the Chinese and western cultural deposits of Macau, mountains and sea pattern and ecological features of Hengqin Island as well as urban and architectural cultural connotations of Lingnan Area, the planning aims to create a multi-leveled and multi-center humanistic campus that develops like a traditional Chinese academy for classic learning.

1.A Multi-centered Layout with Juxtaposition of Teaching and Living

In recent years, the planning of a number of new campuses in China prefers specific functional zones to enable a clear spatial interface and keep a certain spatial distance between the teaching zone and the living zone. This design approach is somewhat beneficial to the spatial image, functional division and management of the campus. However, for universities in Hong Kong and Macau, relatively mixed-use functional zones can better accommodate their needs for humanistic association. Therefore, the design must fully consider integration of the two features and endeavor to achieve the humanized design for easy mutual communication by keeping the integrity of the functional zones and avoiding mutual interference while effectively shortening the spatial distance between the teaching zone and the living zone. Specifically, considering the narrow and long site, the teaching buildings and corresponding living buildings are arranged in a cluster layout to create three academy areas. Each academy clusters with other functions to form the overall campus layout centering on the south-north landscaping axis consisting of ecological lakes and gardens. The living buildings and teaching buildings rely on and closely connect with each other to establish their independent operation systems and combine into a larger overall network at the same time.

2.A Development Strategy Referencing Traditional Chinese Academy for Classic Learning

Academies are a prevalent layout adopted for students' living buildings of universities in Hong Kong and Macau, and architecturally reflect the idea of upholding association, coexistence and harmony in a comprehensive manner, conveying a profound academic and humanistic spirit. Therefore, an academy-like development pattern as the core mode of the cluster not only echoes the sustainable development planning concept, but shows respect to the humanistic tradition of University of Macau. The building clusters form an academy-like development pattern, stressing the functional integrity and comprehensiveness and focusing on spatial variations and humanized atmosphere. The clusters boast their own three-dimensional centers and multi-leveled walking systems to establish independent and efficient operation systems. Thus, full integration of functional spaces and clear-cut hierarchy and varied combinations of garden spaces are successfully realized. This lays a physical and spatial foundation for the growth of clusters and reserves enough room for future development while effectively controlling the spatial scale of the campus and creating multi-leveled and multi-centered campus spaces.

3.Human-oriented Spatial Scale Based on Comfortable Walking Distance

Systematic walking spaces are an important part in the contemporary campus planning. They reflect the deep humanistic care and fit the theme of energy conservation, emission reduction and environmental protection advocated in the planning and building development in the contemporary world. Therefore, the planning, through the design mode of the main vehicular ring roads, establishes separate pedestrian and vehicular traffic systems which operate effectively without mutual interference, which lays a good foundation for all-round multi-leveled walking spaces of the campus. For medium-sized campus spaces, it is entirely feasible to establish a human- oriented traffic system featuring walking. The planning adopts the comfortable walking scale of 300m to control the size of clusters and the distance between to avoid large and improper spaces and meet the requirements of connecting the clusters through the pedestrian axis and creating a perfect and comfortable walking system. Result of multi-leveled pedestrian circulation analysis.

4.A Modern Campus with Ecological Environment and Humanistic Atmosphere

On the basis of the three planning features, i.e. multi-centered layout focusing on both teaching and living, development strategy referencing traditional Chinese traditional academy for classic learning and modern campus with ecological environment and humanistic atmosphere, the multi-level environment and space design can be adopted to finally form a modern campus with ecological environment and humanistic atmosphere. Ecological circulating waters are introduced as the planning highlight to create a multi-leveled ecological environment system through multiple combinations of brooks, lakes, west lands and islands, which can echo the regional environmental features of Macau SAR and Hengqin Island and fulfill the unique waterside feelings of Lingnan Area. In addition, the planning also brings into full play the water resources as the spatial tie, and employs such approaches as the south-north axis organization, academy cluster framed interface control, and landscape design blending with the nature in order to foster the overall environmental atmosphere integrating the rationality and romance and create a modern campus spaces with a graceful and natural ecological environment and a pervasive cultural atmosphere.

Ⅱ .Architectural Design Concept

1.Regional Lingnan Buildings based on Natural Elements

In the building complex layout, the free and flexible courtyard layout is adopted to create the academic atmosphere of the campus in line with the principle of mutual integration and dependence. For example, the central teaching building is designed in view of the master planning of the campus to, together with the library, frame out the iconic square. It opens wide to embrace the ecological lake, and makes a delightful contrast with the university history exhibition hall, forming the core landscape area of the campus. The architectural functional clusters create varied association spaces for students during class break and after school by forming different courtyards and elevated platforms in view of the landscape planning features of brooks and islands. Buildings are designed to present a shape in view of horizontal slopes, with a better harmonization between modern sloping roofs and the environment, and combine to become a beautifully staggered, solid and elegant complex in harmony with the natural environment.

2.Buildings with Focus on Communication Spaces

Responding to humanistic spirit as advocated in the planning concept, the architectural design concept particularly stresses introduction of communication spaces. Specifically, top priority is given to the modern teaching concept by well combining the learning spaces during the class with the communication spaces after class. Creation of multi-leveled ecological communication spaces gives rise to clearly-defined and varied building spaces. Open pedestrian corridors and courtyards are provided inside each building system and between building clusters, so as to offer highly comfortable venues for free communication after teaching. This is another extremely important learning and thinking development method in the modern teaching, by which knowledge and wisdom are refined during the argument between teachers and students, and students themselves.

3.Cost Effective and Energy-Saving Green and Environment-friendly Buildings

Proactively inwards spaces framed by buildings in response to green and environmental protection theme as advocated in the planning smartly integrate with internal and external landscape of the campus. Green platforms, cantilevered stands, recessed sunshading green spaces as well as roof gardens at the vertical traffic nodes and floor top comprise a multi-leveled greening system with varied ecological green spaces. In addition, considering the demand for ventilated environment by referencing the adaptation of buildings in Lingnan Area and South European cities to local conditions, natural wind is introduced through the stilted ground floor and voids in the sky to enable air circulation and enhance the air exchange inside buildings to create an excellent living environment for users. This idea is also extended to the inside of buildings to effectively improve the micro-climate in some areas and relieve discomfort during hot days in South China. In view of planning concepts and climatic environment, buildings are arranged with the front side mainly facing the south and all allow for natural ventilation and daylighting. Energy conservation measures are taken to pursuit eco-friendly green buildings.

4.Building Forms with Regional Features Combining Architectural Styles of Lingnan Area and South Europe

The design incorporates the features of buildings in Lingnan Area and South Europe, and employs the modern approach to flexibly combine such exquisitely selected major spatial elements as corridor, arcade, classic style, garden environment and grey spaces to create the building complex environment in coexistence with the planning concept. The architectural concept is conceived on the basis of traditional elegant style by drawing on advanced design thoughts in the regional, cultural and era nature, so as to especially highlight cultural deposits of campus buildings of University of Macau and showcase the simple and lucid modern style in details and colors as well, hence a combination of traditions and spirits of times.

Ⅲ . Conclusion

Taking full advantage of considerable experiences from the Chinese teaching building studies over nearly a decade and referencing the education features and mode in Hong Kong and Macau, the planning for Hengqin Campus of University of Macau creatively proposes a concept of combining the Chinese and western cultures and incorporates the styles of buildings in Lingnan Area and South Europe, striving to build it into a multi-leveled and multi-center ecological and humanistic campus with unique charm that develops like a traditional Chinese academy.

Source: Journal of South China University of Technology (Natural Science Edition), 2010 Issue 7, Volume 38, P151-154

浙江大学紫金港校区东教学组团

EAST TEACHING BUILDING CLUSTER, ZIJINGANG CAMPUS, ZHEJIANG UNIVERSITY

项目地点：浙江省杭州市
设计时间：2001 年
竣工时间：2002 年
建筑面积：170,000 m^2
曾获奖项：国家级优秀设计项目银奖（2004 年）
中国建筑学会中华人民共和国成立 60 周年建筑创作大奖（2009 年）
建设部优秀建筑工程设计二等奖（2003 年）
教育部优秀建筑设计奖一等奖（2003 年）
广东省注册建筑师协会优秀建筑创作奖：创作奖（2003 年）

Location: Hangzhou, Zhejiang
Design: 2001
Completion: 2002
GFA: 170,000 m^2
Awards:

Silver Award for National Excellent Design Project (2004)

ASC Grand Architectural Creation Award for the 60th Founding Anniversary of PRC (2009)

The Second Prize for Excellent Construction Engineering Design by the Ministry of Construction (2003)

The First Prize of Excellent Architectural Design Award by the Ministry of Education (2003)

Creation Award of Excellent Architectural Creation Award by Guangdong Chapter of Association of Chinese Registered Architects (2003)

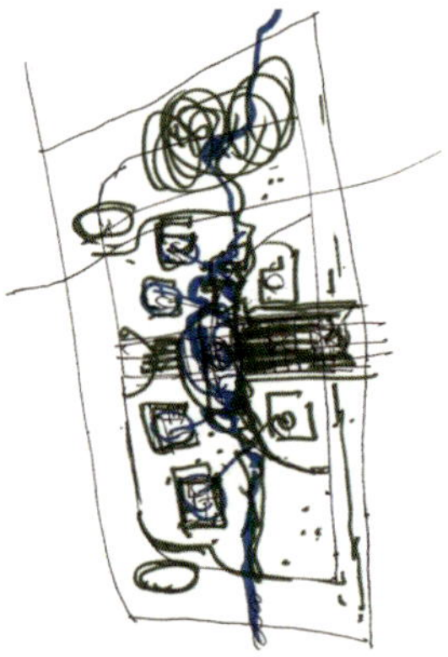

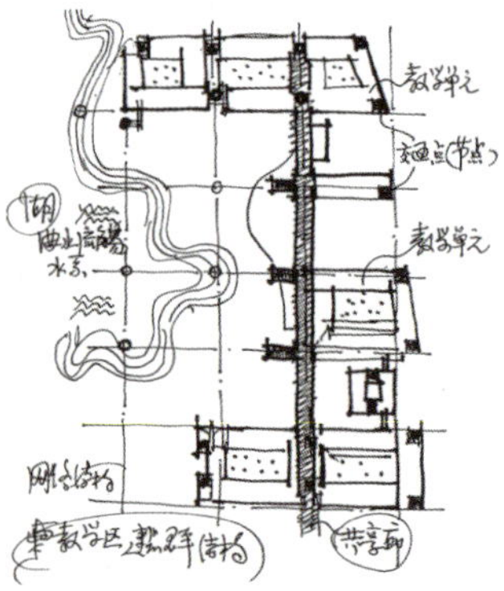

浙江大学紫金港校区东教学组团
EAST TEACHING BUILDING CLUSTER, ZIJINGANG CAMPUS, ZHEJIANG UNIVERSITY

浙江大学紫金港校区东教学组团的设计遵循现代化、园林化、网络化、生态化的设计原则，两组团分别位于主校道的东西两侧，共同围合起校园的教学空间，建筑的总规肌理、平面布局、轴线关系、立面风格等相互联系，和谐统一。靠近水面的建筑做了不同形式的亲水处理，使建筑与地形地貌完美结合。

一条中间主交通轴联系起所有功能区。设计中尤其注重交往空间的位置，各部位走廊均有局部扩宽与立面抽空，内空间与室外的大自然相互沟通。结合“园”的概念进行空间划分渗透，通过架空庭院联系起围绕建筑物周边的“园”，各个“园”大小变化有致，景观各异，又能相互渗透。

The design for the East Teaching Clusters intend to create a modern, garden-like, networked and ecological campus. The two clusters respectively at east and west side of the main road jointly enclose the teaching space of the campus. The buildings appear interconnected, harmonious and unified in terms of fabric, planar layout, axial relation and facade styles. The waterfront buildings are designed with various waterfront amenities to allow for the perfect combination of the architecture and the terrain.

A main traffic axis links up all functional areas. The communication spaces are carefully located. Corridors at different locations are partially widened and penetrated in facade, so that the interior spaces could freely communicate with the nature outdoors. The concept of garden is introduced into the planning for spatial division and penetration. The open-up courtyard links up the gardens around the buildings. The gardens are varied in sizes and views while penetrating into each other.

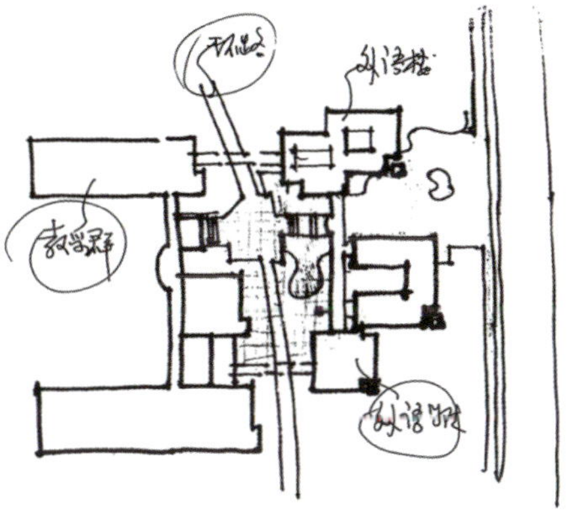

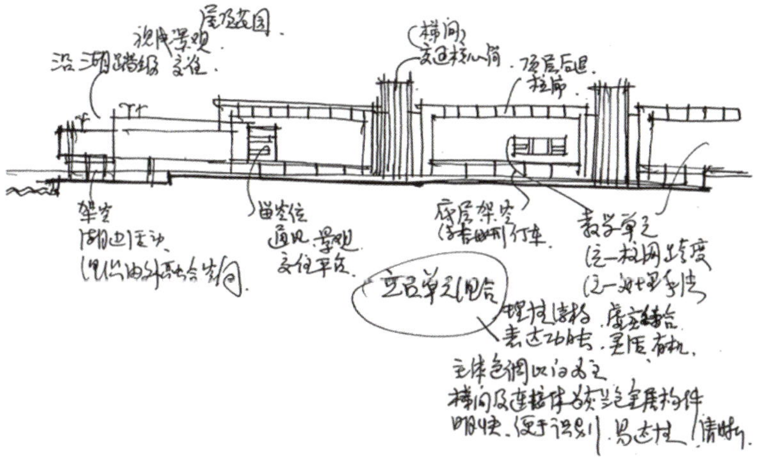

现代教育理念的探索与实践——浙江大学新校区东教学楼群设计

现代社会需要高素质、开拓型、复合型人才，知识经济时代使教育内涵由传统的教师对学生的单向灌输向以学生为主体，以人的发展和素质培养为中心的转化。教育面向现代化、面向世界、面向未来，教育制度迈向多元自主，教育民主化、终身化、多元化已成为 21 世纪高等教育的发展方向，这些变化极大地影响了大学校园的规划建设。适应现代教育的发展，体现现代教育理念的变化，是当前我国大规模校园规划设计首先需要考虑的问题。

浙江大学是我国一所拥有百年历史文化的一流学府。在国家实行高等教育体制战略性调整之际，率先实现四校合并，在杭州紫金港建新校区，总用地面积近 600 hm^2（其中首期约 200 hm^2），学生 5 万多人。这是一所规模尺度非同凡响的综合性大学，华南理工大学建筑设计院通过设计竞赛中选，完成首期总体规划后，继而承担东教学楼群的设计。按照总体规划布局，该楼群由位于主校道两侧的东西两大组团构成，其中西组团包括教学大楼、信息基础实验中心、电工电子实验中心和物理实验中心等 4 个功能单元；东组团为外语教学 2 个功能单元，总面积达 170,000 m^2。在这样一个超大型教学楼群中，如何适应现代教学要求，体现新的教育理念和特点，如何表达百年名校“海纳百川”的文化内涵和江南地域特色，创建一所新型的大学形象，这是我们创作的着重点。

一、网络结构，组团布局

教学楼群位于主校道两侧，构成东西两大组团，采用网络结构布局连成一个整体，共同围起学校的主教学空间。每个大组团以一条贯通南北的纵向主交通轴将各教学及实验功能单元串连起来，在交点处再延伸东西向横轴，轴线纵横交错，网络结构清晰，交通组织一目了然。每个功能单元由标准的教学或实验室、交通核及联廊组成，三者有机组合，层次分明。这种布局，便于识别交通，易达性强，单元构件统一，施工方便，节约投资，同时又能适应学科结构和层次结构的变化，可以不断调整使用功能。当学校规模扩充时，主交通轴可以沿南北两个方向延伸，增加功能单元，做到有机生长，持续发展。

二、建构大学园林，营造育人环境

以规划、地景、建筑三位一体的整体化校园设计为目标，在外部空间设计中，通过群体组合，形成大、中、小三个层次的园林空间：即校级“曲水流觞”中央生态带错落布局围合的公共园林空间、功能单元围合的庭园空间；造园注重与自然地形地质和环境协调，体现江南水乡清秀、雅致、自然的整体情调，强调亲水性，保持生态湿地、丛林和白鹭栖息地；庭园组织要多样化，结合功能分区，合理安排文化小品；建筑空间设计注意与园林相互渗透和联系，首层空间通过平台、坡地、凹廊、室外梯的处理，使学生在各功能单元都能方便到达庭园和湖边；适应生态带水面的水位变化，利用地形设半地下架空层，解决停车及半室内活动场地。校园环境的设计，要从总体上把握，使校园建筑的理性与园林空间环境的浪漫自然结合起来，建构新型的大学园林，营造有高雅文化品位的校园环境。

三、组织多层次的交往空间

学校要为培养创新型、复合型的人才提供各种交往的空间场所，使学生在交往中碰撞智慧的火花，在交融中生长，在交叉中发展。在设计中我们主要从下面几方面考虑：结合网络式布局，组织两条贯通南北的主交往轴，使交通与交往合二为一。其中西组团的主交往轴长 500 多米，宽 10 m，高两层，沿廊布置学生活动中心、展览厅、休息厅、咖啡室、小型会议室及各种学生交往活动场所，空间和造型上注意与使用功能和园林环境、湖景结合，增加活跃气氛；室外结合园林和建筑小品，创造不同特色的交往空间；建筑群向中心湖景跌级形成高低错落的室外休息平台；注重室内外之间的“灰空间”设计，使平台、联廊、敞廊、凹廊、架空层成为学生喜爱的活动场所；重视建筑物内各层交通核、通廊及敞厅的设计，为学生创建一个立体的多层次的交往空间。

四、校园文化与建筑风格

这是一个占地面积数公顷的超大型校园设计，总体规划通过近两千米长的中央“曲水流觞”生态带将校园划分隔成几大功能片区，各大片区的建筑风格不一定强求统一，但求谐调和表达校园文化建筑的个性。本建筑群以开朗清新的现代风格为主调。为了体现大型校园建筑的高雅、大气、开放性和文化特色，我们对建筑群的布局、体型、体量、高度、材料、色彩和格调都做了认真的推敲。如建筑以五层为主，沿湖跌级处理；统一各功能单元和交通核的处理手法，并通过组合排列形成序列，使造型既统一协调，又富韵律感；强调建筑的有序与园林环境灵活的相结合；建筑以淡雅的灰白色为主调，并配以灰蓝绿色金属构件和局部黄色板块，以增加校园的活跃气氛，其目的在于创建一座大型有时代气息和文化品位的校园新建筑。

Exploration and Practice of Modern Education Philosophy-Design of East Teaching Building Cluster in New Campus of Zhejiang University

Modern society calls for quality, pioneering and versatile talents. The way of education undergoes a remarkable shift from traditionally teacher-centered one-way inoculation to student-oriented transformation focusing on personal development and quality cultivation in the time of knowledge-driven economy. Education shall adapt to the modern society, the world and the future, while education system towards pluralism, democratization, lifelong trend and diversity has become the direction of higher education in the 21st century, all of which have great impact on the planning and construction of university campuses. How to adapt to the development of modern education, reflect the change of modern education philosophy are among the priorities to be taken into account from the very beginning when a large-scale campus is planned and designed in China.

Zhejiang University is a top-notch educational institution in China that carries on a brilliant legacy over a century. Taking advantage of the strategic adjustment of higher education in the nation, it merged with three other universities, and a new campus at Zijingang was proposed that covers an area of 600 hectares (about 200 hectares for Phase I) and would house over 50,000 students. It's a comprehensive university of an incredible size. We were chosen from the design competition to first provide the master planning for Phase I development and then the design for the east teaching building cluster Phase I. According to the master plan, the cluster is composed of two parts sitting on both sides of the main campus road, one on the east and the other west respectively. The west part includes four functional units: teaching building, Information and basic experiment center, electric & electronic experiment center and physical experiment center. The east part contains two functional units for foreign language teaching with a GFA of 170,000 m^2. It's the main focus of our project design to, within such a jumbo teaching complex, respond to the modern teaching requirements, showcase the new education philosophy and characteristics, interpret the cultural implication of "Embracing and Encompassing" that the university cherishes as well as the regional characteristics from the perspective of its locality, thus eventually present a brand new image for the university.

Ⅰ. Networked and Clustered Composition

Teaching complex sits on both sides of the main campus road, forming two clusters, one on the east and one west, to be linked up through a networked structure to jointly enclose the main teaching space of the campus. Each cluster connects various teaching and experiment functional units in series via a main longitudinal traffic axis that travels along north to south, while lateral axes are extended at the crossing in east-west direction, a criss-cross of axes and a clear-cut network are thus formed to ensure a clearly-defined traffic network. Each functional unit is composed of standard teaching classroom or lab, traffic core and corridor, which are of organic combination and well-structured. Such composition enables easy traffic recognition and enhanced accessibility. Uniform component means easy construction and lower cost, while the change of discipline structure and layered arraignment are well accommodated, making continuous functional adjustment possible. In case of a campus expansion, the main traffic axis can be easily stretched in both directions longitudinally for added functional units, realizing an organic growth and sustainability.

Ⅱ. Gardenlike University Campus and Ideal Talent-Cultivation Base

Aiming at an overall campus design that integrates planning, landscape and architecture, three levels of garden spaces ranging from the large, medium to the small are established through grouping in the exterior space design, namely the campus-wide "meandering" central ecological belt, the well-distributed and enclosed public garden spaces, and the courtyard space surrounded by functional units. Special consideration is given to match the geological terrain and environment in garden design to manifest the riverside town appeal of delicacy and grace, highlighting the water theme with a vision to preserve wetland, jungle and the egret's habitat. Courtyard components should be diversified, and featured amenities are to be provided in view of functional zoning. Attention is to be paid for architectural space to communicate with garden for penetration and interaction during design. Through terrace, slope and external stairs of concave corridor, ground floor space allows for easy access to the courtyard and lakefront from each functional unit for the students. Parking and semi-indoor event venues are addressed utilizing terrain to build semi-basement open floor adapting to the water level change of ecological belt. Landscaping on campus shall start from the full picture to combine the architectures and environment of the garden space in a rather natural way to build a novel gardenlike campus, shaping a campus atmosphere of high cultural taste.

Ⅲ. Multilevel Communication Spaces

The campus should provide spaces and venues of various kinds to train trailblazing and composite talents, where students share sparking wisdom in the clash of ideas, and develop their talents through interactions. The consideration is mainly given to the following aspects. Two main communication axes in north-south direction are provided in consideration of the networked to mix the traffic and communication. The main communication axis of the west part is over 500 meters long, 10 meters wide and 2 levels high. Students' activities center, exhibition hall, lounge, café, mini meeting room and venues of various kinds are provided along the corridor. From the perspective of space and style, consideration is given to match the function, garden environment and lakeside to enhance the active atmosphere. For outdoors, the garden and architectural furnishing are used to create various featured communication spaces. The building complex cascades toward the central lake view and form the outdoor resting platforms on different vertical levels. . "Grey space" design is given a lot of attention to turn terrace, corridor, thoroughfare, concave corridor, open floor into events venues students frequent. Great effort is also put on the design of traffic core, vestibule, and atrium of each level of the buildings to produce multilevel communication spaces for the students.

Ⅳ. Campus Culture & Architecture Style

It's the design of a super large campus which covers several square kilometers. The campus is divided into a couple of functional areas by the meandering ecological belt in the center that extends for nearly 2 kilometers. The architecture styles of different areas aren't necessarily the same; however,

五、设计工作一点体会

浙江大学新校区首期工程从 2001 年 11 月打桩，到 2002 年 10 月，仅一年时间完成 540,000 m^2 建筑并交付使用，校园已初具规模。近日又被评为教育部优秀设计一等奖，这是中国建筑师共同创作的设计成果。整个设计工作操作有两点值得借鉴：第一，充分发挥和尊重建筑师的作用。校方按大组团分别委托国内有经验的建筑名师主持该组团设计，充分信任，各负其责，并按总体规划定期整体协调。第二，组织落实校方、设计、施工三方紧密配合，有问题及时现场解决。

作者：何镜堂、汤朝晖

文章出处：《建筑学报》2004 年第一期 P36—41

they together signalize the uniqueness of the buildings on the campus in their harmony. The building complex has a main theme of bright and fresh modern style. Focused efforts are made on the layout, shape, weight, height, material, color as well as style of the building complex to convey the elegance, magnificence, openness and cultural features of buildings on this supersize campus. For example, the buildings are mainly in five levels and cascade toward the lake. Coordinated and rhythmical building appearance is achieved by unified approach of each functional unit and traffic core through permutation and combination to form series. Focus is also put on the integration of orderly architectures and changeable garden circumstances. Grey is the main color of the buildings, supplemented by grey blue and green metal components as well as local yellow sections to tone up the active atmosphere on the campus, in an attempt to build an enormous campus of architectures emitting the flavor of the age and cultural taste.

Ⅴ. Reflections on Design

From pilling in November 2001 to October 2002, the Phase I of the new campus of Zhejiang University saw 540,000 m^2 constructed and delivered in merely one year. The campus now takes its initial shape already. The project was recently credited as First Prize of Excellent Design by the Ministry of Education, and it's the shared work of the Chinese architect team involved. The entire design process can serve as inspiration in two aspects: Firstly, put the architects' role into full play and respect them. The university authority engaged experienced and famous architects in the country to take care of the design of each cluster respectively, fully trusted them, set up clear and definite responsibilities for each side, and coordinated from the whole picture on a regular basis according to the master plan. Secondly, the university authority, design team and the building team worked together closely in organization and implementation, when encountering any issue during the construction, they promptly addressed it just on the spot.

By He Jingtang, Tang Zhaohui

Source: Architectural Journal, 2004 Issue 1, P36-41

浙江大学紫金港校区东教学组团

EAST TEACHING BUILDING CLUSTER, ZIJINGANG CAMPUS, ZHEJIANG UNIVERSITY

华南理工大学广州国际校区

GUANGZHOU INTERNATIONAL CAMPUS OF SOUTH CHINA UNIVERSITY OF TECHNOLOGY

项目地点：广东省广州市
设计时间：2017 年
建筑面积：1,400,000 m^2

Location: Guangzhou, Guangdong
Design: 2017
GFA: 1,400,000 m^2

华南理工大学广州国际校区
GUANGZHOU INTERNATIONAL CAMPUS OF SOUTH CHINA UNIVERSITY OF TECHNOLOGY

华南理工大学广州国际校区以“合璧”作为校园总体规划理念，紧扣“中西合璧、博雅合璧、传统与现代合璧、科学与人文合璧”的主旨，一方面提取和延续华工老校区的环境基因，另一方面再现与注入国外著名大学的空间意向元素，构建具有岭南地域特点并符合时代精神的综合性大学国际校区。

Taking “combination” as the main idea of campus master planning, South China University of Technology (Guangzhou International Campus) closely adheres to the purport of “combination of Chinese and Western, well-informed and refined combination, combination of tradition and Modern, combination of Science and Humanities”. On the one hand, it extracts and continues the environmental genes of the old campus of South China University of Technology. On the other hand, it reproduces and incorporates the spatial intention elements of foreign famous universities, so as to construct the international campus of a comprehensive university with Lingnan regional characteristics and in line with the spirit of the times.

华南理工大学广州国际校区
GUANGZHOU INTERNATIONAL CAMPUS OF SOUTH CHINA UNIVERSITY OF TECHNOLOGY

广州大学城华南理工大学教学区

THE TEACHING AREA OF SOUTH CHINA UNIVERSITY OF TECHNOLOGY, GUANGZHOU HIGHER EDUCATION MEGA CENTER

项目地点：广东省广州市
设计时间：2003 年
竣工时间：2006 年
用地面积：818,000 m^2
建筑面积：431,000 m^2
曾获奖项：

· 院系办公实验楼群：
  中国建筑学会中华人民共和国成立 60 周年建筑创作大奖（2009 年）
  国家优质工程银质奖（2006 年）
  中国建筑学会建筑创作奖：佳作奖（2006 年）
  建设部优秀建筑工程设计二等奖（2005 年）
  广东省注册建筑师协会优秀建筑创作奖：创作奖（2005 年）
  广东省优秀工程设计项目一等奖（2005 年）
  第三届中国威海国际建筑设计大奖赛优秀奖（2006 年）
  全国优秀工程设计铜奖
· 公共教学楼：
  广东省优秀工程设计项目二等奖（2005 年）
  广东省优秀建筑设计奖二等奖（2004 年）
· 广州大学城华南理工大学专家楼（大学城中心酒店）
  广东省优秀工程勘察奖三等奖（2009 年）
· 广州大学城华南理工大学校区首期工程：
  广东省优秀工程勘察奖表扬奖（2004 年）
· 广州大学城华南理工大学科技楼 B：
  广东省优秀工程勘察奖二等奖（2007 年）

Location: Guangzhou, Guangdong
Design: 2003
Completion: 2006
Site Area: 818,000 m^2
GFA: 431,000 m^2
Awards:

· Office and Laboratory Building Group
  ASC Grand Architectural Creation Award for the 60th Founding Anniversary of PRC (2009)
  Silver Award for National High-quality Project (2006)
  Honorable Mention of ASC Excellent Architectural Creation Award (2006)
  The Second Prize for Excellent Construction Engineering Design by the Ministry of Construction (2005)
  Creation Award of Excellent Architectural Creation Award by Guangdong Chapter of Association of Chinese Registered Architects (2005)
  The First Prize for Excellent Engineering Design of Guangdong Province (2005)
  Excellence Award, The 3rd China Weihai International Architectural Design Award & Competition (2006)
  Bronze Award of National Excellent Engineering Design
· Public Teaching Buildings:
  The Second Prize for Excellent Engineering Design Project of Guangdong Province (2005)
  The Second Prize of Excellent Architectural Design Award of Guangdong Province (2004)
· Experts Guesthouse (University Town Center SCU Hotel)
  The Third Prize of Excellent Engineering Exploration Award of Guangdong Province (2009)
· SCUT Campus (Phase I) in GZHEMC
  Honorable Mention of Excellent Engineering Exploration Award of Guangdong Province (2004)
· Technology Building B, SCUT Campus in GZHEMC
  The Second Prize of Excellent Engineering Exploration Award of Guangdong Province (2007)

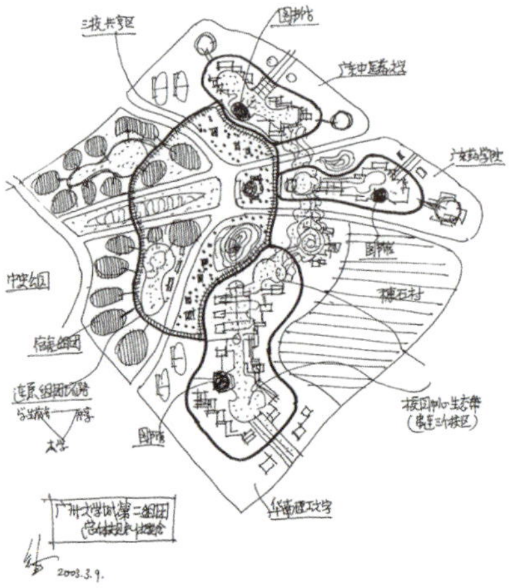

广州大学城华南理工大学教学区

THE TEACHING AREA OF SOUTH CHINA UNIVERSITY OF TECHNOLOGY, GUANGZHOU HIGHER EDUCATION MEGA CENTER

广州大学城华南理工大学教学区
THE TEACHING AREA OF SOUTH CHINA UNIVERSITY OF TECHNOLOGY, GUANGZHOU HIGHER EDUCATION MEGA CENTER

华南理工大学教学区以完整的轴线系统，体现人文地域文脉的延续。轴线对于整体规划结构来说，有着一种控制性的力量，能体现出庄重、理性的稳定构架。同时也与知识理性的教化功能相协调。规划设计以朝向江面和正南正北形成两个方向的轴线，并在中心广场以“知识源泉”为核心，轴线做了巧妙的转折。建筑与外部空间均依托于这条转折的轴线，从而奠定了整体规划环境的基调——校园理性与浪漫山水的结合、庄重科学精神与自由人文精神的结合。

The SCUT campus features a well-established axis system which carries on the cultural and geographical context of the project site. The axis system is able to control and regulate, and finally generate a solemn, rational and stable planning structure. The two axes in the planning, which respectively faces the river and runs in due north-south direction, make a graceful turn at the core, i.e. the Wellspring of Knowledge at the Central Square. Both buildings and exterior spaces are based on the turning axes, which sets the keynote for the entire environment, i.e. the combination of rational campus and romantic landscape, and the integration of serious science spirit and the free humanistic spirit.

广州大学城华南理工大学教学区
THE TEACHING AREA OF SOUTH CHINA UNIVERSITY OF TECHNOLOGY GUANGZHOU HIGHER EDUCATION MEGA CENTER

建筑·空间·场所——华南理工大学新校区院系楼群解读

一、背景

华南理工大学新校区位于广州小谷围岛的广州大学城内，于 2003 年底规划并启动建设，2004 年 9 月份首期工程建成投入使用，新校区于 2005 年底基本建成。院系楼群是新校区的首期工程之一，用地位于校园中心区东侧，由三组院系楼组成，编号分别为 1—17，1—18 和 1—19，与公共教学楼隔湖相望。在规划中校园主要控制轴线在图书馆前广场发生转折，外部空间在此放开，形成校园中心区，由理性规整的公共教学楼、自由灵活的院系楼、庄重高耸的教学主楼共同围合。

三组院系楼为三个相对独立的文科院系使用，功能相似，包括研究室、工作室、办公室、小型报告厅、资料室及其他附属用房。

二、总体布局与体量组合

基地位于校园中心湖西侧，由于规划中心湖水面呈南北长向，东西向不宽，最窄处只有 25 m。为了减少建筑对于水面的压迫感，设计中采用集中与分散相结合的手法化解建筑体量，使建筑隐于绿树丛中，同时也创造出不同尺度、层层渗透的室外空间。每组院系楼通过相同的母题重复和对位关系，将主要的功能用房——研究室和工作室相对集中布置于东侧，形成统一的肌理和外部空间界面，强化三组院系楼的整体性；朝向中心湖的西侧通过小体量建筑层层跌落，形成高低错落的建筑体形，增强建筑的层次感。将行政办公部分、小型报告厅和资料室等独立功能集中布置于几组方形和椭圆形的活跃元素中，与主体部分规整有序的体量灵活穿插咬合。建筑的总体布局在统一中求变化，并最终能够融入校园的整体环境之中。

Building, Space and Site-Interpretation on Design of Faculty Buildings on New Campus of South China University of Technology (SCUT)

Ⅰ. Background

The new campus of South China University of Technology (SCUT), located in Guangzhou Higher Education Mega Center (GZHEMC) on the Xiaoguwei Island, Guangzhou, has been planned and started construction since 2003 and the phase I of the project was completed and put into use on September 2004. The new campus was expected to be basically completed at the end of 2005. As part of the Phase I new campus development, the site for the Faculty Buildings is located on the east of the central area of the new campus and consists of three faculty buildings, numbered 1-17, 1-18 and 1-19 and facing the comprehensive teaching building across the lake. The main control axis of campus is planned to take a turn on the square in front of the library and exterior space opens up here as the central area of the campus, enclosed by the rational and regular comprehensive teaching building, the flexibly flowing faculty buildings and the solemn and lofty main teaching building.

The three groups of faculty buildings are planned to serve three relatively independent faculties of arts with similar functions, including research rooms, studios, offices, small lecture hall, libraries and other ancillary rooms.

Ⅱ. General Layout and Combination of Building Volumes

The site is located to the west of the Central Lake on the campus. The planned Central Lake appears longish in north-south direction but not that wide in east-west direction, with the narrowest point being only 25 m. To mitigate the pressure of buildings on water surface, the building volumes are decomposed in both centralized and decentralized manner, so that the buildings are hidden in woods and cascading exterior spaces of varied scales are created. Through the repetition and contraposition of the same motif on each group of the faculty buildings, major functional rooms like the research rooms and studios are centralized on the east, forming unified fabric and exterior spatial interface and emphasizing the unity of the three groups of faculty buildings; while buildings of small volumes cascade on the west to face the Central Lake, creating varied building volumes and enhancing the

三、开敞空间的组织与场所的营造

现时的新建校园往往由于建设周期短，在设计上只注重实体建筑，而忽略了外部空间的营造，从而与一些看似平淡无奇的老校园相比，缺少了应有的校园场所精神和人文精神。新时期 “环境育人”“以人为本”的新要求需要我们更加注重校园开敞空间的营造，以优美的校园物质环境催生丰富健康、积极向上的校园文化。

设计中我们在湖滨绿化与建筑物之间规划了一系列广场空间，在尺度上控制各广场的大小，利用建筑、绿化等各种元素围合成积极的外部空间，并利用建筑底层的局部架空使各个广场空间隔而不断，形成连续、流动的外部空间。湖滨软质的绿化步行区域面向湖景开放，是人工向自然的过渡，具有充分的开敞性。硬质广场带的步行区域是建筑与环境之间的过渡，依托建筑，具有半开敞性，成为大量人流活动的区域。两个层次的步行区域相区别又紧密联系，提供两种不同的空间场所。

广场带通过起承转合空间序列的设计手法，形成步移景异的空间效果。

起：由校园东西向主联系轴线开始，穿过一组院系楼 1—17 的架空层，进入步行区域。步行区域面向湖景开敞，另一侧湖岸的教学楼群和位于轴线尽端的主教学楼成为远景；水面作为中景；湖滨的绿化为近景，提供丰富的景观层次作为流动空间的起始。

承：穿过架空廊道来到中间的一组院系楼 1—18，长向的广场空间朝向湖面开敞，创造亲切宜人、环境优美的流动空间。

转：绕过 1—18 的展厅，进入在院系楼 1—18 和 1—19 之间的一个过渡空间，逐渐转入中心广场。

合：流动空间巧妙转向最北面的一组院系楼 1—19，空间在此完全打开，结合高低起伏的地形，通过中心集会广场和高低错落的各层平台形成广场带的高潮。

结：通过一条飞桥通往弧形屋顶平台，直指远处的湖心绿岛，在视野上完全打开，成为流动空间有力的终结。

建筑实体与外部空间可以说是一体两面，互为依托，在规整的肌理下，活跃的建筑元素既是空间中的焦点，也是限定空间的元素。通过这种外部空间的分割、渗透与联系，防止出现大而无物，空而不当的消极空间。广场带也因此成为学生课余交往、交流和举行各类活动的平台，成为校园场所精神的物质载体。

四、平面组织与立面造型

由于后期进驻院系的不确定性，在功能要求上仅提出粗略的任务书。考虑到以后使用的适应性与可变性，在平面布局中，主体建筑我们选择 6m×8.5m 的柱网单元，通过单元的组合拆分形成不同大小的房间。每组建筑形成一条南北向的主联系轴线，在横向分出次轴线，形成鱼骨式布局。

保证主要功能用房大部分为南北朝向，并集中布置，创造优良、方便的工作与学习环境。在顺应夏季主导风向的东南侧，采用挖空形成空中休息平台的做法，将主导风引入内庭院，获得良好的通风效果。

由于规划中采用环路的布局形式，车辆交通在外，保证了组团内部良好的步行环境，因此在交通流线组织上，利用原地形东低西高的现状条件，形成半地下车库，机动车辆直接从环路进入车库，减少车辆对中心区的影响。而人行出入口则顺应人流方向朝向广场，实现人车分流。

采用了传统与现代相结合的手法，规整的建筑主体部分采用较为厚重的红色面砖，既传承老校区清水砖墙的建筑风格，又使三组建筑形成了整体统一的背景；湖边的活跃元素采用白色型钢、穿孔铝板与玻璃相结合的做法，强调了轻巧、活泼的特点，视觉效果突出，成为视觉焦点。材质和细部上形成了沉重与灵巧、传统与现代的对比。

五、思考

现代的大学校园是一个有机的整体，无论从内部功能体运作的抽象层面，还是从外部环境和建筑的物质层面，整体性是一个具有活力的校园所不可或缺的条件。以往对校园整体性的理解更多地关注于单一物质实体的形式层面，注重建筑实体的材料、立面手法等视觉性的方面。而缺乏从校园空间、使用者的体验和场所认同等更多方面、更深层次的发掘，从而造成了校园文化和精神的缺失。

从这一角度来讲，华南理工大学院系楼群在摆脱传统的单一建筑设计的局限性，将建筑实体与外部空间作为一体两面进行考虑，在营造校园开敞空间和场所精神这一方面做出了尝试，以期能够看到积极健康的校园文化在此产生！

作者：何镜堂、郑少鹏、郭卫宏
文章出处：《新建筑》2007 年第一期 P37—40

sense of hierarchy. The independent functions including administration offices, small lecture hall and libraries are centralized in several active elements of square or oval shape, which are flexibly interwoven or interlocked with the regular and orderly volumes of main building parts. To conclude, the general layout of faculty buildings showcases the change out of unity and is eventually able to integrate the buildings into the campus environment.

Ⅲ. Organization of Open Spaces and Creation of Places

Recent new campuses are usually built in a short period of time with most attention given to physical buildings and exterior spaces neglected in design. As compared to some old campuses which may seem quite ordinary, new campuses usually lack spirit of place and humanity. The new demands of education by environment and human orientation in the new era require more attention on the creation of open campus spaces and the formation of diversified, inspiring and proactive campus culture through attractive campus environment.

A series of square spaces are created between the lakefront greening and buildings, with the scales of the squares are carefully controlled. Various elements like building and greening are employed to frame and create active exterior spaces, while the partially open-up ground floors allow for the properly divided yet continuing square spaces and the flowing exterior spaces. The softscape of the lakeside tree-lined trails fully open up toward the extensive lake area as the transition between artificial elements and the nature. The hard pavement pedestrian area on squares, as the transition between buildings and the environment and against the backdrop of buildings, however, is of half-open nature and accommodates large amount of pedestrian flow. The two levels of pedestrian areas are differentiated from each other yet closely connected, offering two different spatial spaces.

With the introduction, elucidation, transition and summary of the spatial sequence, the squares are able to present with varied views to visitors as one moves around.

Introduction: Starting from the east-west main axis and passing through the open-up floor of faculty building No. 1-17, one may enter the pedestrian area which opens up toward the lake view. The teaching buildings across the lake and the main teaching building at the end of the axis become the background in a distance, while the waterfront the intermediate view and the lakeside greeneries a close view, offering various hierarchies of landscape to initiate the flowing spaces.

Elucidation: Walking through the undercroft, one may arrive at the faculty building No. 1-18 in the middle. The longish square space opens up toward the lakefront, creating the pleasant and attractive flowing spaces.

Transition: Walking around the exhibition hall of building No. 1-18 and through a transitional space between building No. 1-18 and No. 1-19, one may approach the central square.

Summary: The flowing space turns gracefully to Building No. 1-19 to the north end. At this point, the space is completely open up and reaches a climax along with the undulating landform and via the central square and platforms at varied vertical levels.

Conclusion: A curved bridge leads to an arc-shaped roof terrace, overlooking the green island in the middle of the lake in a distance and fully opening up the view. This design gesture serves as a powerful conclusion of the flowing space.

Physical buildings and exterior space are two inseparable and interdependent parts of one object. With regular fabrics, active building elements are not only the focus of space, but also the limitation of space. Such segmentation, penetration and connection of the exterior spaces help avoid meaningless and negative large spaces. The squares therefore become the platforms for students' after-class contacts, exchanges and events and the physical carriers of the campus spirit.

Ⅳ. Floor Plan and Facade Design

Due to the uncertainty with the final building users, the functional requirements are undetailed in the design brief. To cope with the future adaptability and flexibility, the column grid is decided to be 6m × 8.5m in floor plan of the main building. With free combination and subdivision of the aforesaid column grid, it is easy to realize the rooms in varied sizes. Moreover, each building group forms a north-south main axis and then further develops the secondary axis in transverse direction to form a herringbone layout.

Main functional rooms are in north-south orientation and centralized to offer an agreeable and convenient environment for work and study. In response to the dominant wind direction in summer, the southeast parts of buildings are cut into open air terraces to bring the wind into the interior courtyards and improve natural ventilation.

With the proposed ring road system, the vehicular traffic is outside of the building cluster thus the pedestrian environment inside the cluster is highly ensured. For organization of traffic flow, a semi-basement garage is created by taking advantage of the existing landform conditions of higher altitude in the west and lower in the east. This way the motor vehicles could enter the garage directly from the ring road, mitigating the impact of vehicles on the central area. The pedestrian accesses follow the direction of the pedestrian flow and face the squares, which help separate the pedestrians from the vehicular flow.

Both traditional and modern facade approaches are employed. The main building parts in regular form are clad with relatively heavy red tiles, which not only pay tribute to the architectural style of the old campus featuring fair-faced tiles, but also a way to unify the three groups of buildings into an integral background. The active elements at the lakefront are constructed with white structure steel, perforated aluminum panels and glass, conveying a light and lively features and serving as visual focuses. Hence both the materiality and details present interesting contrasts between heaviness and lightness, tradition and modernity.

Ⅴ. Reflections

Modern university campus is an organic whole, whether in abstract level of internal functional operation or in terms of physical exterior environment and buildings. Wholeness is an essential factor to a vibrant campus. The understanding of the wholeness of campus used to focus on the form of single physical substance, no matter it is the material of physical building or the visual effect of facade treatment. However, campus space, end users' experience, place identity and many more aspects and hierarchies are largely neglected; hence campus culture and spirit are somewhat lost.

The SCUT faculty buildings, with integrated consideration of physical buildings and exterior spaces, have been an encouraging attempt in breaking through the limitation of traditional singular building design and in creating open campus space and place spirit. We expect to see some active and healthy campus culture could grow out of these spaces.

By He Jingtang, Zheng Shaopeng, Guo Weihong
Source: New Architecture, 2007 Issue 1, P37-40

郑州大学新校区
NEW CAMPUS OF ZHENGZHOU UNIVERSITY

项目地点：河南省郑州市
设计时间：2002 年
竣工时间：2004 年
用地面积：308,000 m^2
曾获奖项：
· 总体规划：
教育部优秀勘察设计评选二等奖（2003 年）
建设部优秀勘察设计评选三等奖（2003 年）
· 理科系群：
教育部优秀勘察设计评选一等奖（2003 年）
建设部优秀勘察设计三等奖（2003 年）
广东省注册建筑师协会第二次优秀建筑提名奖（2003 年）
· 核心教学区：
广东省注册建筑师协会第三次优秀建筑创作奖（2005 年）
河南省勘察设计创新奖一等奖（2005 年）
中国机械工业集团科学技术奖三等奖（2005 年）
第九届机械工业优秀工程设计奖二等奖（2005 年）
国家优质工程银质奖（2006 年）
· 图书馆：
国家优质工程银质奖（2006 年）

Location: Zhengzhou, Henan
Design: 2002
Completion: 2004
Site Area: 308,000 m^2
Awards:
· Master Planning:
The Second Prize for Excellent Engineering Exploration and Design by the Ministry of Education (2003)
The Third Prize for Excellent Engineering Exploration and Design by the Ministry of Construction (2003)
· Science Departments:
The First Prize for Excellent Engineering Exploration and Design by the Ministry of Education (2003)
The Third Prize for Excellent Engineering Exploration and Design by the Ministry of Construction (2003)
Finalist of the 2nd Excellent Architectural Award by Guangdong Chapter of Association of Chinese Registered Architects (2003)
· Central Teaching Area:
The 3rd Excellent Architectural Creation Award by Guangdong Chapter of Association of Chinese Registered Architects (2005)
The First Prize of Exploration and Design Innovation Award of Henan Province (2005)
The Third Prize of S&T Award of China National Machinery Industry Corporation (2005)
The Second Prize of the 9th Machinery Industry Excellent Engineering Design Award (2005)
Silver Award for National High-quality Project (2006)
· Library:
Silver Award for National High-quality Project (2006)

郑州大学新校区

郑州大学核心教学区教学楼群位于郑州大学新校区的中心。整个核心区的建筑采用了四周低而中央高的设计，犹如在平原中升起的高台，是对中原“高台建筑”的传统理念的切合。整个西面的建筑沿弧形规划道路逐级上升形成坡道，坡道屋面设置屋顶花园，沿屋面平缓台阶可以从地面到达各栋教学楼。平台花园使原本平面均质的校园空间增加了立体的层次，大大丰富了师生交流活动的空间，沟通了整个教学区的室内外空间。

理科系群为郑州大学理工学院部分系办公楼及专业课教学楼，用地呈南北纵长状，环绕中心布置了生物系、数力系、物理系、材料系、化工系、环保系等六个各自包含教学、研究、行政功能的系馆综合体。

The buildings in the Central Teaching Area at the core of the new campus features a layout where the lower buildings are placed in the periphery while the taller buildings in the center, resembling a rising platform in the plain and responding to the traditional philosophy of high-platform building. The buildings on the west rise gradually all along the arc-shaped road and create a ramp. Roof gardens are placed on ramp roof. Along the gently rising steps on roof, one may arrive at the teaching buildings via the ground level. The roof gardens add levels to the originally flat and homogeneous campus, offer diversified communication and activity spaces to the faculties and students, and realize the communication between the interior and exterior spaces of the whole Teaching Area.

The buildings of Science Departments include offices and specialized courses teaching buildings of some departments from the Institute of Technology. The site appears longish in north-south direction. Around the center of the site, there are six department complexes which accommodate teaching, research and administrative functions of the Department of Biology, Mathematics and Mechanics, Physics, Materials, Chemical Engineering and Environmental Protection.

一次时空交融的建筑体验——郑州大学理科系群设计简介

郑州大学理科系群基地位于郑州大学新校区 A—5—1 地块内，用地面积 57,427 m^2，总建筑面积 76,622 m^2，大约能容纳 5000 名学生进行专业学习。其北面为学校的中心图书馆，西面为公共教学中心，东面为实验楼群。理科系群与即将投入使用的实验楼群共同组成完备的学科组团模块。

理科系群是郑州大学新校区的首期主要建筑，是新校园形成的肇始，其内容包括：生物、数学力学、物理、材料、化工、环保等六个理工科系馆，各个系馆又包括教学、研究、办公三个主要部分。

理科系馆组团的设计有别于传统的单门独院式的系馆楼，体现出一些新的设计理念。

一、以分型为联系模式组织的系馆综合体的概念

理科系群用地呈南北纵长状，环绕中心布置了生物系、数力系、物理系、材料系、化工系、环保系等六个各自包含教学、研究、行政功能的系馆综合体。

这么多的功能单元的结合，是按照分型学的模式来组织成一个整体的：单个的教室、研究室以及办公室是最小的功能单位，这些功能单位分别通过许多的平台、休息厅、交流角等紧密联系成每个系馆中的教学区、研究区与行政办公区；这些教学区、研究区、行政办公区再通过一个多层通高的公共空间和室外庭院来组织成一个较高级的功能单位——系馆；各个系馆再通过一个更高一级的共享大厅以及连廊、庭院来组织成为一个最高级的整体功能单位——理科系群。

以分型为联系模式组织的系馆综合体的最大特点是，同一等级的功能单位都能相对独立以减少干扰，同时相互之间的联系十分便捷。而不同等级的功能单位之间的干扰能够减少到最低限度，有利于形成紧凑而独立的平面。

以该概念设计的理科系群，各个系馆内都分为教学区与研究行政区。由于教室与办公室、研究室对空间尺度的要求不同，从经济实用角度出发，各个系馆的教学区与研究行政区为两栋不同层高、相对独立的建筑，以连廊联系成为整体。每个系馆都有一个共享中庭，使各个功能部分拥有一个共同的交往空间，日常可以举行展览、表演、集会等多种形式的活动，成为系这个大家庭的公共客厅。

六个系馆相对独立，均有独立的出入口与门厅，形象完整。同时，每个系馆都通过一系列的连廊、庭院以及中心的共享大厅联系起来，形成整体而联系紧密的理科系群，有利于形成学科间的交流与资源的共享。

位于六个系馆中央的共享大厅以及平台广场是理科系群中多样性空间的集中体现，也是对传统系馆建筑单一功能的突破。共享大厅内设有供学生活动的网吧、展厅、书店、茶室等，为各个系的师生提供一个具有实质功能内涵的交流区域。共享大厅在首层联系着用地中段的四个系馆，可以通过过厅，到达各个系馆内部。从大厅内可以通过螺旋梯拾级而上，到达利用大厅屋面形成的平台广场。广场周围的系馆、连廊、过街楼等节点使这一空间具有向心性和凝聚力，是整个建筑群的空间核心。此外，由中心广场以及共享大厅所延伸出的一系列广场、庭院，高差错落，丰富生动，尺度宜人；贯穿系群的南北与东西轴线使整个地块的外部空间成为弹性延伸的共享交流系统。

二、重拾学院式街廊的氛围

郑州大学新校区占地广阔，匀质地处理每一个地块并不能带来理想的整体空间。因此我们在总规设计中采用整体低密度，局部高密度的手法。这种规划手法一方面为校园带来了大片的生态绿地，另一方面又在密集的系群综合体内部创造了一种特有的内聚力和亲和感。

理科系群所在地块正是所谓“局部高密度地块”，其容积率为 1.33，建筑密度为 29.8%，低层高密度比较容易创造人性化的外部空间，建筑在这里其本身作为空间界面的意义更甚于作为视觉轮廓总体的意义，因此我们小心处理建筑的每一个界面，尽量使其具有亲和的尺度，并追求小尺度的细腻外在表达，坚持整体的协调，使用者徜徉其间可以有欧洲中世纪“学院街”的空间体验，重新找回步行的乐趣与偶遇交谈的可能。这种空间的体验是我们做该设计的最终要求。

理科系群的设计在空间方面做了大量的考虑，最后的空间体现出许多非凡的视觉效果和特殊体验。每一个空间的视觉景观总是在多视角的层次中延伸、展开、变化，空间的意义大大地延伸了建筑的含义，而更以其连接、围合的“虚空”部分赋予使用者更多的体验，以其群体组合的开放不确定性给予人们更多无穷的回味。连续而流动的室内外空间，打破了功能单一的教学建筑的乏味。透明的玻璃盒、鲜艳的锥体、沿着圆锥螺旋上升的楼梯、古朴的木架亭、笔直的楼梯间、通透的连廊……每个节点都恰如其分地发挥着点睛的作用；空间在不断被点缀中得到转折和延伸。

三、探索中原文化的建筑创新之路

地域个性、文化传承是校园场所精神的主要方面，是师生们对校园的认同感和归属感的根基所在，一个优美的富有诗意的校园将成为师生终身美好记忆的一部分。我们希望通过对理科系群的思考与设计，使之能对今后郑州大学新校区的建设与发展起到一个引导与借鉴的作用，促使新校区建筑的整体、统一，创造优美和谐的校园环境。

对于理科系群本身，我们力图以现代的设计手法与材料来延续中原传统建筑的意境，既尊重河南的地域特色，又具有时代的特征。建筑造型稳重大方，细部丰富，既有北方建筑的挺拔大气，又有南方建筑的流畅细致。各栋建筑虽然造型差异很大，但以统一的细部元素、材料和尺度形成协调，建筑群整体统一不失变化。以仿黏土砖的劈离砖作为外墙主要材料，表达了对周围环境以及传统的呼应，同时大量运用的槽钢、玻璃砖、穿孔钢板等现代材料体现着时代的气息，这种传统和现代材料的对比产生摄人的力度，比单纯地使用传统材料更能表达我们对历史的理解和继承。

在理科系群中漫步，就像在丰富而细腻的空间之中不断回转环绕，转眸之间，在连廊处、台阶处、平台处、庭院处、深深的窗口处，都是师生交流的身影，令人激动的学术创作激情奋发而生。这亦是我们创作者所期冀的建筑空间体验。

作者：陶 郅、陈子坚、郭 嘉

文章出处：《新建筑》2012 年第六期 P120—123

A Time/Space-Integrating Architectural Experience-An Introduction to Design for Science Departments Buildings of Zhengzhou University

Located at Plot A-5-1 of the New Campus of Zhengzhou University, the Science Departments Buildings, with a planned site area of 57,427 m^2 and a planned GFA of 76,622 m^2, would accommodate about 5,000 students. With the Central Library of the University on the north, the Public Teaching Center on the west and the lab buildings on the east, the Buildings of Science Departments, together with the to-be-opened lab buildings, would form a complete discipline cluster.

Buildings of Science Departments represent the main Phase I new campus development of Zhengzhou University as the starting point from which the new campus will take shape. It includes six Science Departments, namely Biology, Mathematics and Mechanics, Physics, Materials, Chemical Engineering, and Environmental Protection. Each department building consists of three components, i.e. teaching, research and office.

Buildings of Science Departments are designed to be different from the conventional detached compound with a single main gate, instead, would showcase some new concepts.

Ⅰ. Concept of Departments Complex Organized in Fractal Model

The buildings of Science Departments appear longish in north-south direction. Around the center of the site, there are six department complexes which accommodate teaching, research and administrative functions of the departments of Biology, Mathematics and Mechanics, Physics, Materials, Chemical Engineering and Environmental Protection.

The combination of these various functional units is based on the fractal model to form an entirety. Single classroom, research room and office are functional units at the lowest level. These functional units, through close connections by a lot of platforms, lounges and socializing corners, become teaching, research and administrative areas of each department. These teaching, research and administrative areas then form an even higher level of functional unit, namely the department complex, through a multi-floor- height public space and an outdoor courtyard. All department complexes then make up the highest level of functional unit, Science Departments Cluster through an even higher level of shared lobby, corridors and courtyards.

The biggest feature of departments complex organized in fractal model is that the functional units of each level are relatively independent to reduce mutual interference, while maintaining an easy and quick mutual connection. The interference between functional units of different levels can be minimized, which is conductive to create a compact and independent floor plan.

For Science Departments designed with this concept, each department is divided into teaching area and administrative/research area. To cope with the different room size required by the classrooms, offices, and research rooms and realize a cost-effective and well-functional project, the teaching area and research/administrative area of each department are placed into two relatively separate buildings of different floor heights, meanwhile are interconnected via corridors. Each department is provided with a shared atrium, offering each functional part a common space for events like exhibition, performance and gatherings, and the entire department a public lobby.

The six departments are relatively independent from one another with separate exits & entrances and hallways of their own, meanwhile, present an integral building image. Furthermore, all departments are linked up through a series of connecting corridors, courtyards and the shared central lobbies, forming a closely-interconnected cluster of Science Departments that is well poised for inter-disciplinary interactions and resources sharing.

The shared lobby and platform square in the center of the six departments are manifestations of the spatial diversity of the Science Departments, also a breakthrough from the singular function of conventional department buildings. Internet café, exhibition hall, bookstore and tea rooms are provided in the shared lobby, offering a real communication space for students and faculty from different departments. The shared lobby on the ground floor connects four departments in the middle segment of the plot, and leads to the inner part of each department building via the gallery. Spiral staircases from the inside of the lobby ascend to the platform square, i.e. the roof of the lobby. Various nodes framing the square, such as the department buildings, connecting corridors and street-crossing arcades, enhance the attraction and cohesion of the square and make it a core space of the whole buildings complex. Moreover, a host of squares and courtyards extending from the central square and shared lobby stagger at different vertical levels in pleasant scales present a vivid and attractive view. North-south and east-west axes run through the departments buildings, and turn the exterior spaces of the entire site into flowing communication system.

Ⅱ.Recapture the School-Block Atmosphere

Due to large expanse of site area, the new campus of Zhengzhou University would not be able to realize ideal spaces through homogenous design of each and every plot. With such understanding, we decide to implement an overall low building coverage in the master plan, with high building coverage just at some specific areas. This planning gives a great deal of ecological green-land, while establishing cohesion and close tie inside the densely distributed department complexes.

The site of the Science Departments is just such a plot of high building coverage in some parts with a planned FAR of 1.33 and building coverage of 29.8%. With low rise and high building coverage, it is easier to create a humanistic exterior space, while the meaning of buildings here as a spatial interface weighs more than that of a visual profile in the whole. That's why we deal with each interface of the building with great care, trying to bring about amicable scale, subtle external expression in a small scale, and an overall harmony of the project. All the efforts intend to give users a spatial experience of college street in medieval Europe, allowing them to recapture the pleasure of a casual walk, encounter and talking. Such a spatial experience is our ultimate goal for the design.

With a lot of considerations and efforts on spatial design of buildings of Science Departments, the finally realized spaces present numerous amazing visual effects and extraordinary experience. The views of the spaces extend, expand and evolve at a multi-perspective level. Consequently, the meaning of architecture is greatly extended by what the space conveys while the "void" connected and enclosed by the buildings offer the users more experience and profound aftertaste with the open uncertainty brought by the combination of the complex. The flowing and continuous indoor and outdoor spaces do away with the monotony of the teaching buildings of singular function. The nodes, such as the transparent glass box, brightly-colored cone, staircase spiraling alongside the cone, primitive wooden pavilion, straight stairway as well as the transparent corridor, work perfectly in adding final tough to the projects, with which the spaces keep turning and extending.

Ⅲ.Exploring Architectural Innovations in Central China

Geographical features and cultural inheritance which dominate the spiritual part on the campus are the origins of students' and faculty's identification with and belonging to the university. An attractive and poetic campus constitutes the fond memories of students and faculty through their entire lives. We hope that the thoughts and design of buildings of Science Departments could serve as a guidance and inspiration to the future construction and development of the New Campus of Zhengzhou University, and contribute to an integral, unified, attractive and harmonious campus environment.

For the buildings of Science Departments, we strive to carry on the connotation of traditional architectures in central China through modern design approach and materials. With stable and generous form and sophisticated details, the buildings on one hand show respect or the local features of Henan province, on the other hand embody the spirit of the times; moreover, combing the magnificence of the northern buildings and delicacy of the southern ones. Though each building distinguishes itself from another in shape, the whole complex stays well-coordinated and coherent as one entirety through uniform detail elements, materials and scale, without sacrificing the diversity. The split tiles made of clay imitation bricks are used as main facade material to resonate with the surrounding environment and traditions; at the same time, modern materials including steel channel, glass brick, and perforated steel panels are used in large amount to showcase the modernity of times. The enchanting strength generated by a contrast between traditional and modern materials, compared to the option of merely using traditional materials only, does a better job in speaking out our understanding and inheritance of history.

Strolling along the buildings of Science Departments is like rotating and turning in a diverse and delicate space. In each turn, under the connecting corridor, by the steps, on the platform, in the courtyard, there are communicating students and faculty, where stimulating insights are sparkling and booming. This is exactly the kind of architectural space experience envisioned and desired by us as architect.

By Tao Zhi, Chen Zijian, Guo Jia
Source:New Architecture, 2012 Issue 6, P120-123

上海大学校本部东区

EAST CAMPUS OF SHANGHAI UNIVERSITY

项目地点：上海市
设计时间：2005—2012 年
用地面积：330,000 m^2
建筑面积：270,000 m^2
曾获奖项：2013 年教育部优秀建筑设计二等奖
2013 全国优秀工程勘察设计三等奖
2011 年广东省注册建筑师协会优秀建筑创作奖
2009 年教育部优秀建筑设计三等奖

Location: Shanghai
Design: 2005-2012
Site Area: 330,000 m^2
GFA: 270,000 m^2
Awards:
The Second Prize for Excellent Architectural Designs by the Ministry of Education (2013)
The Third Prize for National Excellent Engineering Exploration and Design (2013)
Excellent Architectural Creation Award by Guangdong Chapter of Association of Chinese Registered Architects (2011)
The Third Prize of Excellent Architectural Design Award by the Ministry of Education (2009)

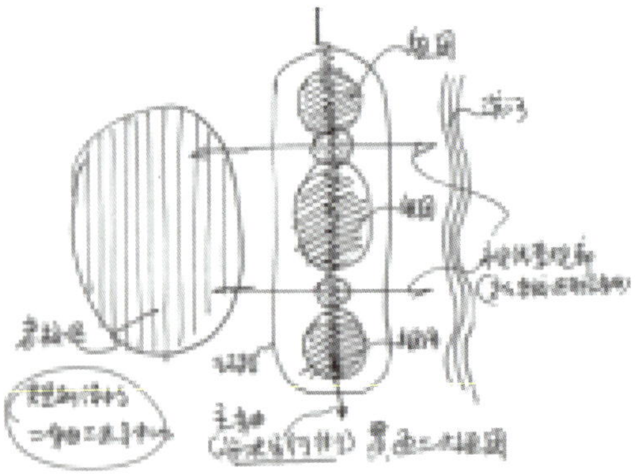

上海大学校本部东区
EAST CAMPUS OF SHANGHAI UNIVERSITY

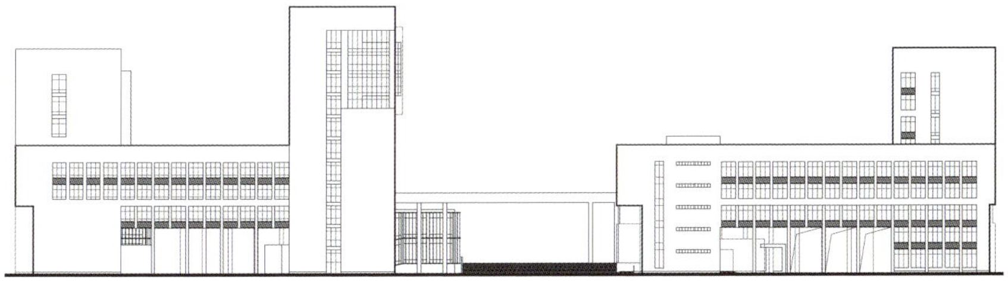

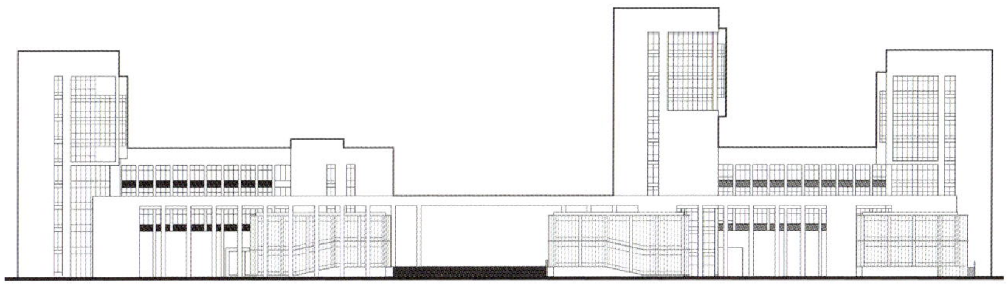

上海大学校本部东区
EAST CAMPUS OF SHANGHAI UNIVERSITY

将园林化设计理念与创新型研究教学模式相结合，以多层次交往园林为中心，设计园林式学院群，以及有利于学科交叉和创新交往的建筑空间和适应研究生培养模式的功能布局，营造园林化的研究生教学区。

提出中心园林—共享平台—研究社区的模式：总体布局采用有利于学科交叉、资源共享的学科组团式布局，改善各专业封闭独立的传统布局，将相近学科的学院以共享园林为中心相邻布置，并在共享空间中设计交往园林和公共资料中心、学科图书馆等公共平台，实现相近学科的资源共享。

The campus planning combines the garden concepts and the innovative R&D teaching mode, and centers on the multi-leveled communication gardens to create the garden-like clusters of campus. Meanwhile, efforts are made to create the building spaces that encourage the cross-disciplinary exchanges and innovative communications, the functional layout that meets the needs of post-graduate education, as well as the garden-like post-graduate teaching area.

The campus planning proposes the mode of central garden-shared platform-research community. The master plan adopts a clustered layout to facilitate the cross-disciplinary exchanges and sharing of resources, and improves the traditional layout which isolates different faculties from each other. With a shared garden at the center, faculties focusing on similar majors are located next to each other. Public platforms such as gardens for communications, public information center and libraries are also included in the shared spaces to realize information sharing between similar faculties.

上海大学校本部东区
EAST CAMPUS OF SHANGHAI UNIVERSITY

大学研究型教学区设计探索——以上海大学本部东区规划为例

中国大学本科教育经历了若干年的规模扩张，在各地建设了数量众多的新校园，与此同时，越来越多的高校向研究型大学转型，在不少定位于研究型大学的高校里，研究生规模已经接近甚至超过本科生。然而，许多新校园的规划设计都没有注意这种变化，仍根据本科教学要求设计，很少考虑到研究生教学的使用要求，以致研究生教学受制于教学空间，在使用中不得不迁就或重新改造这些空间。

研究生教学与本科教学有着相当大的区别，在培养人才层次、教学目的、教学理念、教学形式、活动规律等方面都与本科不同。我们可把研究生教学的特点归纳为：研究性、创新性、团队性、自主性、开放性、实践性、学科交叉性等。研究生教学以科研及创新能力的培养为重点，科研是教学活动中的重心；与本科课堂教学为主的形式不同，研究生培养注重发挥学生的自主性，学生需要自己的研究学习空间；培养过程强调发挥导师与团队的作用，需要有利于导师指导和集体研究交流的空间；培养形式强调产、学、研结合，需要一定的实践场所，同时注重学科的交叉，拓展各自学科的研究范围。这些都决定了研究生应该有与其教学特点相适应，而与本科相区别的教学空间形式。研究生教学空间在校园里的分布一般有三种类型，一种是与本科教学在同一个校区中混合布置；一种类型是由于本科教学迁往大学城新区，而将规模较小的老校区改造为研究生教学区。近年因研究生招生规模的扩大，以及一些大学转型为研究型高校的需要，出现了相对独立于本科教学区新建研究生教学区的第三种类型，如北京中科院研究生院雁栖湖校区、上海大学东区等都属于这种类型。笔者有幸在上海大学东区研究生区设计竞赛中中标并参与实施设计工作，这为我们探索大学研究型教学区的设计提供了机会。

一、项目概况

上海大学本部建于 1997 年，曾规划组织国际竞赛，用地面积约 100 hm^2，属于本科教学区。为满足上海大学建设研究型大学的目标，在本部东面选址建设研究生教学区，占地面积约 33.3 hm^2，建筑面积 240,000 m^2，可容纳约 5000 名研究生。项目用地地势平整，呈南北向长条形，西面与校本部一路之隔，东面为桃浦河，北面为意向中的地铁站，与本部西面研究生宿舍区有主干道连接。

校方提出东区研究生教学区的创新设想，希望其成为研究生教学区的样板工程；要求在总体布局、建筑空间、教学模式上都有所创新，跟本科生教学区有别并适应研究生教学研究、创新、交流等活动的需要。如何创造适应研究生教学使用的校园空间，如何将东区研究生区与本部本科教学区整合为整体，如何在狭长、高密度的用地中规划宜人而有特色的建筑布局和空间环境，这些问题成为此项目设计的关键点，我们尝试在规划、建筑、景观等层面提出一些探索性策略。

二、设计构思——园林式大学研究型社区

1. 研究社区——有利于学科交叉和创新交往的空间网络

提出中心园林一共享平台一研究社区的模式：总体布局采用有利于学科交叉、资源共享的学科组团式布局，改善各专业封闭独立的传统布局，将相近的学科的学院以共享园林为中心相邻布置，并在共享空间中设计交往园林和公共资料中心、学科图书馆等公共平台，实现相近学科的资源共享。同时，适当混合的功能布局，亦利于研究社区氛围的形成。

研究表明，60%以上的创新行为都在非正式交流中产生，设计顺应东区作为研究生教学区的发展定位，在学科群空间设计上通过多层次生态园林、学科共享平台、信息点、景观步行带等场所，创造有利于学科内特别是学科间交流行为发生的一系列空间，促进学科交叉和创新行为的产生。

2. 科研建筑——适应研究生培养模式的建筑空间

与研究生教学相关的主要类型的空间包括：教室、研究生与教师的研修办公空间、实验或实践用房、资料阅览空间、正式或非正式交流空间等。本科教学建筑因要满足课间瞬时大量性交通，一般难以往高层发展；而研究生教学建筑，因其教学性质，研究性空间多于课室空间，人流密度也远低于本科，因此研究生区的建筑有可能向高层发展以节约用地。在上海大学东区设计中，我们尝试采用高低结合的建筑形式，将公共性的课室与实验室布置在低层群楼，而将人流较小的研究生与教师研修办公空间叠合成高层塔楼的形式。

在建筑空间的设计中，充分考虑研究生教学团队性、自主性、开放性、实践性的特点，重点考虑研究生研修、导师办公、学术交流、实验实践几种空间之间的关系。建筑平面根据研究生以学科团队为单位组织架构，每个团队都有自己的实验空间，并与团队的研究空间临近。而每个团队的研究空间，包含了开放型的研究生研修空间和与之联系紧密但又相对私密的导师办公室，还有相应的交流空间。形成一种导师关门做研究，开门指导学生的形式，满足研究生教学的需要。另外，设计致力营造多层次交流空间，研究空间外的开放的廊道和庭院，能够为教学之余的自由交流提供最舒适的场所，使知识与智慧在师生之间，同学之间的思辨交锋之中得到升华。

3. 大学园林——以中心园林为主体构架的布局

创新性、研究性的思维需要自然松弛的外部环境来舒缓压力，更需要工作之余的休闲性非正式交往来为启发创意提供机会。中国园林自古以来就是文人墨客把酒话诗、吟咏其中的交往空间，承载着休闲交往、激发创意的功能。规划借鉴中国园林的功能，在各个学科群中心营造园林，为各组团创造优美的景观中心和交往场所，为科研人员提供接触自然与交往的空间。通过屋顶花园平台、庭园、观景平台等交往空间的营造，校园处处都可以作为师生交流心得，指导学术的第二课堂。而贯通基地南北的园林学街轴，将几个园林中心贯通为空间序列，成为东区主要的规划骨架与开放空间系统。

建筑设计借鉴园林手法，大部分学院建筑以小体量群楼塑造园林化尺度，结合错落的高层研究楼，并以分合有致的建筑、穿插的联廊塑造园林化的空间。由建筑围合而成的各式的院落重重相连，既方便联系又保持了人性化的尺度和富有园林意味的空间肌理。

4. 整体校园——与旧校区及周边城市融为一体的设计

上海大学本部规划特色鲜明，是 20 世纪 90 年代中国大学校园设计的代表作。我们在东区工程中，以整体设计观为指导整合校本部和东区用地，力求在功能和空间上融为整体。南面入口对应于校本部的开敞空间，并将东区行政楼与本部行政楼以架空廊连接；而西北面入口则正对校本部的次入口，考虑校本部的学生和车流主要从这个部位进入东区，规划了对应于本部入口的新旧校区联系轴并直通东面 466,200 m^2 发展用地。同时，东区的空间格局、建筑风格也力求在与本部协调统一的基础上有所创新。

东区规划引入城市设计的手法，在东区天际轮廓控制和与城市景观绿化的融合上，都做了相应的设计。东区项目以低层群楼与高层研究楼结合的设计，既节约用地、形成大片的区内绿化，又形成东区高低错落、变化丰富的城市轮廓。同时以学科为组团的布局，在组团之间形成大片的集中绿化，并与桃浦河绿带相连，与城市生态系统连为一体。

三、总体结构与整体布局

1. 总体规划结构——两轴三区多中心的格局

总体布局结合基地形状和学科群的划分，将几个学院组团从南至北分布，形成两轴三区多中心的规划结构。

两轴——包括南北贯通基地的园林学街轴和东西穿越用地的新旧校区联系轴。其中园林学街轴以人性化的步行尺度为依据，以线带点，形成有利于学科交叉的多中心布局，把校园连成整体。

三区——按学科群划分，由南至北形成人文社会科学、技术学科、生命环境学科三个主要功能区。两个主要人口结合功能区之间空间布置行政楼、图书馆、学生中心、后勤中心等公共建筑。

多中心——各组团以各自的中心园林和公共平台为中心，形成有利于相近学科交流的分区布局。

2. 功能分区与交通系统

人文社会学科区——布置在主入口南面，以图书馆、博物馆为中心，四周为文学、社科、商管等学院。图书馆作为开放式、共享型研究平台，与各学院通联渗透，使整个组团成为有机联系、资源共享的区域。

技术学科区——布置在基地中部，将土木、材料、计算机、通信、机电学科组合成相互渗透、相互联系的学院群。在该建筑群核心布置公共资料中心，实现资源共享。

生命、环境学科区——涉及排放物中有废气，安排于校区最北端，该群体以园林为中心，设计为两个有机联系的单体。

交通系统规划以“人车分流，步行优先”为原则，既考虑新旧校区和未来发展区的有机联系，又保证各区内舒适的步行环境，创造安静的学习和生活环境。贯通南北的景观步行轴及跟它联系的次级步行路网，在各功能区内部组织了舒适、流畅的步行流线，又相互联系连成一体形成完善的步行网络。

四、结语

此方案在上海大学东区设计全国竞赛中中标并得以实施。现在一期约 60,000 m^2 的建筑设计已落成，并获得教育部优秀建筑设计奖，二期学院建筑方案正在实施中，方案也获得广东省建筑创作优秀奖。项目在研究生教学区的规划设计方面，结合研究生教学理念与特点，作了一些积极的探索。我们期待在前两期项目使用中总结经验，在后期项目中改进设计，继续探索。希望此设计能起到抛砖引玉的作用，让更多的同行来共同探讨这个课题。

作者：丘建发、邓剑虹、何小欣

文章出处：《新建筑》2012 年第六期 P120—123

An Exploration into Design of University's Research-Oriented Teaching Area-A Case Study on Planning for East Campus of Shanghai University

A large number of new campuses have been built in China as a result of its undergraduate education expansion program over the past years. Meanwhile, more and more universities are being transformed into research universities. In many of them, the number of postgraduates has grown close to or even greater than that of undergraduates. However, such changes are not reflected in the planning and design of many new campuses built so far. They are still designed in accordance with the requirements of undergraduate teaching with little regard to the needs of postgraduate teaching, making the latter subject to the existing teaching space and have to compromise, or these spaces have to undergo redevelopment to accommodate the postgraduate teaching.

Postgraduate teaching is significantly different from undergraduate teaching in terms of level of talents produced, as well as the purpose, philosophy, form and activity pattern of teaching. Postgraduate teaching is generally characterized by being research-oriented, innovative, team- spirited, autonomous, open, practical and cross-disciplinary, etc. Postgraduate teaching focuses on the fostering of students' scientific research and creative ability, and scientific research constitutes the center of its teaching activities. Different from the classroom-dominated teaching form of undergraduate, postgraduate education attaches great importance to the development of students' autonomy in learning, and students need to have their own space for research and studies. Postgraduate education process stresses the importance of supervisor and team, and requires appropriate spaces that are convenient for supervisors to tutor students and conduct collective research communications. In education mode, postgraduate education emphasizes the combination of production, learning and research, and requires some places for practice while stressing cross-disciplinary communications to expand the scopes of respective disciplines. All of these determine that postgraduate teaching should be provided with spaces that are adaptable to the characteristics of its teaching and distinguished from undergraduate teaching at the same time. The layouts of postgraduate teaching space on campus are generally categorized into three types. The first is the mixed arrangement with undergraduate teaching area on the same campus. The second is the postgraduate teaching area redeveloped from smaller old campus after the relocation of undergraduates to the university city. The third is the newly built postgraduate teaching area relatively separated from undergraduate teaching area as a result of the postgraduate expansion program and the needs of some universities for transformation into research ones in recent years. For example, the Yanqi Lake Campus of Graduate School of Chinese Academy of Sciences in Beijing, and the East Campus of Shanghai University. The author's team had the honor of winning the bid for the design of postgraduate teaching area in the East Campus of Shanghai University and participated in the project design and implementation works, which provides an opportunity for us to explore the design of university's research-oriented teaching area.

Ⅰ. Project Overview

Shanghai University (Main Campus) was built for undergraduate teaching in 1997. An international competition was launched then for the planning of the campus of about 100 hectares. To achieve the objective of making Shanghai University a research university, the postgraduate teaching area is planned east of the Main Campus with an area of about 33.3 hectares and a GFA of 240,000 m^2 to accommodate about 5,000 post-graduates. This north-south site is a flat and longish strip connected with the postgraduate dormitory area in the west of the Main Campus via a main road, and with the Main Campus just across the road in the west, Taopu River in the east and the proposed Metro station in the north.

According to the university authority, the postgraduate teaching area is expected to become a template for future such projects, and is required to be innovative in overall layout, building space and teaching mode, and distinguishable from undergraduate teaching area while meeting the needs of postgraduate teaching, research, innovation, communications and other activities. How to create campus spaces that meet the needs of postgraduate

合肥工业大学宣城校区

重庆工学院花溪校区 *

HUAXI CAMPUS OF CHONGQING INSTITUTE OF TECHNOLOGY*

项目地点：重庆市
设计时间：2003 年
竣工时间：2006 年
用地面积：788,100 m²
建筑面积：449,760 m²
曾获奖项：中国建筑学会中华人民共和国成立 60 周年建筑创作大奖（2009 年）
中国建筑学会第三届中国威海国际建筑设计大赛铜奖（2006 年）
教育部优秀规划设计奖一等奖（2005 年）
教育部优秀建筑设计奖一等奖（2007 年）
全国优秀勘察设计行业奖评选建筑工程二等奖（2008 年）

Location: Chongqing
Design: 2003
Completion: 2006
Site Area: 788,100 m²
GFA: 449,760 m²
Awards:
ASC Grand Architectural Creation Award for the 60th Founding Anniversary of PRC (2009)
Bronze Award, The 3rd China Weihai International Architectural DesignAward & Competition (2006)
The First Prize of Excellent Planning and Design Award by the Ministry of Education (2005)
The First Prize of Excellent Architectural Design Award by the Ministry of Education (2007)
The Second Prize for Construction Engineering of National Excellent Engineering Exploration and Design Trade Award (2008)

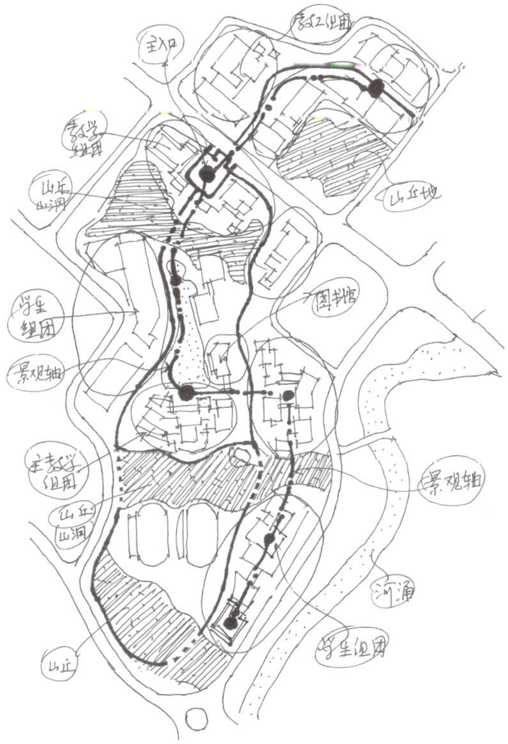

* 重庆工学院于 2009 年更名为重庆理工大学
* Chongqing Institute of Technology was renamed to Chongqing University of Technology in 2009

方案通过依山就势的生态布局来表达一个现代高校与水转山绕的自然格局、人文荟萃的地方与传统相结合的诗意画面，在山体水系的基础上，形成了“三山四水，岛翠墨香”的独特格局，山成为校园的背景和绿肺，水系及其滨水区域则为整个校园景观及活动中心。

建筑群体以顺应、环绕的姿态，更强化了基地优美的地表特征。而岛状组团之间冲沟又将背景山麓的自然景色强有力地渗透到校园中心，保持了生态景观的连续性。

方案通过理性的分析与推敲，又叠加了有机的空间架构关系，将有序的建筑融入有机的大自然。方案建立了东西和南北两条轴线，控制了整个校园的序列格局；各个区块通过灵活的体量组合，轴线变化，形成了灵活多样的空间体验。

Through the ecological layout of mountains, the design scheme portrays a poetic image where a modern university is well integrated with the natural pattern of water and mountains and the local tradition of humanities. On the basis of the mountain and water system, a unique layout featuring “three mountains, four rivers and green island” is formed. The mountains become the background of the campus and the green lungs, while the water system and the waterfronts serve as the landscape and activity center of the entire campus.

The buildings represent a conforming and surrounding posture, which further strengthens the beautiful surface features of the base. The gully between the island groups strongly infiltrates the natural scenery of the background mountain into the center of the campus, maintaining the continuity of the ecological landscape.

Through rational analysis and refinement, the scheme superimposes the organic spatial structure relationship and integrates the orderly architecture into the organic nature. The program establishes two axes of east and west and north and south, which controls the sequence pattern of the whole campus; each block forms a flexible and diverse space experience through flexible mass combination and axis change.

teaching, how to integrate the postgraduate teaching area on the East Campus with the undergraduate teaching area on the Main Campus, how to plan a pleasant and distinctive architectural layout and space environment in the long narrow and high-density site; all these constitute the key points in the design of this project. Here we're trying to propose some exploratory strategies in the respects of planning, building, landscape and others.

Ⅱ .Design Concept-Garden-like Research Community in University

1.Research community-space network that encourages cross- disciplinary exchanges and innovative communications

The mode of central garden-shared platform-research community is proposed. The master plan adopts a clustered layout to facilitate the cross-disciplinary exchanges and sharing of resources, and improves the traditional layout which isolates different faculties from each other. With a shared garden at the center, faculties focusing on similar majors are located next to each other. Public platforms such as gardens for communications, public information center and libraries are also included in the shared spaces to realize information sharing between similar faculties. Meanwhile, the appropriate layout of mixed functional areas is also conducive to the build- up of research community atmosphere.

Studies have shown that more than 60% of innovative behaviors are generated in informal communications. Therefore, the East Campus is designed in line with its positioning as postgraduate teaching area by planning multi-leveled eco-gardens, platforms shared among different disciplines, information point, landscaped walks within the space of disciplinary clusters, thus creating a series of spaces that encourage intra-disciplinary especially cross-disciplinary exchanges, which will facilitate cross-disciplinary communications and innovative behaviors.

2.R&D buildings-building spaces that meet the needs of postgraduate education

The main types of space related to postgraduate teaching include: classroom, research office for students and teachers, lab or practice room, reading room, space for formal or informal communications, etc. Considering the instantaneous heavy traffic of students, it is generally difficult to develop high-rise classroom buildings for undergraduate teaching. For postgraduate teaching, on the contrary, high building is an option for optimal land utilization as the purpose of postgraduate teaching determines that it requires much more research space than classroom space and has much lower density of population than that of undergraduates. In the design of the East Campus of Shanghai University, we experimented with the combination of high and low buildings by providing common course classrooms and labs on the lower podium floors while those research office spaces for postgraduates and teachers in high-rise towers.

In building space design, we have taken full consideration of the postgraduate teaching that is characterized by teamwork, autonomy, openness and practice while focusing on the spatial relations among postgraduate research room, supervisor's office, academic exchange space, and lab/practice room. The building plan is arranged and structured as per faculty teams; each team has its own lab space, which is close to the research space of their own team. The research space of each team includes open space for postgraduate studies, the closely connected while relatively independent supervisors' offices, as well as the corresponding communication spaces. In this way, supervisors will enjoy an independent space for research with door closed, and can directly provide instructions to students when door opened, thus meeting the needs of postgraduate teaching. In addition, the design is committed to creating multi-leveled communication spaces as well as open corridors and courtyards outside the research space to provide the most comfortable places for free exchange of ideas, bringing their knowledge and wisdom further to a greater height in the exchanges and confrontation of ideas among teachers and students.

3.University Garden-A Layout on Backbone of Central Garden Innovative and research-oriented thinking not only requires natural relaxing environment to relieve stress, but also needs opportunities for informal communications in spare time after work to inspire creativity. Since ancient times, Chinese garden has been a place for leisure and recreation, where men of letters are often inspired while exchanging ideas with others or chanting poems over wine. This planning, with reference to the function of Chinese garden, is designed to create gardens in the center of individual clusters to provide attractive landscape center and communication place for each cluster, where researchers will enjoy access to nature and various communications. With rooftop garden platforms, courtyards, lookouts and other communication spaces, both teachers and students will always find themselves in good places where they can exchange ideas. The north-south street axis of the site runs through and link up the several gardens, creating a spatial sequence and constituting the main planning framework and open space system of the East Campus.

By referencing the Chinese gardening techniques, most campus buildings are designed as small-volume podiums, which, in combination with the scattered high-rise research buildings, appropriately combined or separated buildings, and interspersed corridors, shape up the garden-like spaces. The various courtyards enclosed by the buildings are inter-connected in many ways, not only providing convenient access, but also maintaining a human-oriented scale and garden–like spatial fabrics.

4.A Holistic Campus-Integration with Old Campus and Urban Context Shanghai University (Main Campus) has distinctive features in its planning, making it a representative in Chinese university campus design in the 1990s. In the case of the East Campus project, the holistic design concept is employed as guideline to integrate the Main Campus with the East Campus site both spatially and functionally. The southern entrance faces the open space of the Main Campus, with a sky bridge connecting the administration buildings on the East Campus and the Main Campus. The northwest entrance directly faces the secondary entrance of the Main Campus, which serves as the main access for students and traffic from the Main Campus to the East Campus. Accordingly, an axis facing the entrance of the Main Campus is planned to connect the new and old campuses with direct access to the 466,200 m^2 site for future development on the east. Meanwhile, the spatial pattern and building styles in East Campus are kind of innovative while keeping in tune with the Main Campus.

The urban design techniques are employed in the design of East Campus by making appropriate arrangements in the East Campus skyline control and integration with urban landscape. The combination of low-rise podiums with high-rise research buildings in the East Campus project not only helps realize the economic use of the land and create large green space within corresponding area, but also presents a varying urban profile with interspersed high and low buildings on the East Campus. Meanwhile, the layout based on faculty clusters provides centralized green spaces between different clusters, which are connected with the Taopu River greenbelt and then integrated into the urban ecosystem.

Ⅲ . Overall Structure and Layout

1.Overall planning structure-two axes, three zones and multiple centers

In consideration of the topography of the site and the division of faculty clusters, several school clusters are distributed from south to north, forming a planning structure with two axes, three zones and multiple centers.

Two axes-include the north-south garden street axis running through the project site and the east- west axis connecting the new and old campuses. The former, with it humanistic walking scale, links up various nodes all along to create a multi-centered layout that facilitates cross-disciplinary exchanges, and eventually links up campus into an integral whole.

Three zones-three functional zones are divided by faculty clusters from south to north, namely the humanities and social sciences, technology sciences, and life and environmental sciences. Public buildings like administration building, library, students' center, logistics center are placed at the two main entrances and the spaces between the functional zones.

Multi-center-Each cluster centers on its central garden and public platform to form a zoning layout that encourages exchanges between similar faculties.

2.Functional Zoning and Transportation System

Zone for humanities and social sciences is placed at the south of the main entrance. It centers on the library and museum and is surrounded by schools of liberal arts, social sciences, and business management, etc. Library as an open and shared research platform is well connected with each school, making the whole cluster a well-organized resource-sharing area.

Zone for technology sciences is placed in the middle of the site. It brings civil engineering, materials, computers, communication, electrical and mechanical disciplines together into a mutually penetrating and interconnected faculty cluster. At the center of the cluster, a Public data center is for resource sharing.

Zone for life and environmental sciences is placed at the northernmost part of the campus as it may discharge exhaust gas. With the garden as its center, this cluster is designed into two singular buildings that are organically interconnected with each other.

The transportation system is planned to separate the pedestrians from vehicular circulation with priority given to the pedestrians. It takes into account the connection among the old and new campuses and future development area, meanwhile, ensures a comfortable pedestrian environment as well as quiet environment for study and living in each zone. The north-south promenade, coupled with its duly connected secondary pedestrian network, establishes a comfortable and smooth pedestrian circulation within each functional zone, and further creates a complete interconnected pedestrian network.

Ⅳ . Conclusion

This scheme was accepted and implemented as the winning proposal in design competition for the East Campus of Shanghai University. So far the Phase I building development of approximately 60,000 m^2 has been completed and won an award from the Ministry of Education for outstanding architectural design. The architectural scheme for Phase II, which has won the Excellent Architectural Creation Award of Guangdong Province, is being implemented. This project offers great opportunity to do some encouraging studies in the planning and design of postgraduate teaching area by taking into account the postgraduate teaching philosophy and its characteristics. We hope to provide better design in subsequent project phase based on the experiences of the first two project phases and make further exploration in this regard. It is also our hope that this design case would inspire and encourage more peers to join the discussion on this subject.

By Qiu Jianfa, Deng Jianhong, He Xiaoxin
Source: New Architecture, 2012 Issue 6, P120-123

合肥工业大学宣城校区
XUANCHENG CAMPUS OF HEFEI UNIVERSITY OF TECHNOLOGY

项目地点：安徽省宣城市高教园区
设计时间：2012 年
竣工时间：2016 年校区基本形成
建筑面积：总建筑面积：609,400 m^2，其中：一期建筑面积：196,150 m^2，
二期建筑面积：205,350 m^2，三期建筑面积：207,900 m^2。

Location: Xuancheng, Anhui
Design: 2012
Completion: 2016
GFA: The total construction area is 609,400 m^2, of which: the first phase construction area: 196,150 m^2, the second phase construction area: 205,350 m^2, and the third phase construction area: 207,900 m^2.

重庆工学院花溪校区
HUAXI CAMPUS OF CHONGQING INSTITUTE OF TECHNOLOGY

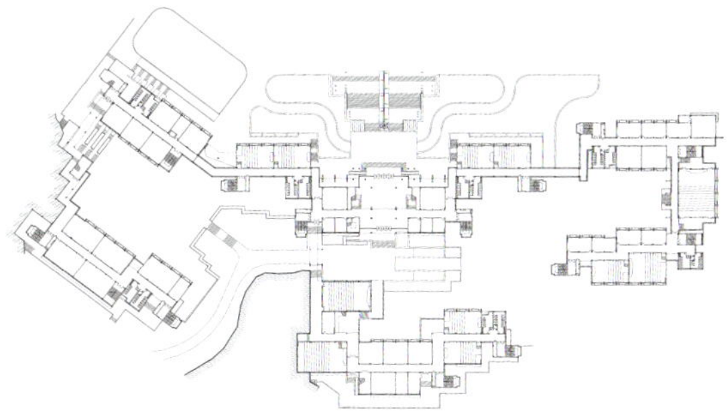

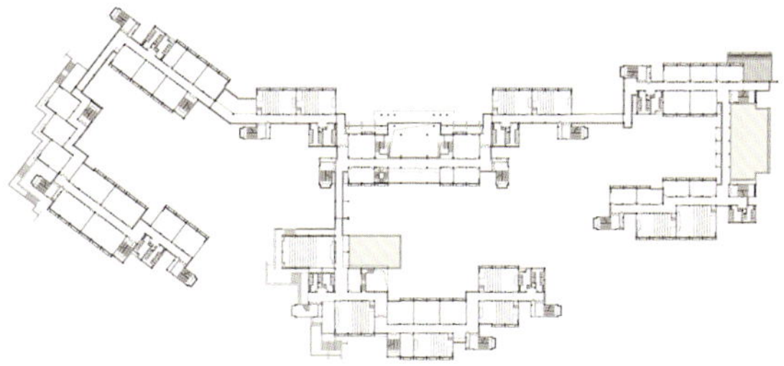

项目设计从基地原生态自然环境出发，利用基地环境中丘陵、河流、池塘等景观元素组织校园规划，形成“建筑—丘陵—建筑—丘陵”疏密相间、张弛有度的规划结构；对洼地原有池塘进行改造，形成大小不一、层层跌落的中心区水体景观；建筑组团局部向花溪河开放，使花溪河景观与校内景观互相渗透，有机融合在一起，形成山、水、建筑一体化的校园空间；建筑形式采用重庆传统建筑手法，结合地形营造错落有致、层次丰富的山地院落空间；景观设计人工与自然结合，多处保留原有植物，以营造自然、生态、文化的校园环境。

Based on the original natural environment of the site, the campus planning properly organizes the landscape elements within the site such as the hills, rivers and ponds, and establishes a well-organized planning pattern comprising architecture-hill-architecture-hill. The previous pond in the low lands are renovated into the cascading central water features in varied sizes. The building clusters partially open up toward the Huaxi River, mingling the river view with the campus view and integrate them to create a campus space integrating hills, water elements and architecture. The traditional architecture approaches in Chongqing are incorporated to create the diverse courtyard spaces in hilly area. The landscape design combines the artificial elements with the nature, and reserves original plants at various locations to present a natural, ecological and culture-oriented campus environment.

重庆工学院花溪校区

HUAXI CAMPUS OF CHONGQING INSTITUTE OF TECHNOLOGY

校园与山水共生——重庆工学院花溪校区规划设计

重庆工学院花溪校区的建设地点位于重庆市巴南区南部新城。用地面积78.81 hm^2，建筑面积约 450,000 m^2。设计规模为在校生 1 万人。整个新校区用地西高东低，属山区浅丘陵地带，地形海拔高度相差 70 多米。用地内平缓的谷地有不少鱼塘与农田，山地地势变化较大，没有大面积的平地。

对于这样一个地形复杂和原生态景观良好的校园规划，我们认为沿用以往那种方正规整的布局方式是不合适的，而应该充分尊重基地原有环境特征及其生态结构，因地制宜，灵活布局。在规划中，我们充分利用丘陵地形及花溪河良好的原生生态环境条件，因地制宜组织建筑布局，并在校园景观中延续重庆的山城传统建筑特征，力图营造一个生态的、充满诗意的山地校园。

一、生态校园

基地环境优美，有山有水，充满诗情画意，我们希望新校园的建设对基地原生态环境的破坏降到最低限度。为了突出校园生态特色，我们通过对基地环境的自然条件的分析和地形地貌特征的研究，萃取了构成基地的三个主要景观元素——丘陵、河流、池塘。

丘陵——基地内部有三条主要的丘陵自西向东伸入基地，其中南地块北部的丘陵已建设成人工化的台地，另外两个保留了自然形态，最南边的丘陵在国防铁路 100 m 宽的控制红线内。在规划设计中我们保留这三个主要的丘陵并且加以利用，把台地丘陵改造成山顶公园，另两个维持其自然形态并进行适当的植物种植，使这些主要的丘陵成为校园的绿色制高点。

河流——基地的东侧有一条景色优美的花溪河，河岸两边是生长茂盛的竹林，竹子是基地内较为有代表性的植物。我们完整地保留了河边的竹林，把学生宿舍组团放在靠河的一侧，以获得良好的景观，并且利用花溪河边的小片平地建设成体育公园，用人行天桥联系与校区的体育区和宿舍区，形成一个方便到达的宜人的运动与休闲区。

池塘——基地平缓的谷地有许多鱼塘，这是基地很有特色的一个景观，我们把这种景观因素结合到校园规划中去，将部分鱼塘改造成为校园园林景观，为师生提供一个宜人的交往场所。

对各个自然要素的合理利用强化了基地原有的特色，在尽可能少地破坏环境的情况下使校园景观得到最大的提升，形成生态自然的校园环境。在一期项目完成之后，我们欣喜地看到基地原有的野生白鹭和一些不知名的鸟群返回了校园园林中生活，使校园充满了自然的气息。

二、诗意校园

为了保留基地原生态的诗情画意般的环境感受，我们通过组织与利用丘陵、建筑与水体的相互关系来取得诗意般的校园空间。

校园南地块校前区的丘陵自然地隔开了城市道路与校内主要教学空间，对内形成相对封闭宁静的教学环境。我们为保护该山体而采用了隧道的形式，不仅保留了山体的自然形态，而且在校园空间上形成“桃花源”般独特的空间感受。

我们把实验楼顺应山势布置在中心园林两侧，加强空间的引导性，并且借鉴中国园林中“廊”的造园手法，利用横跨山体的廊式建筑来增加中心园林空间的渗透与层次变化。中心园林区周边的教学建筑以中部丘陵为背景依山而建，形成高低错落富有韵律与节奏感的空间界面。宿舍组团拉开组团间的间距，退让出丘陵绿地，使得花溪河的自然景观与丘陵绿化呼应，内外景观有机融合。中心园林区水体设计也有别于一般的平地校园，中心园林的水体由原有池塘改造而来，形成大小不一、层层跌落的小尺度园林水景。

在规划中，我们利用地形环境与建筑组织多层次的校园交往空间，其中以丘陵绿地及谷地中部的水体园林组成公共交往空间的主要架构，各个建筑组团与地形结合形成空间丰富的组团园林，形成层层递进的、有条不紊的多层次园林空间结构，为师生提供理想的交往场所。

三、山地校园

由于校区具有明显的山地地形特征，我们通过组织校园景观系统来强化校园的山地特征，利用丘陵等自然元素来建立校园整体结构，进而按照不同学科及功能组织不同功能组团。由于功能组团的组织结合丘陵的形态，保证了在分期建设的过程中，不影响校园的整体空间结构形态。

各组团与丘陵相间的布局使丘陵成为各组团间的绿色景观带与交往空间，形成“建筑—丘陵—建筑—丘陵”疏密相间，张弛有度的校园空间布局，正如中国书画中“疏可走马，密不透风”的概念。同时，校园建筑组团局部向花溪河开放，使花溪河景观与校内景观互相渗透，有机融合在一起，形成山、水、建筑一体化的校园空间。

我们通过控制建筑首层的标高及建筑层数等手段来控制校园的建筑群体效果，使整个校园的建筑顺应地形布置，对外形成高低错落富有节奏感的立面，对内形成空间层次丰富、尺度宜人的山地院落。建筑相对紧凑地以灵活自由的形态布置在丘陵之间平缓的坡地，通过广场、院落、步行道、连廊、平台等建筑元素，使各个建筑彼此之间紧密地联系，并取得丰富的校园空间形态及层次感。 建筑造型借鉴重庆传统的山地建筑形式，利用单坡顶及错落有致的体量变化，形成类似重庆江边特有的房子层层叠叠布置的传统山地景观意象，营造出富于情趣的山地校园形象。

校园道路的设计结合山势地形地貌，减少土方量的开挖，为了保证道路线形流畅，坡度尽量保持在 5% 以内，局部地方为保留丘陵的自然形态采取了开隧道的方式，隧道不长，保证隧道有充足的采光。最初，校方对采用隧道方案在经济等方面有所顾虑，在规划实施的过程中，他们逐渐认识到开山确实过于破坏丘陵景观环境，慢慢地接受了我们的建议。

四、后记

重庆工学院花溪校区经过一年多的建设，目前已经完成了一期项目的建设，二期建设也正在展开。就已建成的效果来说，规划得到了来自学校等各方面的充分肯定和赞赏。

山地校园比平地校园的设计复杂得多，要把“依山而建”的理念变为现实，需要在建设、设计等各个方面付出加倍的努力和辛劳。在设计与建设的过程中，我们的工作得到校方各级领导和工作人员的大力支持与理解，对此深表谢意。同时也希望本文的思考与尝试，对今后山地校园规划提供一些有益的借鉴和参考，不足之处愿与各位同行、同仁共同探讨。

作者：何镜堂，郭卫宏，马明华

文章出处：《建筑学报》2005 年第 11 期 P16—18

Symbiosis between Campus and Landscape-Planning and Design for Huaxi Campus of Chongqing Institute of Technology (CQIT)

Situated in Nanbu New City, Ba'nan District, Chongqing, CQIT Huaxi Campus is planned with a site area 78.81hm^2 and a GFA of 450,000 m^2. It is designed to accommodate 10,000 students. The site of the new campus, high in the west and lower in the east, is classified as low mountainous and hilly area, with an altitude difference over 70 m. There are many fish ponds and farmland in the gentle valley within the site, while there isn't any large area of flat land due to the quite changeable terrain.

As for the planning of such a campus with complicated terrain and favorable original environmental landscape, we believe it is inappropriate to adopt the traditional regular layout, instead the original environmental features and biological structure of the site shall be taken into full consideration to make a flexible arrangement based on local conditions. In the planning we make full use of the hilly area and the favorable original environmental conditions of the Huaxi River to organize architectural layout based on local conditions, and adopt the traditional architectural features of Chongqing for campus landscape, trying to build an ecological and poetic mountain campus.

Ⅰ. Ecological Campus

The site is situated in a beautiful place with mountains and waters, full of poetic attraction. We expect to minimize destruction to the original environment of the site during the construction of the new campus. In order to highlight ecological features of the campus, we extract three main landscape elements comprising the site-hills, rivers and ponds based on analysis of natural conditions and studies of geological features of the site.

Hills-Three hills extend into the site from west to east, of which the one in the north of southern part has been constructed into artificial terrace, while the other two maintain their natural forms, and the one at the end of south is within the 100m-wide building line of national railway. In the planning and design we preserve the three hills and put them to use, renovate terrace hill into a mountaintop park, and preserve the other two with natural forms and give them properly planting, building these hills into some green commanding points of the campus.

Rivers-The Huaxi River is located to the east of the site, and the banks are covered with lush green bamboos as a very typical kind of plant within the site. We perfectly preserve the bamboo forest, and arrange the student dormitory cluster on the river bank to obtain a nice view. And then we build the small area of flatland nearby the Huaxi River into a sport park, with a pedestrian overpass connecting sport area and dormitory area on the campus, forming an accessible and pleasant sport & leisure area.

Ponds-Many fish ponds are noted in the gentle valleys within the site, offering a highly unique view there. We integrate this element into campus planning and make some fish ponds into campus garden, offering pleasant space for interaction of and between the faculty and students.

Rational utilization of various natural elements enhances the original distinctive environmental features of the site, moreover, upgrades campus landscape to the maximum while minimizing destruction to the environment and contributes to an ecological and natural campus. After completing Phase I of the project, we are very glad to find that the original wild egrets and some unknown flocks of birds return to the campus, which makes the campus full of natural breath.

Ⅱ. Poetic Campus

In order to preserve the original poetic environment of the site, we strive to create some poetic campus spaces by organizing and utilizing mutual relation between hills, architecture and water features.

The hills in front of the southern part of the campus separate urban roads from the main teaching space naturally, creating a relatively enclosed and quiet teaching environment. A tunnel is created to preserve not only the natural form of the hills, but also create some Peach Garden-like unique spatial experience.

The laboratory buildings are placed on both sides of the central garden to follow the terrain of the mountains and enhance the guiding nature of the space. The gallery technique in the Chinese gardening is referenced to create a gallery-like building which spans over the hills, thus enhance spatial penetration and hierarchical changes of the central garden. The teaching buildings around the central garden are developed by and against the hills in the middle to create an artistically and rhythm organized spatial interface. The dormitory clusters placed at larger interval set back from the hills and green lands, integrating natural landscape of the Huaxi River with green hills and the internal with the external. Different from the ordinary campus on the flat site, the water feature design of the central garden creates small-scaled cascading water features in varied sized by taking advantage of the water introduced from the renovated fish ponds.

In the planning, the terrain and architecture are used to organize multi-leveled campus interaction spaces, where the green hills and water garden in the center of the valley comprise the backbone such interaction spaces. The terrains are incorporated into the various building clusters to create the diverse garden spaces and a progressive and well-arranged multi-leveled garden spatial structure, moreover, offer ideal interaction places to the faculty and students.

Ⅲ. Mountainous Campus

Since the site features conspicuous mountainous terrain, efforts are made to enhance mountainous features of the campus via campus landscape system, establish the overall campus structure with the natural elements such as the hills, then organize various functional clusters by discipline and function. Since the functional clusters are organized according to the hill shape, it is assured that the entire shape of campus spatial structure will not be influenced during the phased construction.

Due to the interwoven layout between various clusters and the hills, the latter function as green area and interaction space between various clusters, forming a well-organized campus spatial pattern comprising *architecture- hill-architecture-hill*, just like what mentioned in the concept of Chinese calligraphy and painting as *It may be broad enough for riding, or too tight to breathe*. And meanwhile campus building clusters partially open up towards the Huaxi River, mingling and integrating the river view with the campus view to create a campus space boasting hills, water elements and architecture.

The desired effect of the campus building clusters is achieved by controlling the ground floor elevation and the number of floors. The campus buildings are all arranged to follow the terrain, so that it is possible to present a rhythmic and well-proportioned facade toward the outside while forming mountainous courtyard with diverse spatial hierarchy and pleasant scale. Buildings are placed on the gentle slope between the hills in a relatively compact and free-flowing manner, and are closely interconnected via elements such as squares, courtyards, walking path, corridors and platforms, realizing diverse campus spatial form and hierarchy. With reference to the local traditional mountainous building style in Chongqing and by means of single slope roofs and the rhythmically varied building volumes, the buildings cascade toward the riverfront to present the view that is uniquely seen in the Chongqing and portray an attractive picture of a mountainous campus.

The campus roads are designed in view of the terrain to reduce earthwork excavation. For smoothly flowing road alignment, the slope has been kept at no more than 5%. Tunnels are excavated in some places to maintain the hills in natural conditions. The tunnels are not very long so that sufficient lighting can be assured. At first, the university authority was kind of concerned about the cost of tunnel, yet, during the design process, gradually realized the fact that splitting the hills will bring damage to the landscape and environment in hilly area, hence eventually took our advice.

Ⅳ. Postscript

Following more than one year of construction, CQIT Huaxi Campus (Phase I) has been completed, and Phase II is still under construction. As for the completed works, the campus planning proposal has been fully accepted and appraised by the university authority.

The design of a mountainous campus is much more complicated than that of a flat campus. To turn the concept of hillside construction into reality demands tremendous efforts from all parties involved in construction, design and etc. We greatly appreciate the supports and understanding from the university authority and staff during the design and construction process. We also hope that the thoughts and practice mentioned in this article could serve as reference to mountainous campus planning in future. Comments from and discussion with peers are most welcome.

By He Jingtang, Guo Weihong, Ma Minghua
Source: Architectural Journal, 2005 Issue 11, P16-18

资本市场学院
CHINA CAPITAL MARKET INSTITUTE

项目地点：广东省深圳市
设计时间：2017 年
竣工时间：2017 年
建筑面积：20,129 m²

Location: Shenzhen, Guangdong
Design: 2017
Completion: 2017
GFA: 20,129 m²

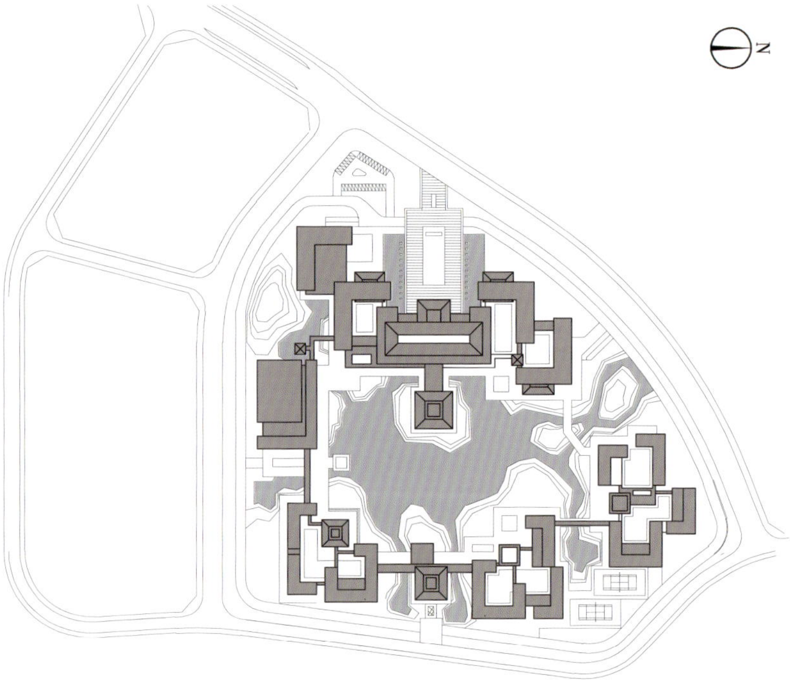

资本市场学院
CHINA CAPITAL MARKET INSTITUTE

场地北靠麒麟山，场地中建筑成组团布置，组团间山水景互相渗透；西侧从水库引水入园，汇聚于校园中心，以此成为校园融山聚水的核心景观格局。寓意着资本学院将吸引汇聚大批来自全国的高端人才，并推动整个资本市场的未来发展。

设计注重创新型多样化的交往空间的营造。创新思维的产生与创新知识的传播有赖于交往行为。交往特别是非正式交往空间，是促进创新产生的重要条件。山、水、建筑与园林空间互相咬合，形成多层次人性化的园林式布局，能够为教学之余的自由交流提供各种舒适的场所。

建筑形象力图塑造具有中国传统文化神韵而又典雅庄重的现代校园建筑群。平坡结合的建筑群体造型体现了时代精神与传统气质。石材，钢、玻璃幕墙等现代的建筑材料与传统园林式布局相结合，表现出整体典雅大气的校园群体形象。同时，将数字化、绿色生态、可持续发展的理念融入建筑的规划、设计和未来的运营管理中。我们以网络化、可生长式的建筑布局实现校园的弹性发展，同时综合运用各种低碳节能环保策略、数字化管理策略打造绿色、节能、智慧校园，营造出一种人与自然和谐共生的学习生活环境。

The site sits against Qilin Mt. on the north, while the buildings on the site are planned into clustered layout with mountain and water features in between. Water is diverted into the center of the campus from the reservoir on the west of the site, realizing the central concept of landscaping, i.e. bringing mountain and water elements into the campus. It is a metaphor for the Capital Market Institute's mission of attracting top talents from all over the country and promoting the future development of the entire capital market.

We intend to create innovative and diversified communication spaces in the design, as the generation of innovative thinking and the spread of innovative knowledge depend on communicative behaviors. Communication, especially that in informal spaces, is an important factor to promote innovation. Here mountains, water elements, buildings and garden spaces interact with each other, together making up a multi-layered and human friendly garden layout that can provide various comfortable spaces for free communication outside classroom.

In terms of building image, the goal is to create a modern campus building complex with both the charm of Chinese traditional culture and solemn elegance. The building clusters adopts both flat roofs and pitched ones, displaying both the spirit of the times and traditional temperament. Modern building materials, such as stone, steel and glass curtain wall, and the traditional garden layout are brought together to create an elegant and generous image of the campus. New concepts, such as digitalization, green ecology and sustainable development are also integrated into the planning, design and future operation of the buildings. We employ the digitalized and sustainable buildings to achieve the resilient campus development, and adopt various low-carbon and energy-saving environmental protection strategies and digitalized management strategies to create a green, energy-saving and smart campus, ensuring a living and learning environment where man and nature harmoniously co-exist.

中山大学深圳校区
SHENZHEN CAMPUS OF SUN YAT-SEN UNIVERSITY

项目地点：广东省深圳市
设计时间：2017 年
建筑面积：2,000,000 m²

Location: Shenzhen, Guangdong
Design: 2017
GFA: 2,000,000 m²

中山大学深圳校区
SHENZHEN CAMPUS OF SUN YAT SEN UNIVERSITY

中山大学图书馆

中山大学深圳校区位于光明新区，一期用地面积 150 hm²，以医科和工科为主，可容纳两万名学生。用地一山矗立，七丘拱卫，新陂头河横贯其中，我们希望这是一所与山水相融的、有利于学术创新的大学校园。

中心山体作为校园的生态绿核，外部生态环境通过指状绿廊引入，建筑嵌在绿带之间。大尺度、高层的建筑组团布置在外围，点式、低层的建筑沿山布置，实现建筑与生态相融。

北面沿岸景观优美，规划把体育馆、活动中心和景观中心布置在这里，形成滨河活力带。同时结合两条雨洪廊道，形成海绵校园的主要骨架。

校园中心由南至北，沿轴线布置了牌坊、中山像、图书馆、礼堂和惺亭，既传承了中大历史文脉，又建立了校园空间秩序。

东西向两条步行带将学科组团、公共教学实验设施、宿舍串联起来。学科组团和公共教学实验楼相邻布置，强调学科交叉、教研融合。

Shenzhen Campus of Sun Yat-sen University in Guangming New District is planned with a land area of 150 hectares for Phase I development. With medicine and engineering as key disciplines, the campus is designed to accommodate 20,000 students. The site has a central mountain surrounded by seven smaller hills, with the Xinbeitou River winding through. Our goal is to create a university campus that well blends with the landscape and inspires academic innovation.

The central mountain serves as the green core of the campus, while the external green corridors are brought into the site via the finger-like green corridors. The buildings are embedded in between the green belts. Larger and higher buildings are placed at the periphery while the lower ones and towers along the mountains, ensuring perfect integration with the eco-environment.

The waterfronts in northern part of the site enjoys attractive natural scenery, where the gymnasium, activity center and landscape center are planned to create a dynamic waterfront area. This waterfront area, together with two stormwater corridors, form the backbones of a sponge campus.

At the center of the campus, a Paifang (Chinese archway), a statue of Dr. Sun Yat-sen, a library, an auditorium and the Xing Pavilion are placed along the central axis from south to north. This is a tribute paid to the tradition of the University and an approach to establish the spatial order of the campus.

Two east-west pedestrian belts connect discipline building clusters, public teaching/lab buildings and dormitories. The discipline building clusters and public teaching/lab buildings are placed side by side to facilitate the crossover of disciplines and integration of teaching and research.

中山大学深圳校区
SHENZHEN CAMPUS OF SUN YAT-SEN UNIVERSITY

中山大学珠海校区
ZHUHAI CAMPUS OF SUN YAT-SEN UNIVERSITY

项目地点：广东省珠海市
设计时间：2016 年
建筑面积：1,600,000 m^2
曾获奖项：2019 年度教育部优秀工程勘察设计奖优秀规划设计一等奖

Location: Zhuhai, Guangdong
Design: 2016
GFA: 1,600,000 m^2
Award:
The First Prize for Outstanding Planning and Design of Excellent Engineering Exploration & Design Award by the Ministry of Education (2019)

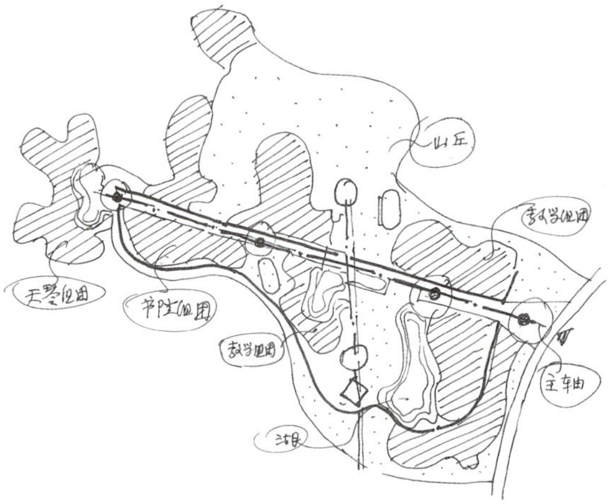

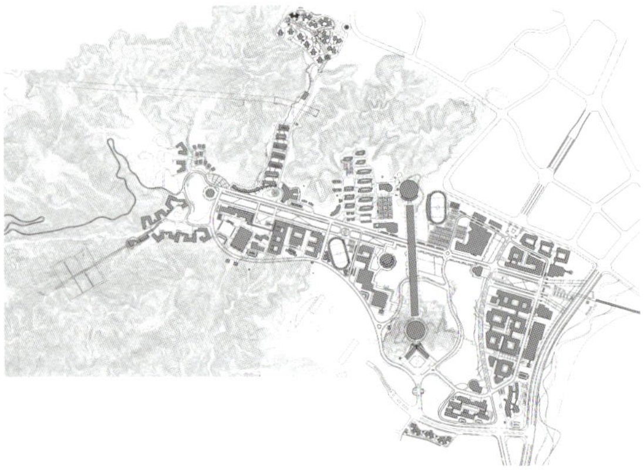

中山大学珠海校区
ZHUHAI CAMPUS OF SUN YAT-SEN UNIVERSITY

项目设计围绕建设世界一流大学的战略目标，规划创新复合的学科布局、营造理性浪漫的活力场所、构建文脉传承的经典空间、打造倚山临海的校园格局。

各学科群内布置有利于促进学科交叉的共享平台，公共建筑如图书馆、博物馆、会堂等散布其间，形成校园活力空间与创新网络。

注重营造环境育人的氛围，精心打造每一处空间特色。校园中围合的庭院、廊道与开放的园林、草坪相结合，理性严谨的学院空间与自由浪漫的山水环境相融合。这些场所空间承载了多样的非正式学习活动，也将为校园师生留下难忘的场所记忆。

在采用先进绿色技术的同时，引入中大百年老校的经典场所特质，以长轴串联中山像、牌坊、草坪等元素形成多进式空间。建筑布局立足岭南地域特点，以水院、架空廊道等营造通透自由的园林空间。将时代特色与深厚的文化地域特色融合，打造世界一流的大学环境。

自然山体与建筑组团相互渗透，临海界面打通山海视线通廊，营造显山露水、朝海开放“山、海、城”的生态校园格局。

Centering on the strategic goal of building a world-class university, the design aims to plan an innovative and comprehensive layout for discipline development, a dynamic place with rational romance, a classic space allowing for inheritance of culture and tradition and a campus embracing mountains and sea.

Shared platforms that promote cross-disciplinary interactions are provided in every discipline building cluster, while public buildings, such as libraries, museums and auditoriums are scattered in between, establishing a dynamic spatial and innovative network on the campus.

Each space is elaborately designed with characteristics to foster favorable learning ambiance. Enclosed courtyards, corridors, open gardens and lawns are interwoven with each other, while rational and precise academic spaces are merged with the free flowing and romantic mountain and water landscape. These spaces are designed to accommodate various informal learning activities and become unforgettable places for the faculty and students.

While employing up-to-date green technologies, elements of classic landmarks of the century-old university are referenced as well. The statue of Dr. Sun Yat-sen, a Paifang(Chinese archway), and lawns are linked up in sequence with a longish axis, forming a multi-sequence space. In view of the local characteristics of Lingnan Region, the building layout is designed in a way to create transparent and free-flowing garden spaces through waterscape courtyards and elevated corridors. In doing so, the spirit of the times is integrated with local cultural features to create a world-class university campus.

The natural mountain and building clusters mutually penetrate into each other. Visual corridors between the mountain and sea are opened up at the seafront, realizing an ecological campus that open up to and well merged into the surrounding mountains, the sea and the city.

广州大学城广东药学院教学区

TEACHING AREA OF GUANGDONG PHARMACEUTICAL UNIVERSITY, GUANGZHOU HIGHER EDUCATION MEGA CENTER

项目地点：广东省广州市
设计时间：2003 年
竣工时间：2004 年
用地面积：381,000 m^2
建筑面积：244,000 m^2
曾获奖项：
· 规划与建筑设计：
  中国建筑学会中华人民共和国成立 60 周年建筑创作大奖（2009 年）
  中国建筑学会建筑创作奖：优秀奖（2006 年）
  教育部优秀规划设计奖一等奖（2005 年）
  教育部优秀工程勘察奖一等奖（2005 年）
· 教学楼与管理楼：
  国家级优秀设计项目铜奖（2006 年）
  建设部优秀建筑工程设计二等奖（2005 年）
  广东省优秀建筑设计奖一等奖（2004 年）
· 多功能体育馆：
  中国建筑学会蓝星杯第五届中国威海国际建筑设计大奖优秀奖（2009 年）
  广东省优秀工程勘察奖一等奖（2009 年）
· 行政办公楼：
  广东省优秀建筑设计奖三等奖（2004 年）
  广东省优秀工程设计项目二等奖（2005 年）

Location: Guangzhou, Guangdong
Design: 2003
Completion: 2004
Site Area: 381,000 m^2
GFA: 244,000 m^2
Awards:
· Planning and Architectural Design:
  ASC Grand Architectural Creation Award for the 60th Founding Anniversary of PRC (2009)
  Excellence Award of ASC Architectural Creation Award (2006)
  The First Prize of Excellent Planning and Design Award by the Ministry of Education (2005)
  The First Prize of Excellent Engineering Exploration Award by the Ministry of Education (2005)
· Teaching Building and Management Building
  Bronze Prize for National Excellent Design Project (2006)
  The Second Prize for Excellent Construction Engineering Design by the Ministry of Construction (2005)
  The First Prize of Excellent Architectural Design Award of Guangdong Province (2004)
· Multifunctional Gymnasium
  Excellence Award, Blue Star Cup · The 5th China Weihai International Architectural Design Award & Competition (2009)
  The First Prize of Excellent Engineering Exploration Award of Guangdong Province (2009)
· Administration Building
  The Third Prize of Excellent Architectural Design Award of Guangdong Province (2004)
  The Second Prize for Excellent Engineering Design Project of Guangdong Province (2005)

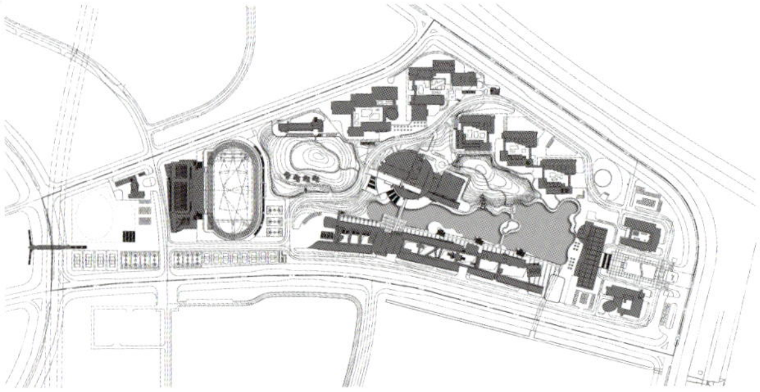

广东药学院教学区地块狭长，建筑面积较大，用地较为紧张。在规划中，我们运用连廊、“巨构”等方法，将各建筑连为一体，形成特色鲜明、整体化的建筑群体。整体化的建筑群体有利于集中建筑用地，留出更大面积的绿化用地，提高校园环境质量；便于设施的共享使用和管理；具有更大的弹性，可根据学科的发展灵活调整各院系的用房；联系更为便捷，师生可通过连廊方便地到达各处。

Due to the considerable planned GFA and the relatively tight land available on the long and narrow site for the campus of Guangdong Pharmaceutical University, we use corridors and "mega-structure" to integrate various buildings into one integral entity and create the distinctively featured and integrated building group. Such integrated building group is able to more effectively centralize the construction land, allow for more green spaces and enhance the campus environment quality; moreover, it also facilitates the facility sharing and management, and offers more flexibility in adjusting the rooms of different faculties in view of actual needs. Also, the corridors provide the faculty and students more convenient connection and easier accessibility to their destinations.

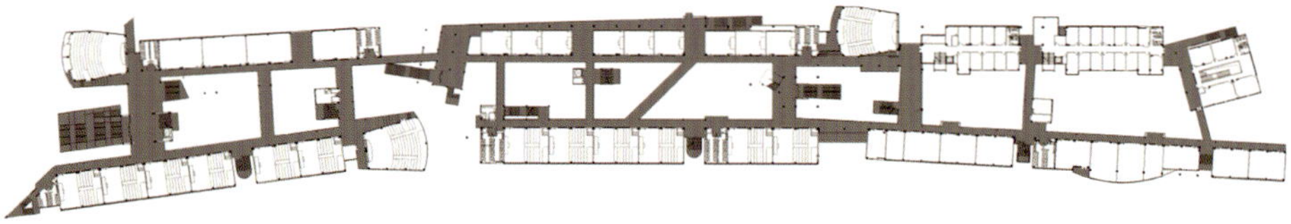

广州大学城广东药学院教学区
TEACHING AREA OF GUANGDONG PHARMACEUTICAL UNIVERSITY, GUANGZHOU HIGHER EDUCATION MEGA CENTER

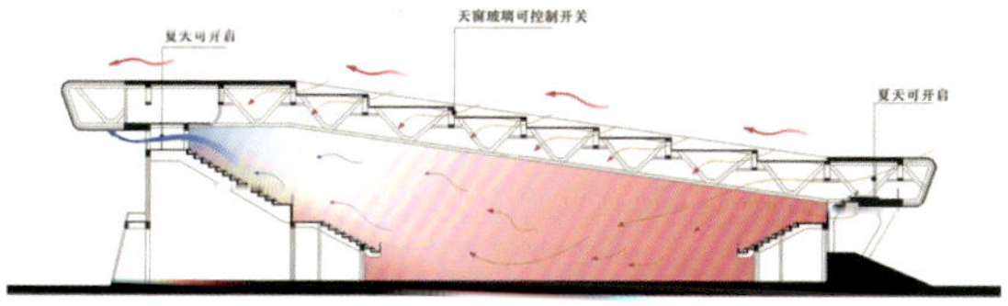
夏天可开启
天窗玻璃可控制开关
夏天可开启

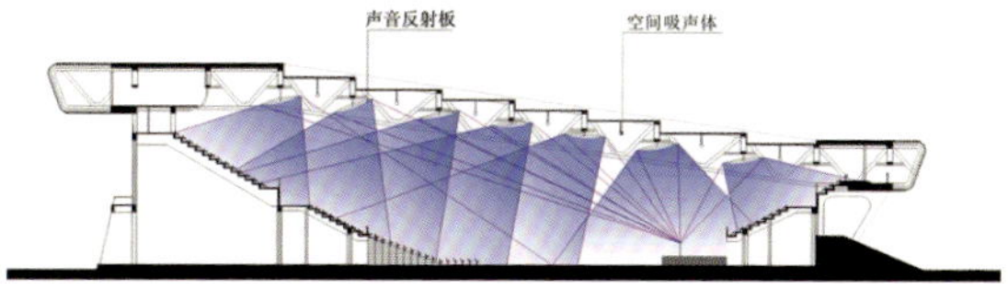
声音反射板
空间吸声体

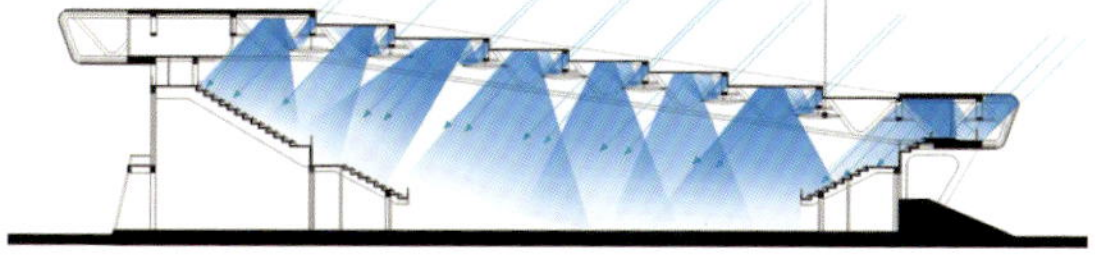
夏天可开启

南京工业大学
NANJING TECH UNIVERSITY

项目地点：江苏省南京市
设计时间：2004 年
用地面积：2,150,000 m^2
建筑面积：600,000 m^2

Location: Nanjing, Jiangsu
Design: 2004
Site Area: 2,150,000 m^2
GFA: 600,000 m^2

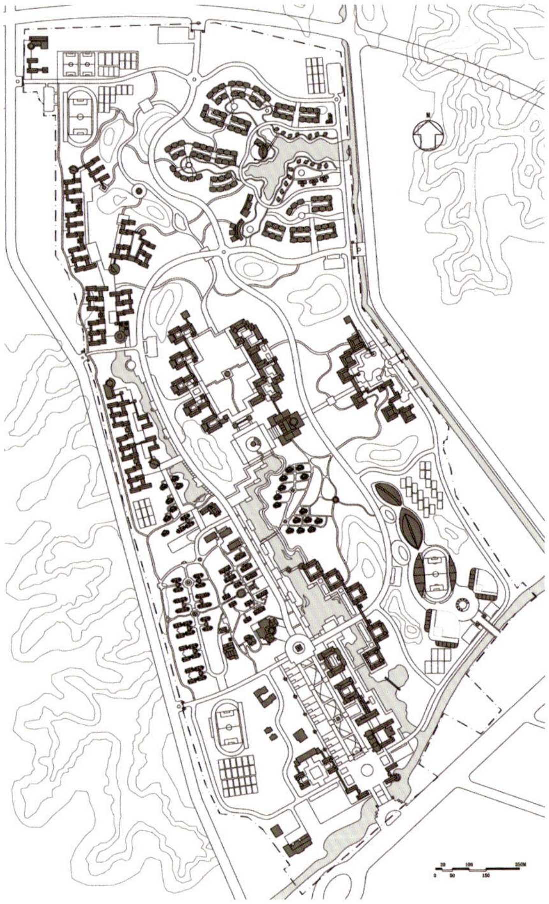

从全局出发充分考虑旧区、新区以及发展用地的关系，将三部分作为一个整体进行规划设计。规划以师生为本，以步行尺度为基准，采用教学区与生活区平行布置的分区，从而较好地解决大型山地校园的联系与使用的问题。各组团分区均以园林为核心，或水面，或山林，成为各组团中主题各异的交往核心，形成以园林为核心的多中心布局。

With a macroscopic view on the relation among the old area, new area and the project site, the project planning regard these three elements as a whole. The planning is oriented to offer convenient conditions to both the faculty and students and takes the walking distance as the criterion. The teaching area and the living area are in two parallel locations, offering satisfactory solution to the connections within a large hilly campus and its uses. Each cluster takes either the garden, the water or the woods as its core. Such core with distinctive themes is usually also the communication center of each cluster. Therefore, a multi-centered layout centering around gardens is established.

南京工程学院
NANJING INSTITUTE OF TECHNOLOGY

项目地点：江苏省南京市
设计时间：2002 年
竣工时间：2005 年
用地面积：1,536,400 m^2
建筑面积：6,190,000 m^2
曾获奖项：教育部优秀规划设计一等奖（2011 年）

Location: Nanjing, Jiangsu
Design: 2002
Completion: 2005
Site Area: 1,536,400 m^2
GFA: 6,190,000 m^2
Award:
The First Prize of Excellent Planning and Design Award by the Ministry of Education (2011)

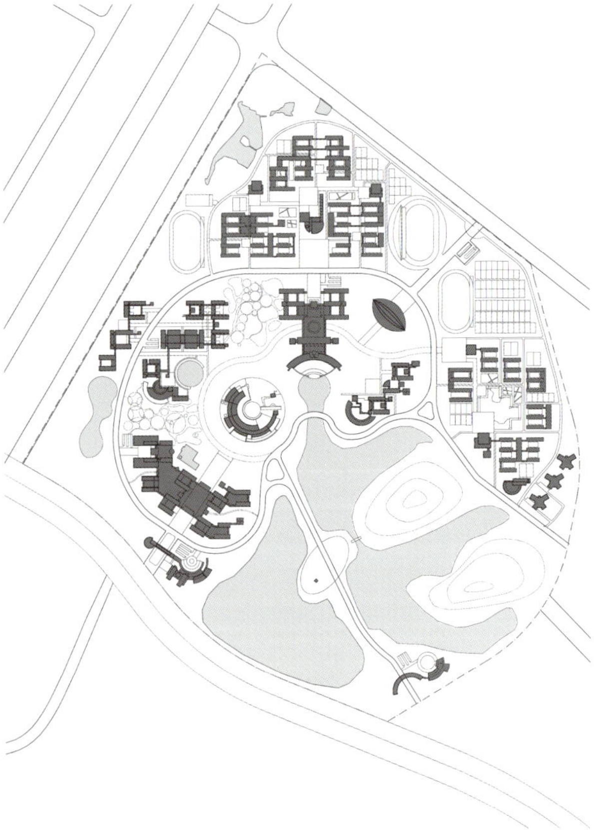

南京工业大学
NANJING TECH UNIVERSITY

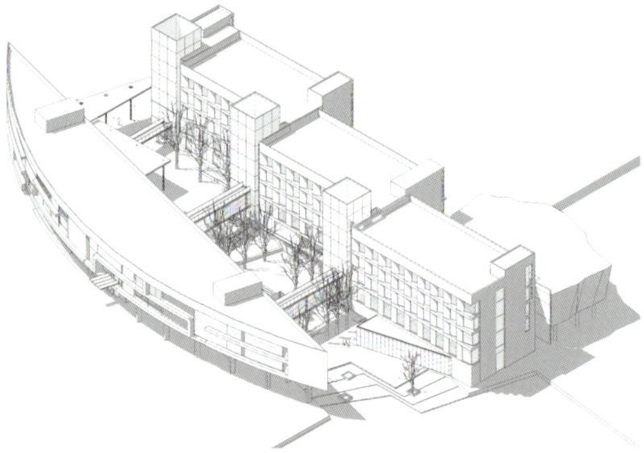

南京工程学院规划设计基于现有地形地貌特点，采用了自由园林式的生态校园布局方式，尊重自然、保护自然、并创造性地利用自然。在校园发展模式上，主张簇群式发展的弹性生长校园模式。使新校区规划成为一个不断生长的动态发展过程，这种模式适应学校分期发展的特点，保证了教育设施的多用途并提高其使用效率。在单体设计风格上，主张体现地域性的现代化工科建筑风格，单体设计手法方面强调了简洁的体量与细腻的钢结构之间的对比，整体的效果和谐而富于变化。

Based on the existing topographic and geomorphological characteristics, the planning and design of Nanjing Institute of Technology adopts a free garden-style ecological campus layout, respecting nature, protecting nature, and making creative use of nature. In the development mode of campus, the flexible growth mode of cluster development is advocated. To make the new campus planning a growing dynamic development process, this model adapts to the characteristics of school development by stages, ensures the multi-purpose of educational facilities and improves their efficiency. In terms of monomer design style, it advocates the regional modern engineering architectural style. In terms of monomer design technique, it emphasizes the contrast between simple volume and delicate steel structure, and the overall effect is harmonious and full of changes.

南京审计学院 *
NANJING AUDIT INSTITUTE*

项目地点：江苏省南京市
设计时间：2003 年
竣工时间：2006 年
用地面积：1,081,000 m^2
建筑面积：398,100 m^2
曾获奖项：
· 南京审计学院教学中心区：
　　教育部优秀建筑设计奖三等奖（2007 年）
· 浦口新校区总体规划：
　　教育部优秀规划设计奖三等奖（2007 年）
· 公共教学楼：
　　广东省优秀工程勘察奖二等奖（2007 年）

Location: Nanjing, Jiangsu
Design: 2003
Completion: 2006
Site Area: 1,081,000 m^2
GFA: 398,100 m^2
Awards:
· Central Teaching Center Area:
　The Third Prize of Excellent Architectural Design Award by the Ministry of Education (2007)
· Master Plan of Pukou Campus:
　The Third Prize of Excellent Planning and Design Award by the Ministry of Education (2007)
· Public Teaching Building:
　The Second Prize of Excellent Engineering Exploration Award of Guangdong Province (2007)

* 南京审计学院于 2015 年更名为南京审计大学
* Nanjing Audit Institute was renamed to Nanjing Audit University in 2015

南京工业大学
NANJING TECH UNIVERSITY

南京审计学院新校区选址于浦口大学城西端，南临长江，北倚连绵起伏的老山山脉。用地连同旧校区共 140 hm^2，建筑面积 398,100 m^2，设计在校生规模 1.5 万人。

如何使校园与校内外山水景观结合，创造生态校园特色；如何营造审计大学严谨、庄重的人文氛围；如何解决山地校园的分区与联系问题都将成为规划的关键。新校区规划正是在充分利用地形的基础上，从使用者出发，将建筑空间和自然人文条件一同考虑，寻找三者的契合点，创造出自然与人文和谐共生的学院氛围。

规划特色：

(1) 因借自然的地域化校园；

(2) 建筑与山水相融的园林中心；

(3) 人性化的多中心模式；

(4) 理性严谨的人文氛围。

The new campus of Nanjing Audit Institute, located in the west corner of Pukou University Town, faces Yangtze River to its south and backs against the continuous Laoshan Mountain on the north. The new campus, together with the old one, totals 140 hectares with a planned GFA of 398,100 m^2 and 15,000 students.

The main considerations of the campus planning include how to integrate the campus and landscapes inside and outside the campus to create an ecological campus; how to foster the precise while solemn humanistic atmosphere; and how to deal with the zoning and connection of a mountainous campus. It is based on the full utilization of landform that the new campus planning takes architecture space, natural condition and cultural context into consideration simultaneously and seeks for balance among the three, thus create the academic atmosphere where the nature and human co-exist harmoniously.

The planning characteristics are as follows:

Ⅰ. a campus bearing characteristics of the region and nature;

Ⅱ. a garden center that integrates buildings, mountains and rivers;

Ⅲ. a humanistic multi-centered model;

Ⅳ. reasonable and precise humanistic atmosphere.

南京审计学院教学建筑群设计

南京审计学院新校区位于南京浦口区，北面是起伏的老山国家森林公园，教学区用地地处老山的余脉与南面长江岸边平地交接形成的脊状山丘地带。用地现状山清水秀，原有的脊状山体与湿地水体相间，在教学区用地上形成山水相融的优美景观。如何使建筑与生态环境融合，如何营造审计学院严谨、庄重的人文氛围与地域特色，成为建筑设计的关键。在教学区建筑设计中，我们对建筑如何能不破坏原有的生态环境，如何与原生山水景观结合、创造生态校园特色的问题反复考虑。在审计学院优美的山水景色前，我们感受到人工环境的美与其相比黯然失色。因此，与其强调某个单体建筑的标志性，不如强调环境与建筑形成的群体效果。山水环境是基地最大特色，建筑应植根于环境，谦逊地与山水相融，教学区最终的感染力应在于建筑融于山水的群体空间，不应在于某个建筑的特异造型。在这个原则的指导下，教学区建筑设计在充分利用地形的基础上，从使用者出发将建筑空间和自然人文条件一同考虑，寻找三者的契合点，创造出自然与人文和谐共生的空间氛围。

一、因借自然的地域化建筑

明南京城建筑布局不拘泥于方正的形制，而是将规整与自然两种传统结合起来，山、水、城融为一体，体现了“因天材，就地利”的设计思想，在中国建设史中别具一格。新校区规划借鉴这种地域化的设计手法，通过对自然条件的因借，营造校园特色。指状的山脊结束于教学区用地，与其并行的几个跌级水塘在此处汇成放大的水面，形成水环山绕的自然景观。教学区建筑群体布局中，我们将用地内原生的山体与水面完全保留下来，建筑没有采用规整的大构图布局，而是采用自由灵活的散点式布局来创造校园的书院气息。各教学建筑分布在山水之间，实现建筑与生态空间的最大程度融合，最终形成了审计学院独有的山水相融的教学中心区空间特色。

二、与环境相融的园林空间

中国园林强调建筑群体的尺度与机理，注重借景、对景等手法的运用。审计学院教学建筑设计采用了建筑与园林环境整体化设计的策略，通过尺度宜人的坡屋顶、错落有致的体量、高低起伏的天际轮廓，形成一种园林化的空间氛围。各教学楼空间向中央生态公园敞开，各建筑都可以引入中心公园优美风景，使建筑内的园林与外部园林空间有机融合。同时，建筑通过空间轴线、建筑空间的围合、视线通廊的设计使教学区形成处处有景、层次丰富的效果。

三、理性严谨的人文氛围

教学区建筑以理性严谨、稳重大方的手法，注重与环境和使用者结合，形成尺度亲切、充满审计院校人文氛围的建筑空间。蓝灰瓦顶、浅色墙身、锈石基座的三段式造型，镶嵌于自然山水间的不同尺度的院落空间与灰瓦粉墙渗透出浓郁的江南书院气息。建筑以方正开敞的院落空间暗喻审计人公正、透明的事业追求，教学区、宿舍区建筑立面在统一中变化，整个建筑群形成风格统一、形式严谨、比例均衡的整体，它与江南书院空间、水乡情境等地域文化元素结合，有利于促成广大师生的心理与文化认同。

作者：丘建发、蒋涛、龙旭水
文章出处：《南方建筑》2009 年第二期 P90-93

Design of Teaching Buildings of Nanjing Audit Institute

The new campus of Nanjing Audit Institute is located in Pukou District, Nanjing, with the continuous Laoshan National Forest Park on its north. The site of the Teaching Area of the new campus is situated in the ridged foothills formed by branches of Laoshan Mountain and the plain on the bank of Yangtzi River to its south. Surrounded by picturesque mountains and river, the site is blessed with beautiful landscape of interweaving ridged mountains, wetland and waters. The keys to architectural design are how to integrate buildings with the ecological environment and how to render the precise and solemn humanistic atmosphere of the University. For architecture design of the teaching buildings, considerations are given to issues like how the buildings could avoid destroying the original eco-environment, and how to build an eco-friendly campus with original landscape preserved to the largest extent. We believed any artificial landscaping efforts would be outshined by the picturesque scenery of the University. Therefore, instead of emphasizing a single iconic building, we decided to emphasize the harmony between buildings and their surrounding environment. The natural landscape with mountains and waters is the most distinct feature of the site and buildings shall be designed modest enough to blend into it. The ultimate appeal of the campus shall be the space formed by buildings harmoniously integrated with the natural landscape instead of the grotesque shape of a certain building. Under the guidance of this principle, it is based on the full utilization of landform that the new campus planning takes architecture space, natural condition and cultural context into consideration simultaneously and seeks for balance among the three, thus create the academic atmosphere where the nature and human co-exist harmoniously.

Ⅰ. A Regionalized Campus Bearing Characteristics of Nature

The layout of Nanjing City, as the capital of Ming Dynasty, has not been strictly square and symmetrical, but rather a combination of the traditional urban grid and the tradition of harmonious co-existence with nature. The integration of mountains, waters and city and the planning concept of "following natural and geographical conditions"is unique in Chinese construction history. The new campus planning, by referring to this local design technique, has taken full advantage of natural conditions to build a distinctively-featured campus. The finger-like mountain ridges end at the site of the teaching area, while the several cascading ponds parallel to them merge here into a larger water surface. Together they form a natural landscape with both mountains and waters. For the layout of the teaching area, the original mountains and waters are completely preserved, while the buildings are flexibly scattered around instead of following any large regular grid to create the academic atmosphere of the campus. The teaching buildings lying among the mountains and waters realize the integration of buildings with ecological space to the largest extent and eventually establish the unique spatial feature at NAU's central teaching area.

Ⅱ. Garden Space Integrated with Environment

Chinese gardens emphasize the scale and fabric of buildings and the approaches like the borrowed scenery and the opposite scenery. NAU's teaching building design has adopted the strategy to integrate the architectural design with the landscape design. The pleasantly-scaled slanting roof, well-proportioned building volumes in varied heights and the undulating skyline are blended into a garden-like spatial atmosphere. The spaces of teaching buildings open up toward the central eco–park to bring in the attractive views into the buildings, realizing the perfect integration between the interior and exterior gardening elements. Furthermore, a campus full of attractive views in diverse hierarchy is created via the spatial axis, enclosed architecture spaces and the sightline design.

Ⅲ. Rational and Precise Atmosphere

Buildings in the teaching area are designed with techniques to convey the values of reason, precision, solemnity and elegance, integrate the buildings with environment and end users, and eventually create the architectural spaces with amicable and humanistic atmosphere. Moreover, the trilogy of blue-gray tiles, light-colored walling and rust stone base, together with the gray tiles and pale walls of the courtyards of varies sizes among the natural landscape, ooze the charm of traditional academies in south China. Buildings featuring square and open courtyard space are the metaphor for the common values of auditors: being fair and square. The facades of teaching buildings and dormitory buildings differs yet with unity and the entire complex is an integrated wholeness with unified style, precise form and well-balanced proportion. The local cultural elements borrowed from traditional academies and water towns in south China correspond to the psychological and cultural identities of the faculty and students.

By Qiu Jianfa, Jiang Tao, Long Xushui
Source: South Architecture, 2009 Issue 2, P90-93

南京审计学院
NANJING AUDIT INSTITUTE

江南大学
JIANGNAN UNIVERSITY

项目地点：江苏省无锡市
设计时间：2002 年
用地面积：2,000,000 m^2
建筑面积：700,000 m^2
曾获奖项：国际设计竞赛专家评选第一名
教育部优秀建筑规划奖一等奖（2003 年）
广东省城乡规划协会城乡规划设计三等奖（2005 年）

Location: Wuxi, Jiangsu
Design: 2002
Completion: 2006
Site Area: 2,000,000 m^2
GFA: 700,000 m^2
Awards:
The First Place of the International Design Competition
The First Prize of Excellent Architecture and Planning Award by the Ministry of Education (2003)
The Third Prize for Urban and Rural Planning and Design by Guangdong Urban and Rural Planning Society (2005)

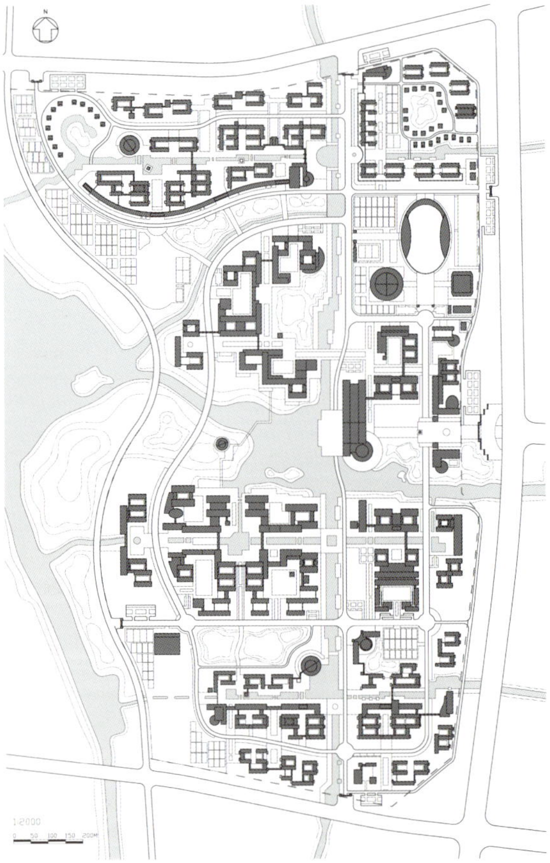

江南大学
JIANGNAN UNIVERSITY

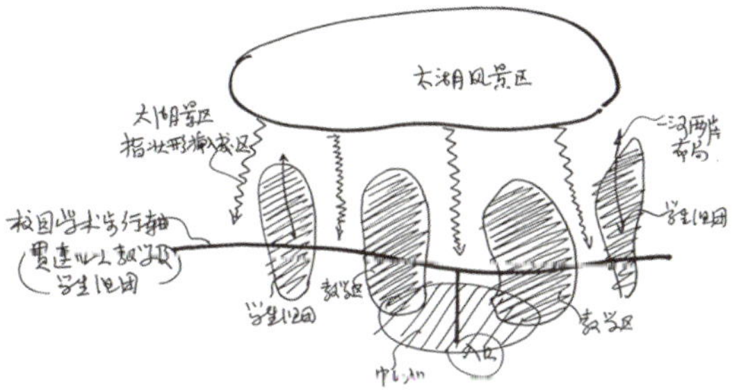

规划设计利用沿中央曲水流觞步行带进行“指状”的布局，在形成校园清晰的功能分区与便捷的流线外，还使校园空间与太湖风景区、长广溪绿化带相互咬合、渗透，有机地融合在一起。“指状”的布局，使各大功能组团呈线形跌宕错落地展开，结合原有水系，形成极具江南水乡街道韵味的校园空间，既延续了江南地域的文脉，也创造了校园特色。

The planning offers a finger-like layout along the central waterfront promenade. This not only realizes a clearly-defined functional zoning and convenient circulation, but also allows the campus space to penetrate into and interweave with the Taihu Scenic Area and Changguangxi Greening Belt. The finger-like layout unfolds the function clusters in a linear and random manner, and, in combination with the existing water system, create the campus space with charm of watery towns to the south of the Yangtze River. This continues the cultural context in the south of the Yangtze River and bestow individuality to the campus.

华南师范大学南海学院 *

NANHAI COLLEGE OF SOUTH CHINA NORMAL UNIVERSITY*

项目地点：广东省佛山市
设计时间：2000 年
竣工时间：2001 年
用地面积：270,000 m²
建筑面积：145,000 m²
曾获奖项：国家级优秀设计项目银奖（2004 年）
中国建筑学会中华人民共和国成立 60 周年建筑创作大奖（2009 年）
中国建筑学会建筑创作奖：佳作奖（2004 年）
建设部优秀建筑工程设计二等奖（2003 年）
教育部优秀建筑设计奖一等奖（2003 年）
广东省注册建筑师协会优秀建筑创作奖：创作奖（2003 年）

Location: Foshan, Guangdong
Design: 2000
Completion: 2001
Site Area: 270,000 m²
GFA: 145,000 m²
Awards:
Silver Award for National Excellent Design Project (2004)
ASC Grand Architectural Creation Award for the 60th Founding Anniversary of PRC (2009)
Honorable Mention of ASC Architectural Creation Award (2004)
The Second Prize for Excellent Construction Engineering Design by the Ministry of Construction (2003)
The First Prize of Excellent Architectural Design Award by the Ministry of Education (2003)
Creation Award of Excellent Architectural Creation Award by Guangdong Chapter of Association of Chinese Registered Architects (2003)

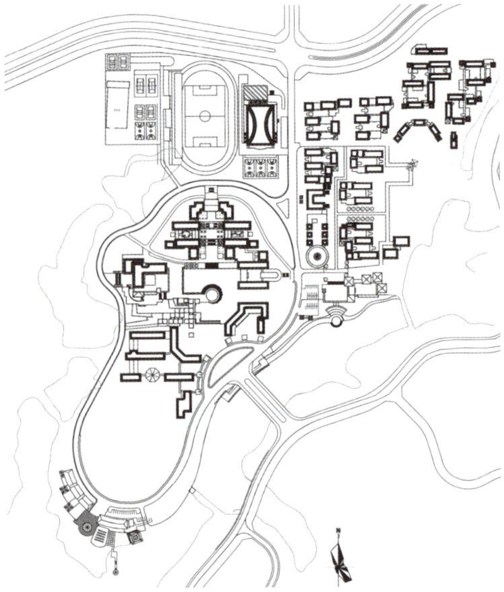

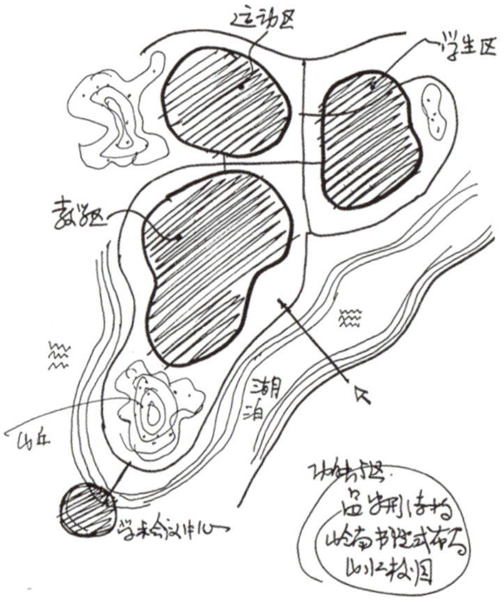

* 华南师范大学南海学院于 2014 年更名为华南师范大学南海校区
* Nanhai College of South China Normal University was renamed to Nanhai Campus of South China Normal University in 2014

华南师范大学南海学院
NANHAI COLLEGE OF SOUTH CHINA NORMAL UNIVERSITY

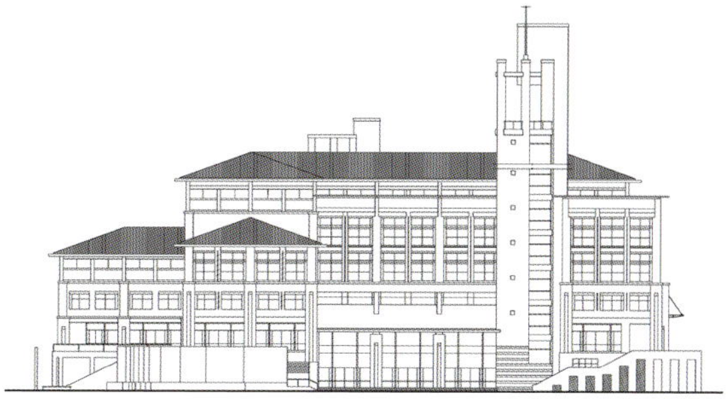

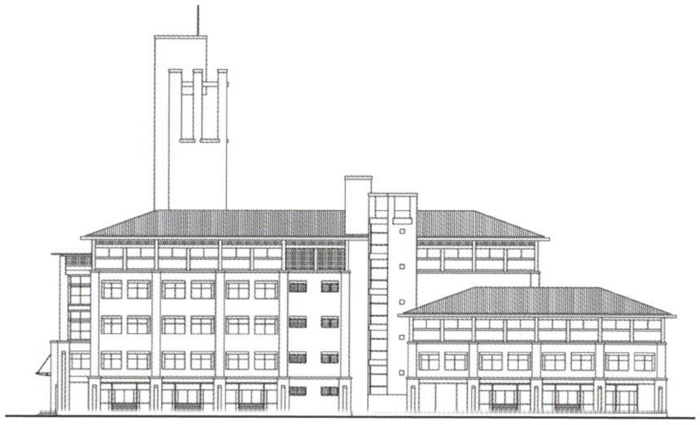

在规划设计中保留了校园内南北两座原生的山丘，作为校园的生态绿核，从而形成了校园的主体结构。建筑围绕绿核布置，使其生态结构尽可能不受人工环境的影响，保持完整与独立。

由于基地以山地为主，在保持自然形态不受破坏的前提之下，将建筑分为四组相对完整的区域，分布于山林之中，因应地形的变化而形成各自的空间特色，彼此间联系便捷而又有所隔离。在建筑设计中，希望通过院落式的布局和富有特色的坡屋顶造型营造浓郁的书院气息。

Two hills in north and south of the campus are reserved as the eco-green core that constitutes main structure of the campus. Buildings are arranged around the green core to minimize the impact brought by the artificial environment to the eco-structure.

As the site features mainly the hilly land, the campus planning, while trying to maintain the natural form of the site, divides the buildings into four relatively complete areas and place them within the mountain forests. The buildings are of their respective spatial features as a result of the changeable terrains, and are conveniently connected to each other while enjoying certain kind of solitude. The architecture design intends to foster highly academic atmosphere through the courtyard layout and the featured slope roofs.

中国矿业大学南湖校区
NANHU CAMPOUS OF CHINA UNIVERSITY OF MINING & TECHNOLOGY

项目地点：江苏省徐州市
设计时间：2002 年
用地面积：1,731,600 m^2
建筑面积：700,000 m^2

Location: Xuzhou, Jiangsu
Design: 2002
Site Area: 1,731,600 m^2
GFA: 700,000 m^2

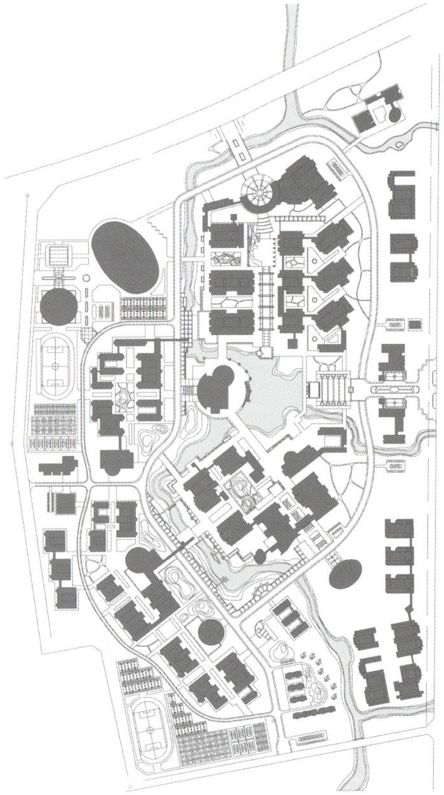

中国矿业大学南湖校区

NANHU CAMPOUS OF CHINA UNIVERSITY OF MINING & TECHNOLOGY

规划以功能分区为先导，布局疏密得当，以多层次、多尺度的组团空间为校园的规划结构体系，并形成以交流、共享空间为核心的校园环境特色。校园位于城市规划的风景区，周边环境依山面水，设计顺应地形高差跌落布局，并将云龙湖水体引入校园，成为重要的景观元素并有效分隔空间，使建筑和空间环境相得益彰。

鉴于中国矿业大学是典型的理工科大学，且地处中原，建筑设计力图创造一种现代、简洁、厚实的风格，并采用方形体块加减的手法来塑造理性化的体量感。在整体统一的基础上，各功能区域的单体建筑形式又各具特色，进一步丰富了校园的肌理形态。

Starting with functional zoning, the plan offers an elaborately devised layout where multi-leveled and multi-scale clustered spaces are created to constitute the campus planning structure and the campus environment is organized around the communication/shared core spaces. As the campus is located in the planned scenic area of the city and embraced by the picturesque water areas and hills, the undulating terrain is respected and followed; meanwhile, the water of Yunlong Lake is introduced into the campus as an important landscape element to effectively separates the spaces and make for a delightful dialogue between the buildings and the spatial environment.

In consideration of the University as a typical university of science and engineering and its geographic location of Central China, the architectural design is aimed to create a modern, minimalistic and solid style, and form a rational sense of volume through addition and reduction of cubic blocks. The singular buildings in the functional areas are of individualized architectural forms while maintaining a kind of overall consistency, further diversifying the fabrics on the campus.

重庆大学虎溪校区
HUXI CAMPUS OF CHONGQING UNIVERSITY

规划方案：
项目地点：重庆市
设计时间：2003 年
竣工时间：2006 年
用地面积：2,460,000 m^2
建筑面积：1,608,000 m^2
曾获奖项：教育部优秀规划设计奖三等奖（2005 年）

教学实验楼群：
项目地点：重庆市
设计时间：2004 年
竣工时间：2006 年
用地面积：35,217 m^2
建筑面积：33,333 m^2
曾获奖项：教育部优秀建筑设计奖三等奖（2007 年）

Master Plan of Huxi Campus of Chongqing University
Location: Chongqing
Design: 2003
Completion: 2006
Site Area: 2,460,000 m^2
GFA: 1,608,000 m^2
Award:
The Third Prize of Excellent Planning and Design Award by the Ministry of Education (2005)

Teaching and Laboratory Building Group, Huxi Campus of Chongqing University
Location: Chongqing
Design: 2004
Completion: 2006
Site Area: 35,217 m^2
GFA: 33,333 m^2
Award:
The Third Prize of Excellent Architectural Design Award by the Ministry of Education (2007)

本规划方案选择的是一种多途径同山丘地形地貌相结合的方法。首先，对中心地区集中的山丘群进行整体保留，并引入水体形成中心生态带的山水环境。其次，对基地中少量集中山丘进行组团保留，形成各个功能区之间的小型山丘绿化；最后，对基地中少量的独立山丘实行单体保留，并使其成为建筑组团之中的特色景观。对山丘的保留使建筑物分南北两侧分别蜿蜒放射而出，形成“非”字状的类似“凤凰展翅”形的规划结构。

第二教学楼及第一实验楼在设计过程中顺应地形起伏的特征，以外部空间的城市设计为核心，创造具有山地特色的多层次的交往空间。结合楼梯、天桥、宽敞的走廊将分栋教学楼联系起来，形成具有独特趣味的动态空间。轻盈活泼的现代山地建筑造型在设计中充分借鉴重庆地区“借天不借地”传统的建筑手法，将建筑底层架空，形成轻盈活泼的山地建筑形象。

The campus planning combines with the mountainous landform via various means. First, all hills clustering in the central area are reserved and water elements are introduced to create attractive views of the central eco area. Second, a small number of free-standing hills within the site are respectively reserved and turned into featured views among the building groups. The reserved hills generate a composition where the buildings meander outwardly on south and north sides, resembling a phoenix with opened wings.

The designs for No.2 Teaching Building and No.1 Laboratory Building follow the undulating landform and center on the urban design of exterior spaces to create multi-leveled communication space with characteristics of mountainous areas. Staircases, foot bridges and broad corridors connect single teaching buildings, forming the uniquely interesting and dynamic spaces. With reference to the traditional architectural technique in Chongqing area that pays attention to the sky instead of the land, the ground floors of the buildings are opened up to shape the light and lively building image up with characteristics of mountainous region.

重庆大学虎溪校区
HUXI CAMPUS OF CHONGQING UNIVERSITY

东华大学松江校区
SONGJIANG CAMPUS OF DONGHUA UNIVERSITY

项目地点：上海市
设计时间：2002 年
竣工时间：2008 年
用地面积：999,000 m^2
建筑面积：400,000 m^2

Location: Shanghai
Design: 2002
Completion: 2008
Site Area: 999,000 m^2
GFA: 400,000 m^2

本规划方案力图塑造出高效舒适的校园交通联系网络和功能完善的建筑组团，从而营造一个活力四射的新校园。在方案中，教学区、实验区、学院区围绕校园中心生态核布置，布局紧凑，各组团之间步行交通联系快速、便捷，大大方便了师生的工作和学习，使教学活动高效运作，建筑的集中布置还能为环境的塑造提供更大的发挥余地，也有利于提高学校发展的灵活性。同时，创造优美浪漫的生态校园也是规划设计中重要的切入点。

方案中，一方面将原有河道张家沂之水引入校园中心区，在校园中心形成一个生态水体，另一方面对张家沂原有河岸线及沿岸景观进行艺术化处理，形成一条滨水景观共享绿化带，整个校园的生态系统就以此“一湖一带”为核心而展开。教学区组团沿湖依据学术次轴采取折线布置，将中心区生态景观最大限度地引入教学组团中；实验区布局紧凑，分为三个相似的组团，组团间为大片的线性绿化带，垂直于中心生态水体，在空间上实现了中心生态空间和实验区之间的相互渗透，线性绿化带是中心生态核在实验区组团的延伸。

The planning scheme strives to create an efficient and comfortable campus traffic network and fully-functional building clusters to develop a vibrant and dynamic new campus. The teaching zone, the experiment zone and the academy zone are centered on the ecological core located in the middle of the campus, presenting a rather compact layout and offering convenient and fast pedestrian connections among the building clusters. This would bring great convenience to the teachers and students for their work and learning and encourage the highly efficient teaching activities on campus. The centralized building layouts not only provide more possibilities in shaping up the environment, but also allow for more flexible university development.

In the planning and design, creating a beautiful and romantic ecological campus is also an important entry point. In order to achieve this, the water from the existing watercourse Zhangjiayi is introduced to the central area of the campus to form an ecological lake; meanwhile the existing banks of Zhangjiayi and the riverfront landscape are artistically treated to create a shared landscaped waterfront green belt. The ecosystem of the campus is then developed around the said “One Lake and One Belt”. The teaching zone zigzags by the lake along the secondary academic axis, interweaving the views of the central area into the teaching zone. The experiment zone in a compact layout is divided into three similar clusters, among which large linear green belts, which are perpendicular to the central lake and function as the extension of the central green, are provided to integrate central green with the zone.

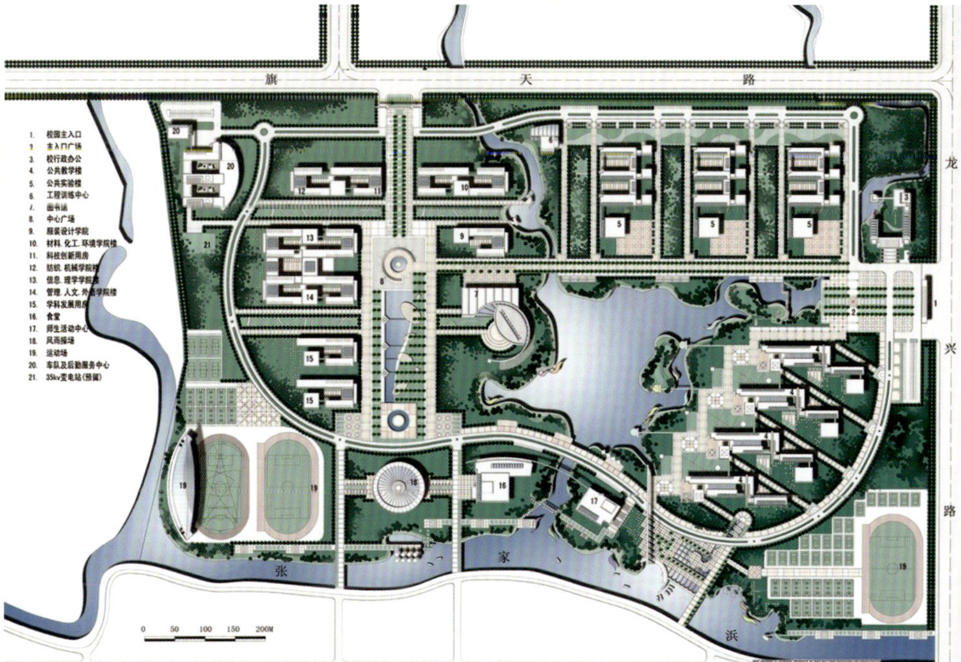

东华大学松江校区
SONGJIANG CAMPUS OF DONGHUA UNIVERSITY

温州肯恩大学
WENZHOU-KEAN UNIVERSITY

项目地点：浙江省温州市
设计时间：2012 年
用地面积：700,000 m^2
建筑面积：306,000 m^2

Location: Wenzhou, Zhejiang
Design: 2012
Site Area: 700,000 m^2
GFA: 306,000 m^2

规划以中国园林水乡意境结合典雅的建筑造型，表达中美校园文化的融合，体现独特的书院校园风貌。充分利用现有自然基地条件，从整个校园生态环境到单体建筑内部，营造多层次的园林空间，展现“山水温州”的地域特色，营造出高雅文化氛围的校园环境，起到“环境育人”的作用。在建筑布局上，突出“前庭后园，特色书院”，形成“前广场，后花园”的格局环境，广场建筑群呼应城市绿化广场轴线，布局严谨有序；依山而建的学院建筑群延续传统书院空间，布局轻松自由。

The planning intends to integrate the campus cultures of China and the U.S. and embody the unique features of an academy-like campus by blending elegant building forms into an environment of Chinese gardens and waterside sceneries. Natural conditions of the site are given full play in the design. Multi-leveled garden spaces are created not only in the larger ecological environment of the campus but also in the interior of the singular buildings, so as to present the local features of Wenzhou, a city of mountains and waters, create a campus with an elegant cultural atmosphere and promote education undertaking in a proper environment. In the architectural composition, the ideas of forecourt, back garden and featured academy are referenced, forming a spatial layout consisting of a square in the front and a garden at the back. The building clusters in the square, in a strict and order layout, echo with the axis that runs through the urban greenery square. Those constructed by the hillside are arranged in a rather easy and free layout, creating some traditional academic spaces on campus.

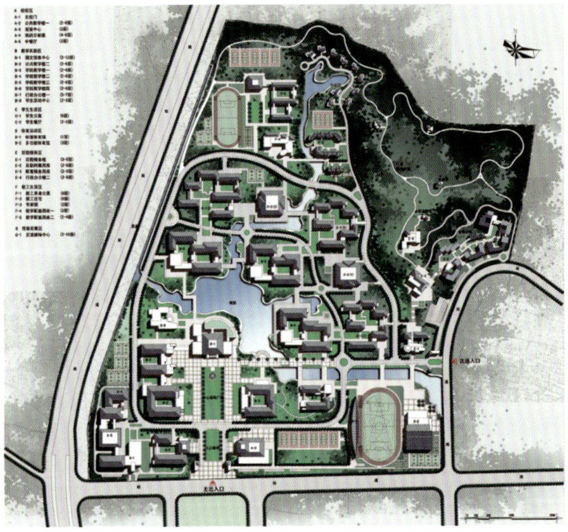

泰州中学
TAIZHOU HIGH SCHOOL

采用传统书院中轴对称的序列空间布局模式，整体规划以中国传统书院的结构为依托，并融入现代校园空间特征，营造出“一带两轴两院四分区”的多元渗透规划格局，其中南北贯通的文化主轴，空间层层进深，从文化石到图文信息中心再到文化亭，每处空间都设置相关的文化视觉焦点和文化主题。校园以礼仪性的书院主空间为主轴，再融入错落有致的书院园林空间，空间层层相套开合有度，传达出重教尚文、外儒内道的精神内涵。校区中的教学区和办公区采用庭院式空间布局模式，分设荟雅院、尚礼院、崇儒院、达理院和敬师院。

建筑造型以现代的手法表现出传统的意蕴，整体风格精致、典雅，实现现代和传统的有机结合，重点表达出校园的文化性和时代感。图文信息中心位于校园的中心位置，建筑立面暗含字母“H”之形，建筑形体上错落的窗洞和木百叶模拟图书放置在书架上的形态，同时将图书馆首层局部抬高架空形成学术交流和观景平台。整栋建筑端庄典雅，成为校园的视觉焦点和标志性建筑。学生公寓和学术交流中心沿湖而设，强化校园后区空间氛围。各种自然元素渗透其中，局部点缀亭台楼榭，烘托出校园静谧典雅的氛围。从校园规划到建筑单体应既能传承校园的文脉，亦能满足现代教学功能以及审美的需求，表达出时代感和文化性，力求体现泰州中学继往开来、从容大气的特征。

In a centrally symmetric layout of traditional academic buildings, the overall planning further integrates modern campus spaces into the basic structure of traditional Chinese academic buildings, presenting a diverse and penetrative framework consisting of one belt, two axes, two courtyards and four zones. The north-south cultural axis runs through layers of spaces, from the cultural stone to the library and information center, and then to the cultural pavilion, each designed with cultural visual highlights and cultural themes. The ritual academic space, as the main axis of the campus, is further integrated with the well-organized and appropriately-interconnected academic landscape spaces, demonstrating the spiritual dimensions of advocating literacy and education and integrating Confucian and Taoist. Teaching and office spaces are designed in a courtyard-style layout and divided into Huiyayuan, Shangliyuan, Chongruyuan, Daliyuan and Jingshiyuan respectively.

The building captures the traditional aesthetics with modern expression. The intricate and elegant overall style shows the organic integration of modernity and tradition, highlighting cultural dimension and underlying trend of times. The library and information center is positioned in central campus, with building facade indicating a vague shape of letter H, and the staggered window openings and wooden louvers resembling books on shelves. At the same time, the first floor of the library is partially elevated as a platform for academic exchanges and landscape viewing. The solemn and elegant building is the centerpiece and landmark of the campus. Students' dormitory and academic exchange center by the lake reinforce the vibe of back space. With various natural elements distributed throughout and pavilions sporadically scattered, a tranquil campus environment is fostered. Both campus planning and singular building design should both transmit the cultural heritage and meet modern teaching functions and aesthetic purposes with modern sense and cultural character, so as to fully demonstrate the calm and generous Taizhou High School inheriting the past and exploring the future.

广东省河源市特殊教育学校
HEYUAN SPECIAL EDUCATION SCHOOL, GUANGDONG

项目地点：广东省河源市
设计时间：2017 年
竣工时间：2018 年
建筑面积：9,383 m^2（含地下建筑面积 1,984 m^2）

Location: Heyuan, Guangdong
Design: 2017
Completion: 2018
GFA: 9,383 m^2 (Including a below-grade floor area of 1,984 m^2)

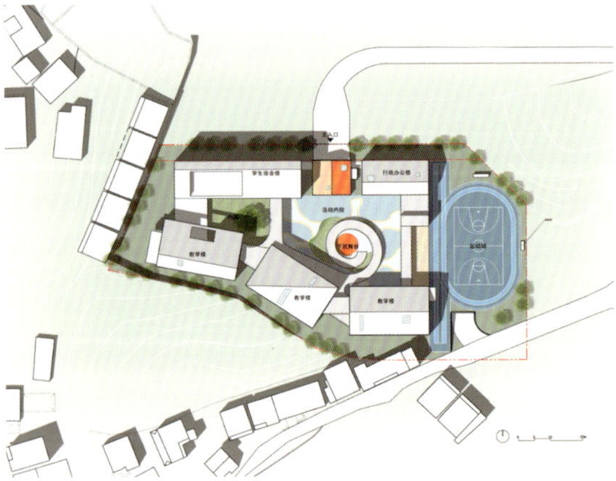

广东省河源市特殊教育学校
HEYUAN SPECIAL EDUCATION SCHOOL, GUANGDONG

村中“村”

学校招收的学生大多来自于用地周边的居民。自由紧密排布的小房屋、曲折的村道是孩子们最熟悉的元素。设计从“村落”的原型入手，将学校按照使用功能拆分为若干个小体量建筑。各体量顺应用地边界自由布置，最大可能围合成内向的活动院落。低层高密度的校园空间特质、灵活的体块布局与周边村落相得益彰。从村落到学校，空间尺度自然过渡，增强学生对校园空间的认同感。

校中“家”

随着城市的发展，周边民居“命运未卜”。学校的建筑语言力图为孩子们保留最初“家”的记忆：各功能体量采用不同的坡顶形式，形成独一无二的小房子，增强标识性；立面设计上，建筑选用与周边浅色调民居相呼应的白色，东西山墙也采取与民居同尺度的方洞，自由散落在白墙之上，在体现民居特色之余不乏现代感。各个小房子通过自然柔和的连廊联系为整体，好似蜿蜒的村道般在建筑之间流动。

"Village" in Villages

Most of the students enrolled in the schools come from the surrounding dwellings. Therefore, they are most familiar with the elements of the small, freely and closely arranged houses and the winding village roads. Starting with the prototype of the "village", this design divides the school into several small-sized buildings according to different functions. Each building is most likely to be integrated into an inward courtyard for activities by being freely arranged along the boundaries. The low-rise and high-density campus space and the flexible block layout consort with the surrounding villages. Consequently, the space naturally transits from villages to schools, enhancing students' sense of identity for the campus space.

"Home" in Schools

With the development of the city, the fate of surrounding houses is unknown. The architectural language of schools seeks to preserve the original memories of "home" for students: each building adopts different roof forms to create a unique small house, strengthening its identification; As for the facade design, the buildings are painted in white, which echoes to the surrounding light-colored houses, and the east and west gables are carved with the same square holes, freely scattering on the white walls, as the residential houses, which is no lack of modernity in embodying the characteristics of the residential houses. Moreover, the small houses are connected as a whole by a natural soft corridor which flows like a meandering village road in buildings.

广东省河源市特殊教育学校
HEYUAN SPECIAL EDUCATION SCHOOL, GUANGDONG

六盘水民族中学高中部

LIUPANSHUI MINZU HIGH SCHOOL

项目地点：贵州省六盘水市
设计时间：2014 年
竣工时间：2016 年
建筑面积：159,679 m^2

Location: Liupanshui, Guizhou
Design: 2014
Completion: 2016
GFA: 159,679 m^2

六盘水民族中学高中部位于教育城东南侧，为一所能容纳6000人、120班的省级示范性高中。学校片区为山地、丘陵地区，地势起伏明显。为了减少对自然的破坏和节省建设开支，本设计并未大面积地改造地形，而是在遵循尊重自然、尊重本土特色的前提下进行，打造与自然融为一体，形成具有地域特色的人文建筑景观。在建筑布局上，整个设计并没有刻意追求轴线。布局以顺势为法，空间以错落为趣。

Liupanshui Minzu High School is a provincial demonstration high school of 6,000 students and 120 classes located in the southeast of Education City. The site is located in mountainous and hilly region and features undulating terrain. In order to reduce the damage to nature and to save construction costs, we do not transform the terrain on a large scale, but on the premise of respecting nature and local characteristics, creating humanistic architecture and landscape with regional characteristics. In the layout, The building layout does not deliberately follow any axis; instead, it responds to the site conditions to create intriguingly staggered spaces.

六盘水民族中学高中部
LIUPANSHUI MINZU HIGH SCHOOL

常州田家炳高级中学
CHANGZHOU TIANJIABING SENIOR HIGH SCHOOL

项目地点：江苏省常州市
设计时间：2014 年
竣工时间：2017 年
建筑面积：70,962 m^2

Location: Changzhou, Jiangsu
Design: 2014
Completion: 2017
GFA: 70,962 m^2

常州市田家炳高级中学位于古运河畔、同济桥堍，设计灵感来源于中国传统建筑群院落空间，以方格网和轴线来控制建筑群体的生成，形成有序的建筑秩序。本案借鉴中国传统规划布局方式，采用“一心两轴多点”的形式来组织整个校区的规划设计，通过轴线、对称、均衡等手法强化校园的秩序感，使整个校区规划布局疏密有致、虚实相生、秩序井然。

Changzhou Tianjiabing Senior High School is located on the bank of the ancient canal and Tongji Bridge. The design is inspired by the courtyard space of traditional Chinese buildings. The square grid and the axis control the formation of the building group and form an orderly architectural order. This project draws on the traditional Chinese planning and layout method, adopts the form of "one heart, two axes and multiple points" to organize the planning and design of the entire campus, and strengthens the sense of order of the campus through the methods of axis, symmetry and balance, so that the layout of the entire campus is dense and accurate, relatively and orderly.

中国地质大学（北京）校园总体规划方案设计
CAMPUS MASTER PLANNING FOR CHINA UNIVERSITY OF GEOSCIENCES (BEIJING)

项目地点：北京市
设计时间：2019 年
建筑面积：706,000 m^2

Location: Beijing
Design: 2019
GFA: 706,000 m^2

该项目在中国地质大学现有校区的基础上进行设计，校园现状有多个开放空间和轴线序列，但缺乏联系，难以形成连续高效的步行网络，应加强各开放空间之间的联系，形成连续复合的校园室外交往结构。

方案提取现有片段化的公共空间和轴线关系，拆除部分杂乱分布的老建筑，梳理校园公共空间界面。加强各部分公共空间之间的步行交通联系，形成开合有序的公共空间脉络和整体统一的校园形象。结合校园文化打造多个开放公共空间，塑造有场所记忆的景点。

项目充分利用地下空间，发掘校园的最大建设可能性。通过在新建教学楼、宿舍、绿地及广场下方进行大规模的地下空间开发，为校园增加了接近 20 万 m^2 的建筑面积。将地质大学打造成复合研究型、生态节能型、创新示范型校园，引领北京高校改扩建先河。

The project is designed on the existing campus of China University of Geosciences(Beijing). There are many open spaces and axes in the campus, but it is difficult to form a continuous and efficient walking network due to the lack of connection. It is necessary to strengthen the connection between the open spaces and form a continuous and compound outdoor communication area for campus.

The scheme extracts the existing relationship of public space and axis in the campus, demolishes some old disorderly buildings, and reforms the campus public space interface. Strengthen the pedestrian traffic connection between all parts of the public space, and form an orderly public space and an overall unified campus image. And we combine with the campus culture to create a number of memory scenic spots in the open space.

By making full use of the underground space, we can explore the maximum construction possibility in the campus. Through the large-scale underground space development under the newly-built teaching buildings, dormitories, parklands and squares, we have nearly 200,000 m^2 construction area more for the campus. The University of Geosciences will be built into a compound research-oriented, ecological energy-saving and innovative demonstration campus, leading the transformation and expansion construction of universities in Beijing.

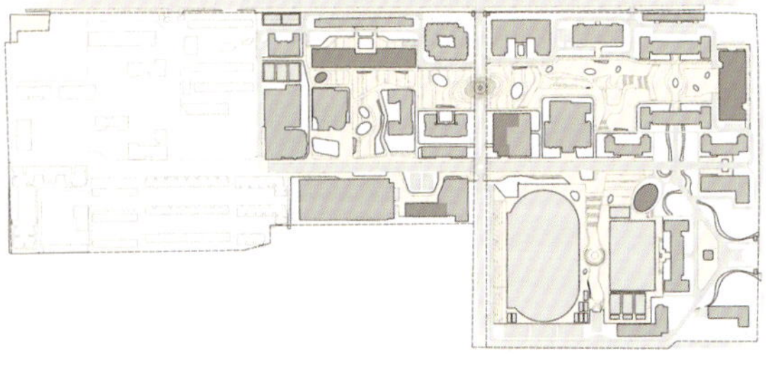

中国地质大学（北京）校园总体规划方案设计
CAMPUS MASTER PLANNING FOR CHINA UNIVERSITY OF GEOSCIENCES (BEIJING)

天津科技大学泰达校区规划设计

PLANNING AND DESIGN FOR TEDA CAMPUS OF TIANJIN UNIVERSITY OF SCIENCE & TECHNOLOGY

项目地点：天津市
设计时间：2012 年
竣工时间：2014 年
用地面积：1,203,653 m^2
建筑面积：1,004,974 m^2

Location: Tianjin
Design: 2012
Completion: 2014
Site Area: 1,203,653 m^2
GFA: 1,004,974 m^2

天津科技大学泰达校区规划设计既有新建基地，又有旧基地扩建以及功能置换改造，如何处理好众多不同的现状条件以及现有元素，使三个割裂的校区整合为一体，是设计面临的最大挑战。通过以下四点设计构思，使得三个校区重新整合为各功能空间一气呵成的整体校园：一体化的校园格局——通过东西走向的校园人文轴线串连起三大区；核心共享的校园资源——在校园重心设计了中央的核心共享绿化区域，带动各区联动发展；多层次的校园空间——各空间环环相连，营造多层次的人文氛围；可持续的发展规划——综合考虑日后校区发展，连通东西轴线，形成多核心的校园人文礼仪轴线。

The planning and design of TEDA Campus involves new buildings, existing building expansion and functional replacement. Hence, it poses the biggest challenge in design to properly tackle the existing conditions and elements thus combine the three disconnected campuses. Four main concepts are developed in design. First, create an integrated campus layout with the east-west humanistic axis linking up the three main zones. Second, realize sharing of campus resources by designing a shared green zone in the center of the campus to drive interactive development of the zones. Third, form a multi-leveled campus spaces which are inter-connected logically to form a diverse and highly humanistic atmosphere. Fourth, establish a sustainable development plan with comprehensive considerations to future campus development, e.g. linking up the east axis and the west axis and forming a humanistic ceremony axis on campus with multiple cores. The above four design concepts help integrate the three separated campuses into a complete one in which functions and spaces appear to be created at one go.

方太大学
FOTILE UNIVERSITY

项目地点：浙江省宁波市
设计时间：2017—2018
用地面积：46,870 m²
建筑面积：63,848 m²

Location: Ningbo, Zhejiang
Design: 2017-2018
Site Area: 46,870 m²
GFA: 63,848 m²

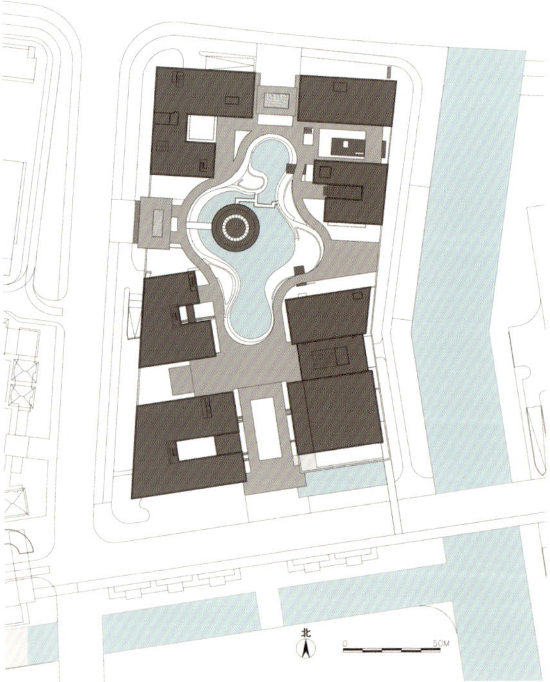

方太大学的设计以儒道思想作为出发点，使企业的儒道文化及儒家管理模式在建筑空间中得以转译。儒道思想强调环境育人的重要性，设计从传统中国园林中获取灵感，通过现代的手法提取传统建筑的院落、庭园、敞廊等空间元素，在符合企业大学使用功能的条件下，塑造具有传统文化内涵的空间层次。

建筑的外轮廓布局方正且遵循秩序，通过隐含的轴线序列隐喻传统文化中的礼仪准则；中央庭院以曲廊组织建筑群落，充分呼应中国传统园林“境贵乎深、不曲不深也”的视觉想象和思想意境，同时形成连续多变的公共交往空间，适应功能需求。

Based on Confucianism and Taoism, which emphasize the importance of the environment's nurture of people, the design proposal of Fotile University interprets the Confucianism spirit of the company and Confucian management model in architectural spaces. Inspired by the traditional Chinese gardens, we utilize various spatial elements in traditional architecture such as courtyards, gardens and corridors with modern techniques to establish a spatial hierarchy with rich cultural connotation within the functional framework of the university.

The buildings have straight and regular layout, with the sequences of the hidden axes implicating the ritual rules in traditional culture. Building blocks are organized with the zigzag corridors in the central courtyard, fully demonstrating the visual and ideology of "winding path leads to profound scenes" pursued in the traditional Chinese gardens. In doing so, the continuous and varied public spaces are formed to meet the functional needs.

方太大学
FOTILE UNIVERSITY

广东以色列理工学院
GUANGDONG ISRAEL INSTITUTE OF TECHNOLOGY

项目地点：广东省汕头市
竣工时间：2015 年
建筑面积：90,500 m^2

Location: Shantou, Guangdong
Completion: 2015
GFA: 90,500 m^2

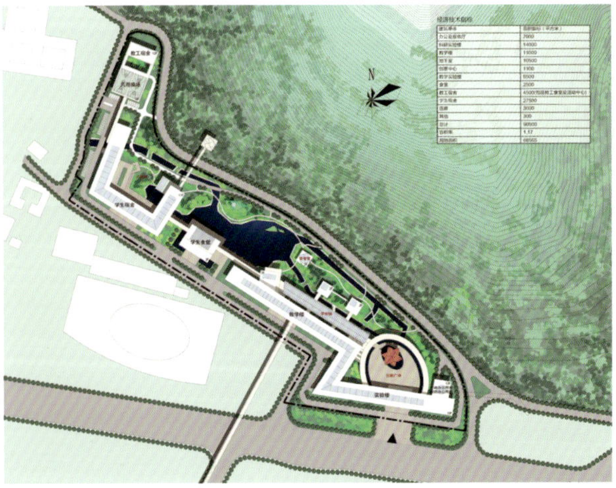

广东以色列理工学院
GUANGDONG ISRAEL INSTITUTE OF TECHNOLOGY

新型的国际性合作大学应当是传承校园历史文化、独具空间特色的个性化校园。通过研究分析，我们总结出了拱券与叠涩、光影和序列、浅色立面等以色列现代建筑的特有风格，并将其作为融入地域文化的承接点。

校区地形极具特色，用地狭长，场地较为平坦。设计将主要功能建筑沿城市干道形成条状布置，宽度约 20 m，满足教学实验的功能平面要求。建筑造型呈起伏的山形，与北侧的桑浦山互相呼应形成山谷之势，新颖的山形建筑造型又突出了以色列理工学院世界一流大学所具有的勇于创新的校园风格。建筑中部以学生食堂将教学区与生活区区分，既创造了建筑的节奏感，又避免了对已建成的汕头大学交流中心的视线遮挡，与汕头大学融为一体。建筑通过架空、平台、连廊、空中花园将绿色引入，构成了立体、活跃的研究型校园氛围和空间感受。低碳节能技术的引入以及一系列适宜生态技术的采用，将新校区打造成示范性的可持续发展的绿色生态校园。

A new type of international cooperative university must be a unique one that not only carries on the heritage of the original university but also has its own characteristics in space. Following studies and analysis, we decided to incorporate the unique elements of modern Israeli architecture into the design, such as arches and stacking, light and shadow, sequence, and light-colored facade and have them integrated with the local culture.

The long and narrow site is quite flat, and major functional buildings are arranged along the urban road in a belt layout of about 20 m wide to ensure the functional requirements of teaching and experiments. The building form is an imitation of the undulating mountain, which not only echoes to the Sangpu Mt. on the north but also demonstrates a unique and innovative campus style that Israel Institute of Technology has as a world-class university. In the center of the site, a student canteen separates the teaching and lab area from the living area, creating a rhythm of architecture, avoid blocking views to the already built Exchange Center of Shantou University, and making the site fully integrated with the campus of the University. With elevated ground floor, platforms, corridors and sky gardens, the greenery is introduced into the site, fostering a dynamic research-oriented campus ambiance and spatial experience. The introduction of low-carbon energy-saving technologies and a number of ecological technologies makes the new campus a model of green ecological campus that supports sustainable development.

广东药科大学云浮校区
YUNFU CAMPUS OF GUANGDONG PHARMACEUTICAL UNIVERSITY

项目地点：广东省云浮市
设计时间：2017 年
竣工时间：2019 年
用地面积：120 hm^2
建筑面积：408,000 m^2

Location: Yunfu, Guangdong
Design: 2017
Completion: 2019
Site Area: 120 hm^2
GFA: 408,000 m^2

广东药科大学云浮校区选址于云浮市西江新城组团的文教片区内。校园紧邻云都大道、云信大道、康盛路等城市主要干道。附近有即将建成的高品质住宅小区，以及城轨站、客运站等重要交通设施。城市生态廊道穿越场地，周边山体、绿地、水体等丰富的景观要素为新校区的建设提供了得天独厚的自然条件。

Yunfu Campus of Guangdong Pharmaceutical University is located in the cultural and educational area of Xijiang New Town, Yunfu. The Campus adjoins the main urban trunk roads such as Yundu Avenue, Yunxin Avenue and Kangsheng Road. Premium housing estates and key transportation facilities including an inter-city rail station and a bus passenger station will be completed in the adjacent locations. An urban green corridor running through the site and the surrounding mountains, green space and water bodies provide rich landscaping elements for the new campus.

广东药科大学云浮校区

海南大学海甸校区更新改造

RENEWAL AND RECONSTRUCTION OF HAIDIAN CAMPUS OF HAINAN UNIVERSITY

项目地点：海南省海口市
设计时间：2017 年
建筑面积：1,310,000 m²

Location: Haikou, Hainan
Design: 2017
GFA: 1,310,000 m²

海南大学海甸校区更新改造

RENEWAL AND RECONSTRUCTION OF HAIDIAN CAMPUS OF HAINAN UNIVERSITY

海南大学

1. 容城纳海

设计充分发挥校园原有区位优势，将校园与城、海相融合。结合校园的发展需求，与周边城市空间协同发展。同时改变校园原有封闭的空间格局，打开校园南侧的用地界面，强化南向校园形象入口，形成向海开放的纳海形态。

2. 整体校园

通过适宜尺度的景观开放公共活动带将校园东西两湖紧密联系；结合道路交通组织优化，强化校园的南北轴线形象与空间，串联校园的各个空间节点，打造脉络清晰的校园复合“十字形”空间架构，形成网络化的整体校园空间。

3. 最美热带校园

结合整体校园空间结构的升级优化和校园用地功能的调整，推进校园景观环境和绿化植被的整体意境塑造，通过若干特色景区的规划设计，营造具有浓烈热带风情的美丽校园环境。

4. 地域风貌绿色校园

吸取海南的地域特色、建筑文化和空间文化特色，结合绿色建筑改造，创造地域风貌特征明显、生态节能兼并的绿色校园。

5. 交往性创新校园

在校园的人流汇集点、景观轴带穿插植入学习、运动、休闲、餐饮、社团活动等设施，形成多元复合、有利于交往的研究型校园。同时整合校园各处可建设用地，预留“产学研”发展空间，鼓励校园创新输出。

6. 可持续发展校园

综合考虑校园现状建筑质量及用地规划的布局，对部分校园功能及建筑进行功能的置换与合并，腾挪出更多的校园可建设用地和多用性建筑。同时，对校园的建设进行合理的分期，确保校园核心的结构稳定，形成由内向外的可持续发展校园。

Ⅰ. A campus embracing the city and the sea

The design gives full play to the advantages of the location of the Campus and integrates it with the city and the sea. Aiming at coordinated development with surrounding urban spaces, it changes the previous enclosed spatial layout by opening up the southern interface of the campus. In this way, the southern entrance of the campus is emphasized and a welcoming gesture to embrace the sea established.

Ⅱ. A holistic campus

An open and landscaped public activity belt in attractive scale establishes close connection between the two lakes in the east and west of the campus. The optimized road traffic system emphasizes the presence and space of the north-south axis which connects various spatial nodes of the campus into a clearly articulated cross-shaped spatial structure and a networked and holistic campus space.

Ⅲ. A beautiful tropical campus

With the upgraded and optimized spatial structure and adjusted land use on the campus, the overall artistic design of landscape and greening is refined. Several featured scenes are planned and designed to create a beautiful tropical campus environment.

Ⅳ. A green campus with local features

The design incorporates the features of local culture, architecture and space in Hainan and employs the green building technologies to create a green campus with distinctive local features and energy-efficient functionality.

Ⅴ. An innovative campus for communications

At public gathering nodes on campus, the landscape axis is interspersed with facilities for learning, sports, leisure, F&B and community activities to cultivate a diverse, integrated and research-oriented campus that facilitates communication and exchanges. At the same time, available construction lands on campus are reserved as spaces for "industry-university-research" development to encourage outputs of campus innovation.

Ⅵ .A sustainable campus

Considering the quality of existing campus buildings and the site layout, some campus functions and buildings are replaced and combined to release more space for development of multi-purpose buildings. The well planned phased construction ensures a stable core structure of the campus and a sustainable campus from inside out.

海南大学观澜湖校区规划方案设计

PLANNING AND DESIGN FOR MISSION HILLS CAMPUS OF HAINAN UNIVERSITY

项目位置：海南省海口市
设计时间：2020 年
用地面积：449,934.18 m^2
建筑面积：36.30 万 m^2

Location: Haikou, Hainan
Design: 2020
Site Area: 449,934.18 m^2
GFA: 363,000 m^2

设计以创新姿态延续校园文脉，对标国际高水平校园建设，适应海南城市旅游文化特色、热带气候特征和独特的场地地质地貌环境，以打造创新示范型、集约复合型、特色生态型校园为总体定位。规划形成“一环一带多中心”的结构，依托开放连续的生态景观区布置公共服务设施，居于核心的学习共享中心涵盖了公共教学、学院实验、阅览、会议、校行政办公等多样功能，环形建筑形态彰显了校园的标志性、国际性、现代性，集约复合的空间模式，有利于促进学科交叉共享和现代教育理念的引入。校园内部主要机动车道呈复合环状布置，步行游览系统结合建筑布局和景观节点营建，构筑出科学有序的交通体系。单体设计对地形高差和现状地质巧妙利用，形成立体化的景观空间和活动场地，并应对热带地区建筑对遮阳通风和生态节能的需求，运用多样的、经济的被动式节能手段，打造因地制宜、绿色生态的校园空间环境。

Benchmarking against world-leading campuses, the design innovatively continues the cultural and historical context of Hainan University and responds to the local tourism culture and tropical climate, as well as the unique geology and geomorphology of the site. The project aims to create an example of innovation-oriented and ecological campus with intensive and mixed-use functional layout. The overall planning structure is featured by "one ring, one belt and multiple centers". Public service facilities are provided in combination with the open, continuous ecological landscape area. The shared learning center in the core comprises various functions such as public teaching, experiment, reading, conference, school administrative office, etc. The circular architectural form becomes the icon of the international and modern campus, while the intensive and complex spatial form enables better interdisciplinary sharing and the implementation of modern education philosophy. Main motor vehicle lanes on the campus are planned into a compound ring layout, while the pedestrian tour system is provided in view of the architectural layout and landscape nodes. Together, they contribute to a reasonable and orderly traffic system on the campus. Singular buildings are designed to tactfully utilize elevation difference and existing geological conditions, creating multi-leveled landscape and activity spaces. The demands of buildings in tropical zones for shading, ventilation and energy conservation are addressed through diverse and cost-effective passive energy-saving methods, which make the green campus well suit the local conditions.

海南大学观澜湖校区规划方案设计
PLANNING AND DESIGN FOR MISSION HILLS CAMPUS OF HAINAN UNIVERSITY

青岛大学胶州校区
JIAOZHOU CAMPUS OF QINGDAO UNIVERSITY

项目地点：山东省青岛市
设计时间：2017 年
用地面积：214 hm^2
建筑面积：1,680,000 m^2

Location: Qingdao, Shandong
Design: 2017
Site Area: 214 hm^2
GFA: 1,680,000 m^2

现代书院制大学：一处诗意栖居的文化场域，具有自治自洽的生活方式和雍容博雅的文化氛围。

“讲于堂，习于斋”的书院式大学，是实现通识教育，才学兼修的理想大学模式。这与青岛大学着重“立德树人”的诉求高度契合。方案提取了西方书院大学中的方院、长廊、塔楼、小镇四个经典元素。突显书院教育模式中师生从游导引、求学问道、自由开放的教学传统。我们将一个院系学科视为拥有共同志趣的学者社群，以此为基础形成书院。青岛大学胶州校区设置五组书院。每个书院都包含教学、科研、住宿、餐饮、运动等功能，有公共共享设施和精神象征，每个书院都是具有独特性格的社区。

现代德式风格：一所风格鲜明的特色名校，吸纳青岛山海灵气，传承青岛大学深厚历史底蕴。

青岛，地处胶东半岛，黄海之滨，深厚的齐鲁文化底蕴与近现代西方文明在这里交流碰撞，孕育出独特的城市文化。青岛大学胶州校区应当延续青岛独特的建筑风格，力求实现对古典德式建筑风格的现代演绎。建筑组合强调错落有致、视线对景、庭院围合。屋顶形式采用红色筒瓦，与米黄色花岗岩墙面共同形成青岛典型城市意象。立面构图采取古典比例和横三纵五处理手法。在重点建筑和重点界面借鉴古典建筑拱廊空间，形成个性鲜明的青岛大学建筑风格。

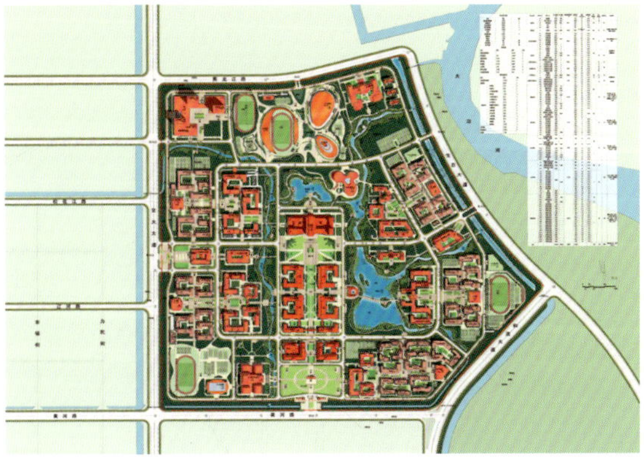

A modern college-university: a poetic habitat and learning environment with autonomous and self-consistent way of living and graceful cultural atmosphere.

A college-university is believed to be an ideal university model that emphasizes general education and the integration of learning and practice. It is highly compatible with the mission of Qingdao University to foster virtue through education. Four classic elements of Western-style college-universities are employed in the design scheme: the Mob Quad, the cloister, tower and small town. Highlighting the free and open learning tradition maximizing teachers' role of guidance and influence and students' pursuit of knowledge and truth, the academy is established with each school as a community of scholars who share common interests. Jiaozhou Campus houses five colleges, each of which provides teaching, research, accommodation, catering, and sports functions and has its own public facilities and emblems. Besides, each college is established as a community with unique characters.

Modern German architectural style: A distinctively featured campus that incorporates the tradition of Qingdao City and carries on the profound legacy of Qingdao University.

Qingdao is located in the Jiaodong Peninsula on the coast of the Yellow Sea. It is the place where the cultural heritage of the ancient states of Qi and Lu in Zhou Dynasty interacts with modern Western civilization and gives rise to a unique urban culture. In this context, Jiaozhou Campus of Qingdao University is expected to carry on the city's unique architectural style and present a contemporary interpretation of the classic German architectural style. In the design, the building clusters are elegantly staggered to create the opposite scenery and enclosing courtyards that are often found in traditional Chinese gardens. Red semi-circular roof tiles in contrast with the beige granite facades are used, portraying a typical urban image of Qingdao city. Classical proportion and a layout with three horizontal and five vertical circulations are adopted in the facade design. Arcade spaces in classical architecture are referenced in the design of major buildings and interfaces to highlight the distinct architectural style of Qingdao University.

青岛大学胶州校区
JIAOZHOU CAMPUS OF QINGDAO UNIVERSITY

哈尔滨工程大学青岛校区
QINGDAO CAMPUS OF HARBIN ENGINEERING UNIVERSITY

项目地点：山东省青岛市
设计时间：2017 年至今
用地面积：1,550,000 m²
建筑面积：1,630,000 m²

Location: Qingdao, Shandong
Design: 2017 to now
Site Area: 1,550,000 m²
GFA: 1,630,000 m²

项目设计立足于青岛城市的地域特色与哈尔滨工程大学（以下简称“哈工程”）校园的现状特征，与校区自然景观相融合，营造倚山临海、与城市紧密相融的校园环境，体现大学的社会责任。在规划建设、设施共享、教育培训、文化活动等方面，加强校区与城市的联系。校区设施功能能够支撑建设世界一流大学的需求。

传承哈工程的历史文化特色，弘扬哈工程精神。新校区规划在校园环境布局上致力于与老校区相呼应，继承哈工程传统，彰显哈工程特征，丰富人文气息。

借鉴中国传统院落式格局，延续哈工程校园的大院式特征，以东西向中心轴线与南北向次轴线为骨架，组织院落式的校园。融入青岛山海城市的特色，校园中心轴线形成与山海相生的景观轴线，将山景、海景融入校园基地内，形成景观绿廊。西侧与山体相融合，是大珠山与校园景观的相互衔接和融合。同时从交通流线和视觉景观上与海滨地带紧密相连，沿滨海路建筑界面环抱海滩，形成与海相生的滨海校园。

建筑在延续端庄典雅的中式格调的基础上，融入现代的金属、玻璃材料，以及遮阳、节能技术，体现新校区的创新与活力。

Based on the regional characteristics of Qingdao city and the current status of the Harbin Engineering University (referred to as HEU), it is in harmony with the natural landscape of the campus, creating an environment that is close to the sea and closely integrated with the city, reflecting the university's social responsibility, planning and construction, facility sharing, and education. Training, cultural activities, etc., strengthen the relationship between the school district and the city. Campus facilities cater the needs of building a world-class university.

Carrying on the historical, cultural and spiritual legacy of HEU, the new campus is planned to echo with the old one in environment and layout, so as to reflect the HEU tradition, characteristics and rich humanistic atmosphere.

With reference to the patterns of traditional Chinese courtyards, the new campus continues the characteristics of the existing HEU courtyards and develops a courtyard-style layout based on the framework of an east-west central axis and a north-south secondary axis. The central axis of the campus reflects the characteristics of Qingdao as a city of mountain and sea, and forms a landscape axis to echo with the mountain and sea views. The landscape axis brings views into the site and forms a green landscape corridor. On the west, the new campus is integrated with mountains, making the campus landscape part of the Dazhu Mountain. Meanwhile, the new campus is closely connected with the seafront in traffic circulation and visual landscape. Buildings along the Bin Hai Lu are planned to embrace the beach, creating a coastal campus that truly interacts with the sea.

While continuing the dignified and elegant Chinese architectural style, the campus buildings employ modern materials like metal and glass, as well as shading and energy-efficient technologies to showcase the innovation and vitality of the new campus.

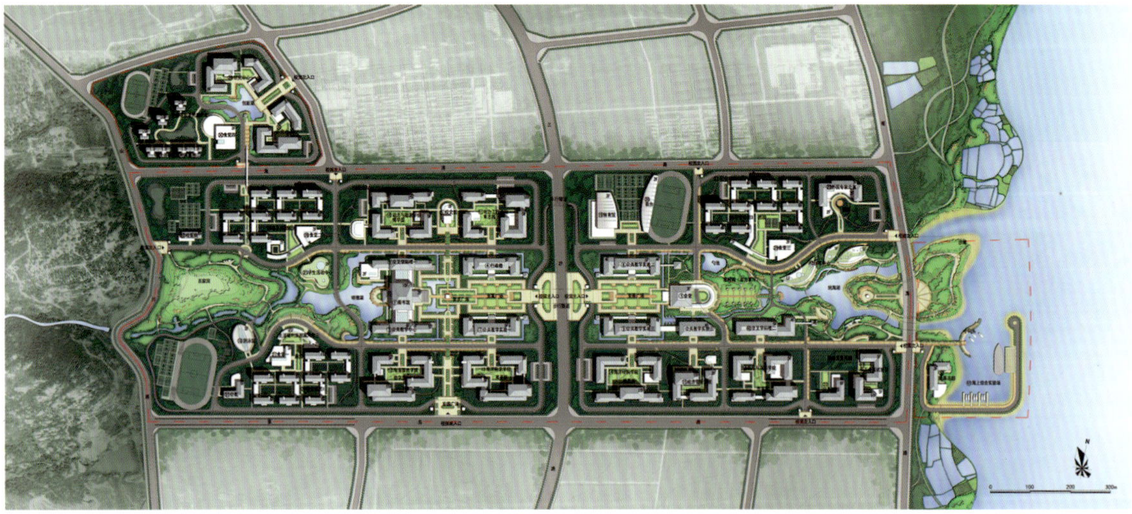

哈尔滨工程大学青岛校区
QINGDAO CAMPUS OF HARBIN ENGINEERING UNIVERSITY

中南财经政法大学武汉学院新校区规划设计
PLANNING AND DESIGN FOR NEW WUHAN CAMPUS OF ZHONGNAN UNIVERSITY OF ECONOMICS AND LAW

项目地点：湖北省武汉市
设计时间：2011 年
竣工时间：2011 年
用地面积：627,800 m^2
建筑面积：414,600 m^2

Location: Wuhan, Hubei
Design: 2011
Completion: 2011
Site Area: 627,800 m^2
GFA: 414,600 m^2

本校区设计以人舒适的步行尺度为基准，因循基地特征，形成主教学区、学院区、宿舍运动区“品”字分区结构，布局紧凑、密度适宜、尺度亲切，为师生的出行提供了便利。途中优美的绿化园林成为重要的交往场所，推动了人与人之间的交往活动。园林布置借鉴中国传统的建筑布局手法，营造校园湖区生态中心，并以中心湖面为核心，将几个园林中心贯通为空间序列，作为整个校区主要的规划骨架与开放空间系统。校园里既有轴线对称、严谨有序、体现理性的书院群落空间，也有适度开放自由，体现文艺的园林式建筑布局，自然地将人工环境与自然环境融合起来，理性与浪漫的情怀相互交织、彼此相融。提出中心园林—共享平台—研究社区的模式，将学院组团以共享园林为中心相邻布置，并在共享中心空间中设计生态园林和公共资料中心等公共平台，实现学科间的资源共享，利于研究社区氛围的形成。

Based on the comfortable walking distance, the campus planning and design responds to the site conditions with a triangular layout that accommodates the main teaching zone, the academic zone and the dorm & sports zone. Such a compact layout of appropriate density and pleasant scale allows the faculty and students to conveniently move around on campus. Beautiful green gardens along the roads become important communication venues and facilitate the interpersonal communications. Traditional Chinese architectural layout is referenced for the garden layout, i.e. a lake is created as the ecological center of the campus to link up the several garden centers to form a spatial sequence that becomes the primary planning framework and the open space system of the entire campus. The campus includes both the academic clusters and spaces, which are axis-symmetrical, precise and orderly to well fit into the rational feature of science study, as well as some open and carefree garden-like buildings that are suitable for liberal arts. Such layout spontaneously combines the artificial environment with the natural one, meanwhile, unites the rational aspects with the romantic elements. As per the proposed pattern of "the central garden-the shared platform-the research community", the academic clusters are centered around and next to the shared garden, while the public platforms like the eco-garden and public info center are placed in the shared central space, thus realize the inter-disciplinary resource sharing and foster a favorable atmosphere for the research community.

中南财经政法大学武汉学院新校区规划设计
PLANNING AND DESIGN FOR NEW WUHAN CAMPUS OF ZHONGNAN UNIVERSITY OF ECONOMICS AND LAW

前海合作区前湾十单元学校项目
SCHOOL IN UNIT 10 OF QIANWAN, QIANHAI NEW DISTRICT

项目地点：广东省深圳市
设计时间：2017—2019 年
建筑面积：139,240 m^2

Location: Shenzhen, Guangdong
Design: 2017-2019
GFA: 139,240 m^2

前海合作区前湾十单元学校项目方案融合环境育人的理念，致力于塑造具有学校价值观和前海精神的教学环境。规划设计打破用地限制，让国际学校与民办学校共享场地，实现统一整体的校园空间格局。

建筑体量向西南面河道公园层层跌落，形成与城市景观的良好关系。校园空间向河道公园敞开，将滨河公园景观引入场地，主要的教学生活空间均可共享滨河景色。

建筑空间传承了岭南建筑的空间特征，采用庭院式的布局，骑楼架空、通风廊道、多层次的架空及遮阳空间等岭南元素，结合立体化的绿化策略，营造了多层次的岭南园林体验。

School in Unit 10 of Qianwan, Qianhai New District integrates the concept of cultivating talents with inspiring environment and is committed to creating a learning environment with the school's values and Qianhai spirit. The planning and design breaks the land restriction and allows international schools and private schools to share the space, so as to achieve a unified overall campus spatial pattern.

The volume of the building falls to the southwest of the river park, forming a good relationship with the urban landscape. The campus space is open to the river park, where the landscape of the riverside park is introduced into the venue, so the main teaching and living spaces can share the riverside scenery.

The architectural space inherits the spatial characteristics of Lingnan architecture, and adopts the layout of courtyard, elevated building, ventilation corridor, multi-leveled overhead and sunshade space and other Lingnan elements. It combines the three-dimensional greening strategy to create a multi-leveled Lingnan garden experience.

前海合作区前湾十单元学校项目
SCHOOL IN UNIT 10 OF QIANWAN, QIANHAI NEW DISTRICT

广东番禺中学长隆学校

CHIMELONG CAMPUS OF GUANGDONG PANYU MIDDLE SCHOOL

项目地点：广东省广州市
设计时间：2020 年
竣工时间：2022 年（预计）
用地面积：41,300 m^2
建筑面积：48,500 m^2

Location: Guangzhou, Guangdong
Design: 2020
Completion: 2022 (expected)
Site Area: 41,300 m^2
GFA: 48,500 m^2

广东番禺中学长隆学校是一所定位为面向未来的现代化的九年一贯制公办学校。学校周边绿化环绕环境优美，基地东北侧为长隆野生动物园，西南侧为体育公园。

设计顺应现有的基地形态，以“生态绿谷，游习乐园”为出发点，通过东西连贯、高低起伏的教学综合体，高效有机地融合了师生的教学与生活空间，形成趣味盎然、层叠错落的城市绿谷。

“长”在公园之上的，是一座连绵起伏的教学综合体，不仅保证了良好的日照需求，同时还围合出性格各异的多层次院落空间。在这个连绵起伏的山形中，设置不同高度的空中平台、连廊，结合特色功能教室形成自由院落，为师生提供休息活动空间。建筑的底层部分架空，结合开放与半开放教学活动的布置，是校园非正式教学的集中地。

建筑的屋面被充分激活，这里将是师生贴近自然的一处静地，也是鸟瞰城市的一个平台。作为科学农场，延伸学生课外教学活动，是探索自然、尊重自然的科普实践场地。

学校地处岭南，为了应对湿热多雨的气候特征，设计采用覆土屋面、立体遮阳、底层架空、空中绿化、透水铺装等手法，共同打造绿色生态校园。

Chimelong Campus of Guangdong Panyu Middle School, a future-oriented modern 9-year public school, is nestled in a beautiful green environment with Chimelong Safari Park on the northeast and a sports park on the southwest.

Following the existing site conditions for a “green eco-valley and a paradise for fun and learning”, we integrate the study and living spaces of teachers and students effectively and organically through a continuous and undulant east-west teaching building complex, creating a multi-leveled green urban valley full of fun!

The undulant teaching building complex “growing” in the park not only ensures ample daylighting but also encloses multi-leveled courtyard spaces with distinctive characteristics. This hilly form is inserted with sky platforms and corridors at different levels, which integrate the classrooms for special purposes into free courtyards, providing relaxing and activity spaces for teachers and students. The ground floor of the building is partially elevated for open and semi-open teaching activities, offering a gathering space for informal teaching on the campus.

The building roof is fully activated to create a tranquil space close to nature for teachers and students, and open up a platform for a panoramic view of the city. It will also serve as a science farm to extend students’ extracurricular learning and a science practice base for students to respect and explore nature.

In response to the typical hot, humid and rainy climate in Lingnan Region, where the campus is located, soil-covered roof, multi-leveled sunshade, elevated ground floor, sky greening, permeable paving etc. are adopted to realize a green eco-campus.

柳州市委党校搬迁工程

RELOCATION PROJECT OF PARTY SCHOOL OF CPC LIUZHOU MUNICIPAL COMMITTEE

项目地点：广西壮族自治区柳州市
设计时间：2017 年
竣工时间：2019 年
建筑面积：59,960 m^2

Location: Liuzhou, Guangxi
Design: 2017
Completion: 2019
GFA: 59,960 m^2

以“中国特色的行政院校”为设计理念，最大限度利用原有水体及地形地貌，打造富有韵味的中式园林。以“地域化、园林化、生态化”为设计原则，留出大片的绿化和水面，为创造绿色生态校园创造了良好的基础。

With the design concept of “administrative colleges with Chinese characteristics”, the design makes full use of the original water bodies and topography to create a rich Chinese garden. Following the design principle of “localization, gardening and ecologicalization”, the large greening and water surface are reserved to create a green and ecological campus.

南京航空航天大学天目湖校区
TIANMUHU CAMPUS OF NANJING UNIVERSITY OF AERONAUTICS AND ASTRONAUTICS

项目地点：江苏省溧阳市
设计时间：2018 年
竣工时间：建设中
建筑面积：621,400 m^2

Location: Liyang, Jiangsu
Design: 2018
Completion: Under Construction
GFA: 621,400 m^2

1. 与城市相互融合，形成校城共享的城市校园。
2. 实现校园内部学科之间的共享联通，形成整体的校园公共空间。
3. 延续江南水乡文脉，营造校园的人文特色，实现“环境育人”的教育理念。
4. 营造绿色、生态、可持续的海绵校园。

The project is designed to integrates with the city to form the urban campus shared by the school and city, and realizes the sharing and communication between the internal disciplines of the campus to form an overall campus public Space. It continues the cultural context south of the Yangtze River, embodies the humanistic characteristics of the campus, and realizes the educational concept of “cultivating talents with inspiring environment”. The goal is to create a green, ecological and sustainable sponge campus.

北京工业大学本部总体规划调整

MASTER PLANNING ADJUSTMENT FOR MAIN CAMPUS OF BEIJING UNIVERSITY OF TECHNOLOGY

项目地点：北京市
设计时间：2013 年
竣工时间：2014 年
用地面积：811,000 m²
建筑面积：719,439 m²

Location: Beijing
Design: 2013
Completion: 2014
Site Area: 811,000 m²
GFA: 719,439 m²

北京工业大学本部总体规划调整设计是在一个相对完整的校园基础上进行规划调整，面临的挑战不同于新建校园。因此，设计根据校园现状与“十二五”规划文件，确立北京工业大学校园“面向世界、研究创新、学科融合”的发展定位；结合现代校园的发展趋势，提出了“城市校园、研究校园、整体校园、人文校园、活力校园、景观校园”这“六大校园”的设计构思，从而解决了校园现状各区割裂、城市界面不完整、空间体系不连贯等问题，实现了整体校园的有效更新。同时，通过对图书馆进行改造，重新焕发校园核心空间的活力。

The master planning adjustment is to tackle a relatively complete campus, which poses a challenge different from a new campus. The campus development positioning is thus established to be “international vision, research innovation and inter-disciplinary integration” in view of the existing campus status and the 12th Five-Year Plan. To respond to the campus development trend, six main concepts are proposed, i.e. “urban campus”, “research-oriented campus”, “holistic campus”, “humanistic campus”, “energetic campus” and “landscaped campus”, to properly address the existing problems with the campus, such as fragmentation, incomplete urban interface and discontinuous spatial system, and realize the effective campus renewal. In the meantime, the core space on campus is rejuvenated through reconstruction of the library.

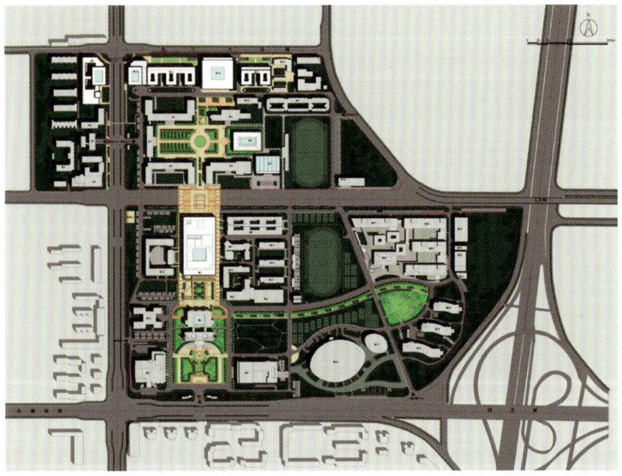

北京工业大学本部总体规划调整
MASTER PLANNING ADJUSTMENT FOR MAIN CAMPUS OF BEIJING UNIVERSITY OF TECHNOLOGY

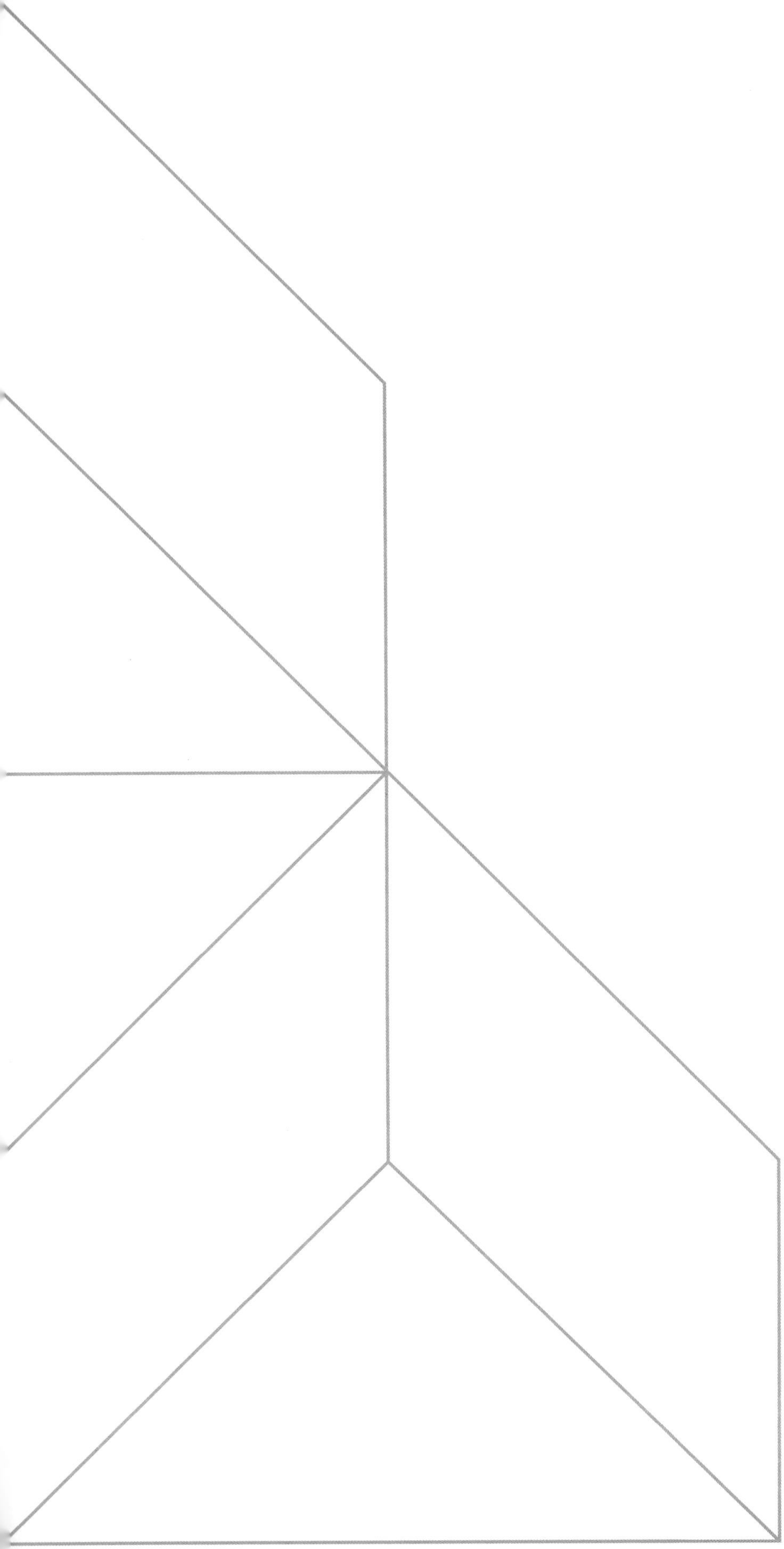

校园单体建筑设计
ARCHITECTURAL DESIGN OF CAMPUS BUILDINGS

Library / 图书馆

Teaching & Laboratory Building / 教学实验楼

Campus Characteristic Building / 校园特色建筑

Sports Venue / 体育馆

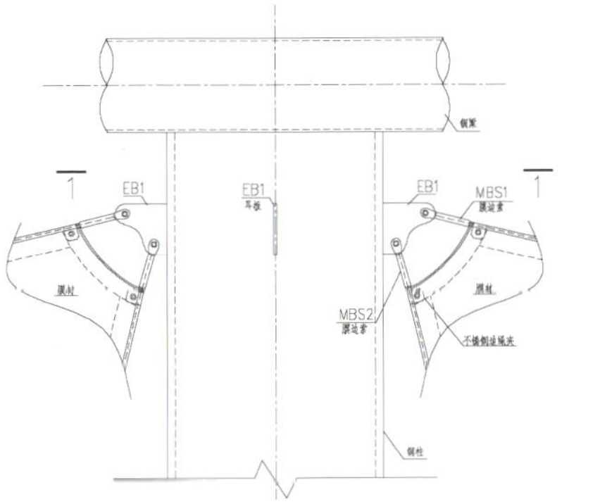
1
1
钢架
EB1
EB1
耳板
EB1
MBS1
膜边索
膜材
膜材
MBS2
膜边索
不锈钢边绳夹
钢柱

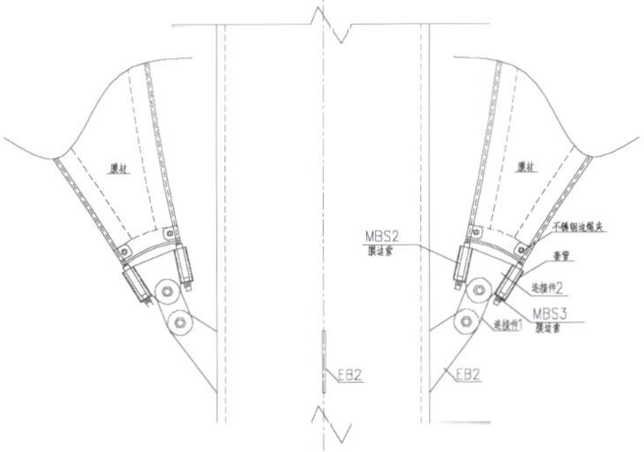
膜材
膜材
MBS2
膜边索
不锈钢边绳夹
套管
连接件2
MBS3
膜边索
连接件1
EB2
EB2

福州大学图书馆
LIBRARY OF FUZHOU UNIVERSITY

图书馆
LIBRARY

福州大学图书馆
LIBRARY OF FUZHOU UNIVERSITY

项目地点：福建省福州市
设计时间：2002 年
竣工时间：2005 年
用地面积：15,000 m^2
建筑面积：35,396 m^2
曾获奖项：2007 年度第五届中国建筑学会建筑创作奖佳作奖
2007 年度教育部优秀建筑设计一等奖
2008 年度全国优秀工程勘察设计行业奖建筑工程一等奖
2009 年全国优秀工程设计奖银奖
中国建筑学会中华人民共和国成立 60 周年建筑创作大奖

Location: Fuzhou, Fujian
Design: 2002
Completion: 2005
Site Area: 15,000 m^2
GFA: 35,396 m^2
Awards:
Honorable Mention of the 5th ASC Architectural Creation Award (2007)
The First Prize of Excellent Architectural Design Award by the Ministry of Education (2007)
The First Prize for Construction Engineering of National Excellent Engineering Exploration and Design Trade Award (2008)
Silver Prize of National Excellent Engineering Design Award (2009)
ASC Grand Architectural Creation Award for the 60th Founding Anniversary of PRC

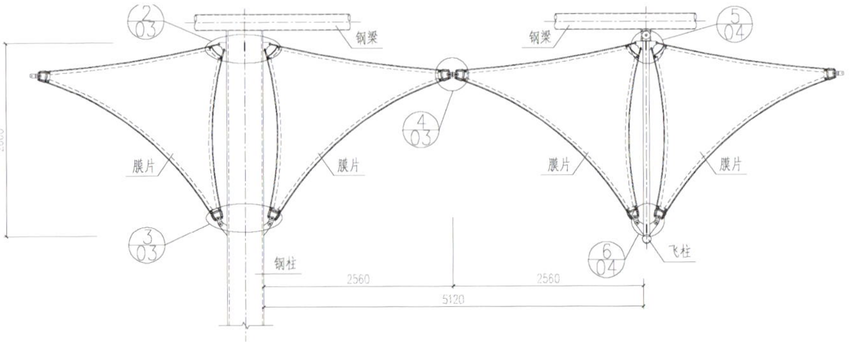

福州大学图书馆藏书 120 万册，固定阅览座位 3500 个，是福州大学的标志性中心建筑。

图书馆的建筑设计从校园空间的特色出发，借鉴福建围楼及其他中国传统建筑以“庭院”虚空间为中心的布局模式，创造出立体开放、多重构成的创新型图书馆核心空间形态。

图书馆的设计，还采用了“门禁内面积最小化”的创新设计理念，将阅览室等因为书籍管理而需要封闭的区域集中布置，而将其他不需要进行书籍管理的区域，如电子阅览、展览厅、学术报告厅、书店、咖啡厅等，解放于门禁系统之外，使这些区域能面向整个校园全天候开放，从而使图书馆即使在闭馆的时间，仍然充满活力，也使图书馆真正成为校园生活的中心场所。

Library of Fuzhou University, with 1.2 million volumes of books and 3,500 fixed seats, boasts the central landmark on the campus of Fuzhou University.

The architectural design of the library, in view of the campus' spatial features, references the layout of the local Hakka Round House in Fujian Province and the traditional Chinese architecture, i.e. to center on the void of the courtyard, and create a three-dimensional, open and multiplex core space of the library.

The library design adopts the innovative design concept, i.e. to minimize the access control area. To be specific, it means to centralize the areas which require access control for book management (such as reading space). While other areas which do not involve the book management, such as electronic reading, exhibition, academic lecture hall, bookstore, coffee shop and so on, are placed outside of the access control system and can be open to the entire campus all day long. This makes the library a place full of vitality and truly the center of campus life, even when the library is closed.

福州大学图书馆

LIBRARY OF FUZHOU UNIVERSITY

建筑元素的创作与空间表达的意义——福州大学图书馆建筑创作手法例析

传统建筑经常利用屋檐、梁、柱、门窗、栏杆等传统构件进行艺术化创作，从而塑造建筑物的风格和个性。而对于现代主义建筑"装饰就是罪恶"的创作取向中，这种装饰功能分离的设计手法已经渐渐遭到淘汰。然而，一些现代建筑又以其过于冷漠、粗犷、缺乏人文关怀而备受诟病。

通过福大图书馆的设计过程及其建成效果进行反思，笔者认为，建筑创作仍旧可以依赖于建筑构件的艺术化塑造来进行，但是"构件"的定义应该演变为"元素"，即创作对象范围由于建筑技术的提高而变得更为广泛，从特定的传统构件可以演变为各个建筑所特有的元素，例如采光构件、灯具、遮阳系统甚至是水暖电的功能组件；创作对象逐渐脱离其装饰性特征而变得个性化，从而更好地为建筑的空间精神服务，通过对一些创新性建筑元素的创作，形成建筑物的自我风格。倘若说建筑是凝固的音乐，那么这些元素就是一首凝固的音乐里头特别显眼或者不断重复的音符，是这些音符确定了整首旋律的风格和基调。无论是经典的圆舞曲或者是激昂的摇滚乐，都需要有特定的音符去体现和传载。

福州大学图书馆的项目，从设计的最开始，我们就选择了"创造空间"而不是"设计立面"的建筑创作道路。从校园的整体规划空间考虑，方案选择了非常规整的正方形轮廓，以体现其中心性和唯一性。对于一个外形方正的简单体块来讲，空间比立面更为重要，因此，如何塑造一个有活力有生气的中心空间，是该项目重点考虑的目标。

我们提出了"门禁系统最小化"的设计概念，将不涉及书籍管理的功能，如咖啡、书店、自修室、多媒体阅览等，尽量独立在门禁系统之外，使图书馆即使在闭馆的时间也是一个充满活力的校园生活中心。同时根据功能、流线将体块化整为零，从而创造出一个具有场所精神的、全天候开放的中心空间。而单单是功能的赋予并不足以塑造一个具有感性吸引力的动人空间，因此，我们对建筑元素进行艺术化的演绎，从而增加了空间的艺术感染力。

位于二层正方形的平台几乎连接了以上所有功能，形成了多义的空间，涵盖了多种功能，包括门厅、大堂、检索、休息、展览、咖啡厅等。从二层的方形平台可到达各个门厅，也可以拾级而上通过直跑梯到达咖啡厅和三层露台，也可以到达书店，或者进入大堂，可通过旋转楼梯到达各层阅览平台，或者通过内部旋转楼梯到达一层的展览大厅，从展览大厅也可以到达学术交流中心。从交通上和功能上，二层方形平台都是具有复合、核心意义的。在这个平台上，我们创造了以下的建筑元素。

一、象征白鹭齐飞的帆拱造型

方形中庭一半为室内一半在室外，十字形的钢柱以 7.5 m 的方形柱网形式界定了整个空间领域感。垂直的帆拱形拉膜结构在界定了空间的同时，在造型上如同一只只展翅腾飞的白鹭一般，在提供遮阳的同时，其斑驳的光影效果及独特的空间造型也给整体空间带来了唯美的艺术享受，给建筑本身的结构赋予了鲜活的生命，并随一天当中的时间变化而变化，为大厅室内外都提供了变幻的魅力。

庭屋面下采用轻巧活泼、流畅的膜结构室内吊顶，吊顶屋面选择法拉利膜材料装饰。本工程膜体面积约为 1,500 m^2，整个图书馆膜结构项目由 74 根飞柱、342 片单元膜体组成，膜边界均以直径 8 mm PE 索膜边索作为连接构件，然后用连接件连接起来作为一个整体，所有连接件均采用直径 16 mm 高强螺栓连接。

膜伞底部与飞柱及中心柱的连接节点、膜四周固定节点、膜边角部固定节点、脊索与膜连接点、膜分缝处节点等关键节点均作了优化设计，优选了膜的剪裁及拼接方法，借助计算机裁剪技术，达到了美观大方，经济适用的效果，使这项膜结构的施工获得了圆满的成功。

二、十字形钢柱

中庭的外边尺寸为 45 m × 45 m，如果按网架的做法，整个屋面可以独立支撑在几个独立柱上，但是带来的效果平淡、普通，空间界定模糊，没有视觉的吸引力。因此经过多轮的方案比选，我们采用了钢框架结构，通过固定的轴网尺寸上重复的钢柱，有效地界定了中心方形空间的范围，增加了空间的层次和视觉的震撼力，同时屋顶的结构方式采用最简洁明了的框架梁式体系，将重点突出在下面的帆拱造型上。方形的钢架轴网跨越了室内和室外，和各个入口形成 45 度的交错形态，使整个空间形成交错、斜切的立体效果。25 个钢柱在二维空间上统一了室内外节奏，而在三维效果上又拔高了空间的高度感，使整体空间形成哥特式般飞腾的向上感。钢柱作为一个重要的结构、造型元素，我们也进行了特殊设计，强调了纵向的线条的细腻感，使之具有丰富耐看的细部造型。

三、采光井兼照明灯

平台上的斜向玻璃幕墙是分割室内外的透明界面。为了强调这个主要界面，我们希望能有一些重复性的元素，脱离该透明界面而如同雕塑一般进行线性的点缀，以丰富平台空间，也强化主入口。因此，我们沿玻璃幕墙依次设计了点状排列的采光井灯柱，由于平台下是展厅，因此，该灯柱在白天是首层展览大厅的自然采光井，在夜晚又为平台广场提供了灯光照明效果，熠熠生辉，成为建筑元素的艺术化创作结合实际功能使用的一处范例，使技术与艺术相结合、实用与感官美相统一，并符合建筑艺术的审美特征。

四、校园中心标志——钟塔

从校园整体规划来看，图书馆位于教学区中心，北侧和环形教学楼形成中心广场，可举办多种校园文化娱乐庆典活动。因此，在北侧，即教学区中心，我们设计了一个三角形的塔楼，成为校区中心的标志。塔楼的平面形式与图书馆整体构图原则相符，为正方形所对角切割形成的直角三角形，塔顶三面悬挂 LED 指针挂钟，铿锵深沉的钟声也为校园平添了几分诗意和浪漫。钟塔不仅为校中心区提供了标志性的观赏物，在二层平台及室内多个角度都可以看到钟塔，通透的玻璃幕墙让人感觉大堂延伸到室外，钟楼、咖啡厅也一一成为大堂的景观。

五、锥形体

大厅正中为一圆锥体，如雕塑般镶嵌在共享中庭上，从外旋弧形楼梯可到达三层平面，或也可从内旋楼梯到达一层展览大厅。内、外旋梯的设计目的，是为了有效地将首层的展厅部分独立出门禁系统，而同时又保持空间的连续。圆锥体外表面镶嵌原木，保留原木断面的年轮纹样，并利用两种厚度营造出凹凸的肌理，达到非常独特的观感效果。从中庭可以通过共享空间仰望整个圆锥体，其创新的造型和肌理既与石材取得和谐搭配的效果，又与洁净闪烁的玻璃幕墙和钢结构产生明显的对比和衬托。

六、墙面与窗统一的细部装饰条

图书馆的设计在立面处理上主要是采用实虚对比、精致细部的手法。大面积的干挂锈石板和晶莹剔透的蓝灰色玻璃产生材质和体量上的视觉对比，在每层层线上，150 mm 的凹型装饰条从实面一直贯通到玻璃窗和幕墙上，既加强了横向的舒展性，也增加了立面的节奏感，令巨大的体量拥有精致动人的细部。

七、廊与桥

在二层平台上，3 条廊桥飞跨其上，将屋顶绿化平台、室内阅读空间、电子阅览空间链接起来。三个连桥分别采取了"桥"和"廊"的处理手法，一来是满足功能的实际需要（从室内到室外和从室内到室内），二来也使二层平台空间更具空间变化，加强了上下层空间的对话。线性的"廊"与"桥"和二层整体空间形成 45 度的交角，如同从柱网中穿梭而过，在效果上也带来了多维度的视觉变化。

通过福大图书馆的创作，我们充分认识到建筑元素在建筑空间表达上的特殊意义，元素创作的重要性是举足轻重的。

1. 建筑元素的创造有助于建筑空间的秩序化表达。

建筑空间是三维的，而空间秩序增加了时间的维度，是四维的。空间秩序有赖于参观者的共同创造，是由参观者穿越其中时所经历的，随着人的感知而不断演变。建筑元素作为空间的重点性特征被强化出来，一般会成为空间的标志物和引导物，这些标志性引导因素一旦确立，就会形成强化的空间秩序，使空间产生不断的深度与层次的变化，让参观者有重点性地被引导和体验。

2. 建筑元素加强了建筑造型的对比性与均衡性，塑造了特定风格和语言。

建筑造型主要是建筑的体量形成的，然而对建筑元素的恰当控制，能加强建筑造型的对比，使空间更具有易于识别和理解的角度，让参观者更易于体会设计的意图。建筑元素的特征化处理，也能够辅助塑造建筑物特定的风格和建筑语言。

3. 建筑元素创造了建筑空间的体验性知觉总和。

建筑元素通过在空间中的累积不断强化了建筑空间的秩序、材料与肌理的对比、光影与色彩的构成，以此影响着建筑空间的效果，并积累形成参观者在空间的一系列感受，即体验性知觉总和。同样的建筑空间设计如果缺少元素的艺术化创作和点缀，那么就会形成完全不一样的空间氛围和知觉感受。

总的说来，建筑元素并不仅限于围护建筑空间的一些基本构件，对于各类不同的建筑类型和建筑形式和空间重点而言，建筑元素的创造是无穷无尽没有界限的，但是并不能有泛滥的风格和追求。建筑元素必须产生于建筑物的自身需求，为了达到一定的设计目标而被设定，且其特征都必须是围绕着建筑物表达的意图和设计初衷而服务。无论是传统建筑构件元素或者创新元素的创造和设计，都能对建筑空间气氛、造型风格等起到画龙点睛的作用。

作者：陈子坚、郭 嘉

文章出处：本文曾发表于《新建筑》2010 年 03 月

Creation of Architectural Elements and Meanings of Spatial Expressions-Analysis on Architectural Creation Approach of Library of Fuzhou University

Eaves, beams, doors, windows, banisters, and other traditional components are often employed in artistic creation of the traditional buildings to shape up the style and character of a building. However, under the mantra of modernistic architecture that "decoration is a sin", this design approach that separates the decoration from the functionality has been phased out. However, some modernistic buildings are widely criticized as being excessively cold, rough and lacking in humanistic care.

Through reflection over the design process for the Library of Fuzhou University (hereinafter referred to as the "Library") and the outcomes thereof, the author considers that artistic shaping of architectural components could still be relied on for architectural creation but the concept "component" should be redefined as "element", in which case the range of objects for creation has widened due to advancement in architectural technology, and specific traditional components can be transformed into particular elements of the buildings, such as daylighting components, light fittings, shading systems, or even functional components for water, heat and power supply. The objects of creation gradually cast off the decorative attribute and are personalized to better serve the spatial spirit of the buildings. Some innovative architectural elements are created to form the individualized styles of the buildings. If architecture is frozen music, then these elements are the particularly salient or repeated notes in a piece of frozen music and set the style and keynote for the entire melody. Whether it is a classical waltz or a passionate rock song, specific notes are needed to embody and carry the music.

From the beginning of the design for the Library, we take the approach of "creating space" instead of "designing facade" for architectural creation. In view of the overall campus planning, a perfectly neat square footprint is selected to present the centrality and uniqueness of the Library. For a simple block of square shape, the space is more important than the facade, which makes it a significant objective to create a dynamic and lively central space for the project.

The Library implements the design concept of "minimized access control system", which is to place non-book-management-related functions, such as cafes, bookstores, study rooms, multimedia reading rooms, etc., outside the access control system as much as possible, so that the Library will remain a vibrant center of the campus life even outside the opening hours. Besides, the block is divided into different parts in view of the functions and circulations to create a 24-hour central space with genius loci. Simply endowing functions is not enough to create a sensuously attractive space and therefore, we give an artistic presentation of the architectural elements to add an artistic appeal to the space.

The square platform on the second floor connects almost all the functions mentioned above and forms a poly-semantic space of multiple functions, including foyers, lobby, retrieval, lounge, exhibition, café, etc. From this platform, visitors can walk into the foyers and book stores, or ascend the straight stairs to the café and the terrace on the third floor, or enter the lobby, or take the helix stairs to the reading platform on each floor or the internal helix stairs to the exhibition hall on the first floor and then to the academic exchange center. The square platform on the second floor is invested with composite and core meanings either in terms of circulation or function and therefore, we create the following architectural elements thereon.

Ⅰ. Pendentives Symbolic of Flying Egrets

The square atrium is half indoor and half outdoor, with cross-shaped steel columns arranged in a 7.5 m square grid to mark out the entire space. In addition to defining the space, the vertical pendentive structures of tensioned membrane are each shaped like a flying egret which, on one hand serves as shading elements, on the other hand provides s dappled light and shadow effect and unique spatial shape that make the entire space a source of splendid artistic enjoyment and inject vitality into the structure of the building. Constantly changing with the time of the day, the pendentive structures endow the indoor and outdoor space of the lobby with varied charm.

A light, dashing and smooth indoor suspended ceiling of membrane structure is installed under the atrium roof which is decorated with Ferrari membrane materials. The entire membrane structure of the Library is composed of 74 struts and 342 unit membranes, around 1,500 m^2 of membrane in total. PE cables, 8 mm in diameter, are fixed at the edges of each membrane as connection components whereby the membranes are pieced together with connectors which are further joined by 16 mm-diameter high strength bolts.

Optimized design is conducted for the connection nodes between the bottom corners of the membrane canopies and the struts and center columns, the perimeter fixing nodes and corner fixing nodes of the membranes, the connection points between the cables and the membranes, the nodes at the seams of the membranes, and other critical nodes. Coupled with the optimized designs for the membrane cutting and joining methods and the computer-aided cutting techniques, a graceful, well-functional and cost-effective membrane structure is achieved and the membrane construction is a success.

Ⅱ. Cross-shaped Steel Columns

The atrium measures the outer dimension of 45 m×45 m. Should the space trusses be employed, the entire roof can be rested on several standalone columns, but the outcome would be banal and plain, with no clear definition for the space and no visual appeal at all. Therefore, after several rounds of comparisons of designs, we choose the steel frame structure, which effectively defines the boundaries of the central square space and increases the spatial layers and the visual effect through arrangement of identical steel columns at fixed intervals along the axial network; meanwhile, we use the simplest and clearest frame beam system as the roof structure to set off the pendentive structures below. The square axial network of steel frames covers both the indoor and outdoor areas and crisscrosses the entrances at an angle of 45 degrees, thus adding a diagonal and crisscross spatial effect to the entire space. 25 steel columns unify the indoor and outdoor rhythms across the two-dimensional space and visually heighten the three-dimensional space, breathing a souring Gothic feeling into the entire space. As an important structural and shaping element, the steel columns are specially designed to emphasize the delicacy of its vertical lines-details that add lasting appeal to the columns.

Ⅲ. Light Wells and Lighting

The sloping glass curtain wall on the platform is a transparent interface that separates the interior from the exterior. To highlight this main interface, we wish to add some repetitive elements which are arranged like sculptures in linear pattern away from the interface as decoration to spice up the space above the platform and give prominence to the main entrance. Therefore, we design along the glass curtain wall some light wells/columns in dot array. Since the exhibition hall is below the platform, these light columns serve as natural light wells for the exhibition hall on the first floor in the daytime and provide lighting for the platform square at night. Such a dazzling element is a paradigm of integrating artistic creation and practical functions in the use of architectural element to achieve combination of technology and art and unity of utility and sensory beauty, and embodies the aesthetic attributes of architectural art.

Ⅳ. Center Landmark of Campus-Clock Tower

According to the campus master plan, the Library is located at the center of the teaching area, with its north side joining the circular teaching building to frame the central square, a perfect place for cultural, recreational and celebration activities on the campus. Therefore, a triangular tower is designed at the center of the teaching area on the north as a central landmark on the campus. The planar geometry of the tower is designed in line with the general composition principle of the Library as an equilateral right angled triangle cut along the diagonal from a square. With LED pointer wall clocks on three sides of the top of the tower and the sonorous sounding of the bell, the tower adds a poetic and romantic flavor to the campus. The clock tower is a symbolic ornament for the central area of the campus that is visible from the second-floor platform and many angles inside the buildings. Its transparent glass curtain wall visually extends the lobby to the outdoors, including the clock tower and the café part of the lobby view.

Ⅴ. Cone

Right in the middle of the lobby is a cone, which is fixed onto the shared atrium like a sculpture, with the helix stairs on its exterior leading to the third floor and the helix stairs in its interior leading to the exhibition hall on the first floor. The interior and exterior helix stairs are designed to effectively separate the exhibition hall outside of the access control system while maintaining the continuity of the space. The exterior of the cone is clad with raw wood tiles that retain the cross-sectional growth ring profiles and have two kinds of thickness for creation of an uneven texture as well as a unique visual effect. The entire cone is exposed to the view from the atrium below through the shared space. Its innovative shape and texture not only match harmoniously with the stone materials but also sharply contrast with and set off the clean and glittering glass curtain wall and steel structure.

Ⅵ. Decorative Strips as Details to Unify Wall Surface and Windows

The facade design of the Library features contrast between the solid components and void as well as the refined details.. Large area of dry-hang rusty stone panel constitutes visual contrast in terms of materiality and massing to the glittering blue gray glass. The 150 mm concave decorative strips embedded between floors run from the solid wall surface all the way through the glass windows and curtain wall to visually enhance the horizontal dimension, strengthen the rhythm of the facade, and add appealing and delicate details to the massive building volume.

Ⅶ. Corridors and Bridges

There are three corridor bridges spanning over the second floor platform, linking the green roof platform, the indoor reading space and the electronic reading room space together. Three linking bridges take the forms of "bridge" and "corridor" to meet the practical functional requirements (to allow for movement from the interior to the exterior and vice versa), introduce more spatial variations to the space above the second floor platform, and strengthen dialogue between the upper and lower spaces. The linear "corridors" and "bridges" are arranged at an angle of 45 degrees with the entire space of the second floor, as if running through the column grid and bringing about multidimensional visual changes.

Through the design for the Library, we fully understand the special meanings of architectural elements in the expression of architectural space and the exceptional importance of element creation.

1.The creation of architectural elements is conductive to the orderly expression of architectural space.

Architectural space is three-dimensional whereas spatial order has one more dimension, that is, time, and is therefore four-dimensional. Spatial order relies on the visitors' participation in the joint creation in that it is experienced by the visitors walking through the space and therefore constantly changes with their perceptions. Architectural elements highlighted as important features of the space usually become marking and guiding objects of the space, which, once established, will strengthen the spatial order, incessantly generate changes in depth and hierarchies of the space, and provide the visitors with specifically guided experience.

2.Architectural elements strengthen contrast and balance in an architectural shape and create special style and language.

Architectural shape is primarily comprised of building volumes, while proper control of the architectural elements could strengthen contrast therein, render the space more identifiable and understandable attributes and help the visitors comprehend the design intents. The featured architectural elements are also helpful for creating unique building style and architectural language.

3.Architectural elements create an aggregation of experiential perceptions of the architectural space.

Architectural elements, via their accumulation in the space, consistently strengthen the spatial order, the contrast between materials and tectonics, and the composition of light/shadow effects and colors of the building, and thereby affect the experiential effect of the architectural space and add up to a series of experiences of the visitors, that is, an aggregation of experiential perceptions. In the absence of artistic creation of and decoration with architectural elements, even the same design of architectural space would generate a completely different spatial atmosphere and perceptual feelings.

In general, architectural elements are not limited to some basic components for enclosure of an architectural space. As for different architectural types and forms and different spatial emphases, the creation of architectural elements is endless, but it is undesirable to have excessive styles and pursuit thereof. Architectural elements must be originated from the demands of the building itself and created to achieve specific design objectives, with all the characteristics thereof woven around and aimed to serve the intentions of the building and the original purposes of the design. The creation and design of architectural elements, whether they are tradidional architectural components or innovative elements, can add a critical finishing touch to the atmosphere, shape and style of an architectural space.

By Chen Zijian, Guo Jia

Source: New Architecture, March 2010

武汉理工大学南湖校区图书馆

LIBRARY OF WUHAN UNIVERSITY OF TECHNOLOGY (NANHU CAMPUS)

项目地点：湖北省武汉市
竣工时间：2016 年
建筑面积：47,557 m^2

Location: Wuhan, Hubei
Completion: 2016
GFA: 47,557 m^2

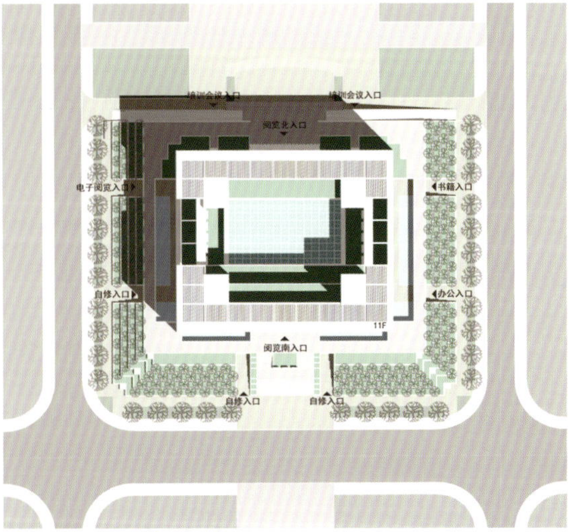

武汉理工大学南湖校区图书馆
LIBRARY OF WUHAN UNIVERSITY OF TECHNOLOGY (NANHU CAMPUS)

一、楚风汉韵

1．筑楚台

图书馆位于平坦宽阔的轴线中心，是整个校园的标志性建筑。建筑必须有足够大的体量创造具有控制力的广场界面。因此，设计将首层设计为基座一五级的跌台绿化，图书馆主体立于高台之上。

2．传统木构件的现代演绎

图书馆主入口通过对传统斗拱、排架的拆分和重组，以钢结构构架演绎传统木构的形态。东西立面覆以木色金属板，并将校园历史文化通过抽象篆书文字镂刻之上。将楚文化进行抽象和演绎，使历史底蕴在新建筑上得以延续和传承。

二、书山绿谷

设计提取传统院落的精粹，以立体庭院的方式营造绿谷的意向。玻璃中庭悬挂绿色垂幔，形成对直射阳光的有效遮挡，也营造出绿意盎然的中庭效果。同时在首层基座跌台绿化设置雾喷改善图书馆建筑的微气候。

Ⅰ. Style of Chu Kingdom in Han Dynasty

1.Chu-style platform building

The library is located in the center of the flat and broad axis as the landmark of the whole campus. The building must be large enough to create a powerful square interface. Therefore, the first floor is designed as a foundation base with five level greening, on which the main body of the library stands.

2.Modern interpretation of traditional wooden frame

The main entrance of library uses the steel structure frame to interpret the traditional wood structure by division and reorganization of the traditional Dougong and Brackets. The east-west facade, covered with wood colored metal plates, is imprinted with the campus heritage in seal characters. It also presents the abstract Chu culture, continuing and inheriting the historical background in the new building.

Ⅱ.Green valley within the campus

With reference to the traditional courtyards, the design intends to create a green valley as a three-dimensional courtyard. The green curtains hanging in the atrium effectively blocks the direct sunlight and creates a green atrium. Meanwhile, the fogging effect of the cascading greening plants on F1 helps improve the microclimate of the library.

武汉理工大学南湖校区图书馆

LIBRARY OF WUHAN UNIVERSITY OF TECHNOLOGY (NANHU CAMPUS)

钱学森图书馆
QIAN XUESEN LIBRARY

项目地点：上海市
设计时间：2009—2010 年
竣工时间：2011 年
用地面积：9,300 m^2
建筑面积：7,960 m^2

Location: Shanghai
Design: 2009-2010
Completion: 2011
Site Area: 9,300 m^2
GFA: 7,960 m^2

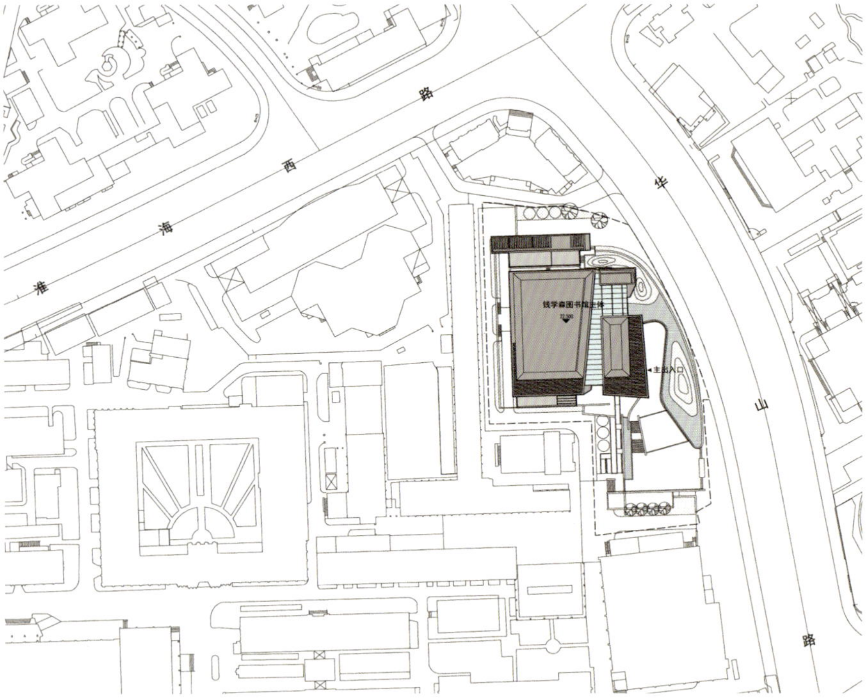

钱学森图书馆
QIAN XUESEN LIBRARY

战略科学家的成功之道
EY TO SUCCESS OF A STRATEGIC SCIENTIST

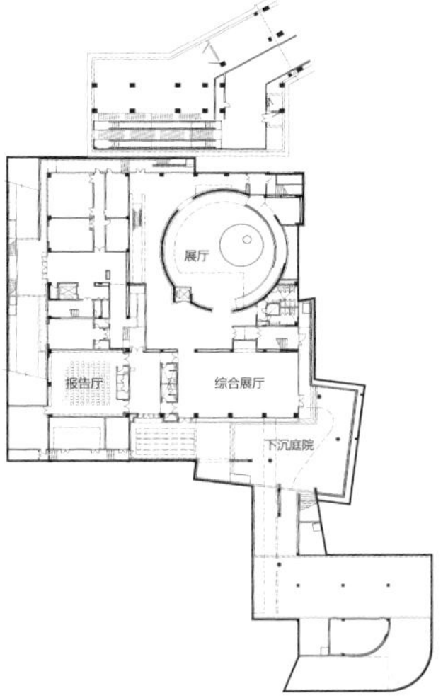
展厅
报告厅
综合展厅
下沉庭院

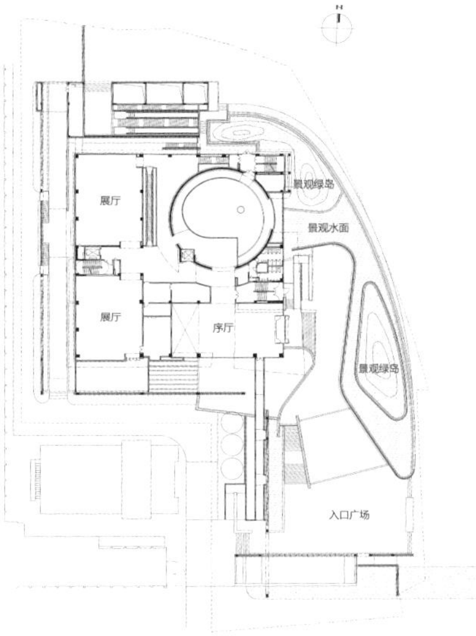
展厅
景观绿岛
景观水面
展厅
序厅
景观绿岛
入口广场

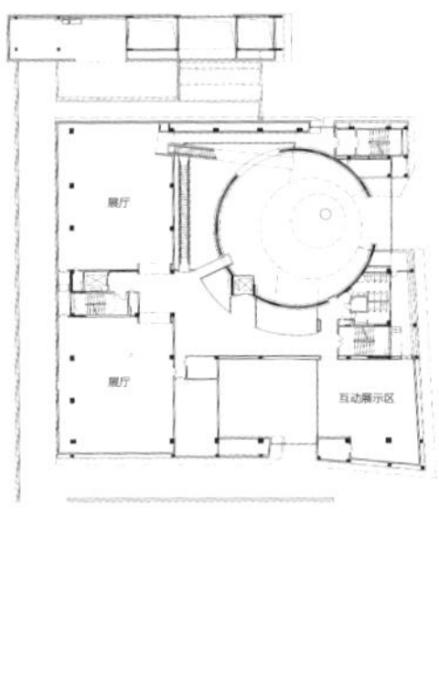
展厅
展厅
互动展示区

建筑基地位于上海交通大学徐汇校区与城市之间的转角地块。

通过对钱老一生事迹的研究与概括，设计提出了“大地情怀、石破天惊”的概念。

以“方正的石头”寓意钱老心系祖国大地的赤子情怀。方正平直的建筑体量呈向外伸展的态势，简洁有力，抽象表达在钱老贡献一生的戈壁滩上的风蚀岩意象。

以“裂开的石头”之中迸发出东二甲火箭的建筑空间场景，寓意钱老领导下的“两弹一星”伟大事业是犹如“石破天惊”般的历史事件。“石头”沿校园道路的延长线从中部裂开，面向城市道路展开最大裂面，“V”字形同高玻璃面透出东二甲导弹实物，“石头”立面的肌理抽象而巧妙地呈现钱老的亲切形象，犹如深情地注视着东二甲导弹。拟像与实物、平面与纵深的交织形成时空对话的场景，突出了人物与其事业的共同主题。

建筑外墙以红灰色为主调，延续了百年徐汇校区的建筑历史文脉。

The site is located at the corner between Shanghai Jiao Tong University Xuhui Campus and the city.

The design concept is defined as Love of Land and Rock Split from Inside, which respectively implies the patriotism and the remarkable achievements of Qian Xuesen (also known as Tsien Hsue-Shen).

The Square Rock symbolizes Qian's patriotic sentiment and high moral character. The square and straight building volume stretches outward in a concise and powerful manner, which serves as an abstract representation of the wind-eroded rock in the Gobi Desert where Qian devoted himself to.

The Split Rock appears to burst open from an origin point, the building space where the real object of DF-2A missile is on display. This serves as a metaphor that the research and development the nuclear bomb, missile and artificial satellite directed by Qian are of great historical significance, and make one feel as if the Rock is split from inside by the overwhelming energy of the missile, one of Qian's achievements. The Square Rock is split along the extension line of the campus road and opens up the largest crevice in the facade facing the city. The DF-2A missile is visible to the outside through the glass facade at the V-shaped crevice. The facade fabrics vividly present a smiling portrait of Qian who is gazing at the missile with much emotion. The juxtaposition of simulated image and real object, as well as juxtaposition of plane and depth, establish a dialogue of time and space, highlight the theme of the architecture.

The exterior wall features cervinus tone, inheriting the historical architecture context of the centennial Xuhui Campus, Shanghai Jiao Tong University.

李政道图书馆
LI ZHENGDAO LIBRARY

项目地点：上海市
设计时间：2012 年
用地面积：2,852.7 m^2
建筑面积：6,500 m^2

Location: Shanghai
Design: 2012
Site Area: 2,852.7 m^2
GFA: 6,500 m^2

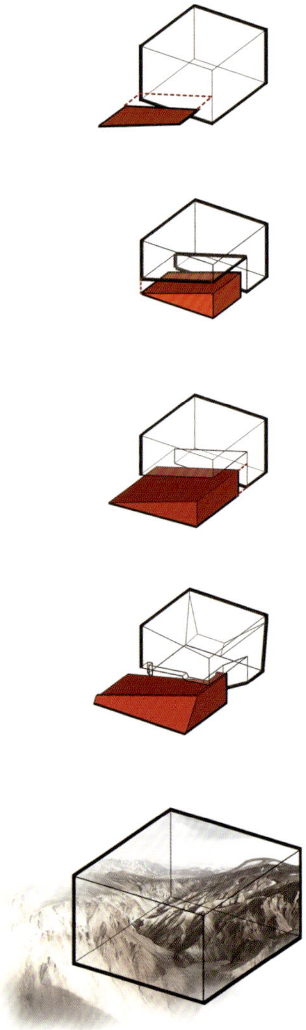

本设计借鉴吴冠中先生《对称乎，未必，且看柳与影》的画作，旨在建筑上呼应李政道先生的理论研究成果，演绎出由对称与非对称共同构筑的美妙平衡；同时立足于李政道先生三十一岁便获得诺贝尔物理学奖的辉煌成就，取用“诺贝尔山”的意象，意在激励青年学生和科技工作者坚持不懈、勇攀科学高峰。

设计在对称稳定的体量中引入动感的切割，并最终生成上下叠置的两个单元。位于下方的为三菱体，位于上方的为带切角的方体，其内包含展览、库藏、阅览、办公、科研等功能。方体之内嵌入中庭，为建筑引入天光的同时成为汇聚各种活动的核心区域，为使用者创造层次丰富的交流场所。

Inspired by Wu Guanzhong's “Symmetry? Not necessarily. Look at Willow and Shadow”, this design aims to echo the theoretical research results of Mr. Li Zhengdao in architecture and deduce the wonderful balance constructed by symmetry and asymmetry. Based on the brilliant achievement of Mr. Li Zhengdao who won the Nobel Prize in physics at the age of 31, this design takes the image of “Nobel mountain” to encourage young students and scientists to persevere and climb the scientific peak.

The design introduces dynamic cutting into the symmetrical and stable volume, and finally generates two overlapping units, which are three diamond body at the bottom and square body with cutting Angle at the top, including exhibition, library, reading, office, scientific research and other functions. The square body is embedded into the atrium, which introduces sky light into the building and becomes the core area to gather various activities, creating a multi-level communication place for users.

李政道圖書館

北京工业大学图书馆
LIBRARY OF BEIJING UNIVERSITY OF TECHNOLOGY

项目地点：北京市
设计时间：2015 年
建筑面积：40,463 m^2

Location: Beijing
Design: 2015
GFA: 40,463 m^2

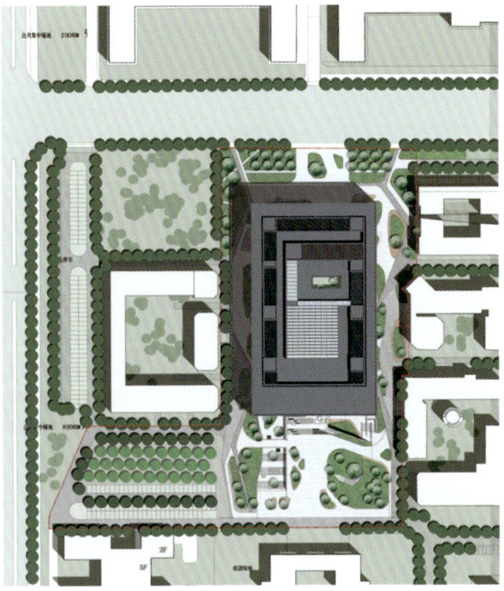

北京工业大学图书馆
LIBRARY OF BEIJING UNIVERSITY OF TECHNOLOGY

在校园的总体规划方案中，图书馆正处于南北轴线的中心点。为了加强整体校园轴线关系和空间序列，重塑校园礼仪轴线，改扩建后的图书馆将成为校园融合交汇的重要节点。同时为师生之间、同学之间提供交流交往的平台，碰撞出知识的火花。

空间构成以博古架为灵感，赋予建筑"博古汇今"的概念，寓意图书馆亦是存放知识智慧的容器，同时借取博古架形态"精""巧""宜"的特点，融合到设计中，通过对不同功能分区的分析和划分，将功能空间，天井、采光天窗及交通核有机组织与组合。受简牍的启发，抽象其肌理形成灵动活跃的立面形态，产生丰富的光影效果，提升建筑的文化内涵。

In the overall planning of the campus, Library of Beijing University of Technology is at the center of the north-south axis. In order to strengthen the relationship and spatial sequence of the whole campus axis and reshape the campus etiquette axis, the rebuilt and expanded library will become an important node of campus fusion and intersection, which also provides a platform for communication between teachers and students.

The structure of space is inspired by Antique Shelves, which endows architecture with the concept of "conversant with ancient and modern learning". It implies that the library is also a container for storing knowledge and wisdom, while borrowing the fine and skillful concept of Antique Shelves form. Through the analysis and division of different functional zones, the functional space, patio, day-lighting skylight, and traffic core are organized and combined. Inspired by bamboo slips, we abstract its texture to form a dynamic facade form, produce rich light and shadow effects, and enhance the cultural connotation of architecture.

北京工业大学图书馆
LIBRARY OF BEIJING UNIVERSITY OF TECHNOLOGY

重庆师范大学大学城校区图文信息中心

LIBRARY AND INFORMATION CENTER OF CHONGQING NORMAL UNIVERSITY (CHONGQING UNIVERSITY TOWN)

项目地点：重庆市
设计时间：2006—2007 年
竣工时间：2007 年
用地面积：12,677 m²
建筑面积：58,409 m²
曾获奖项：蓝星杯第五届中国威海国际建筑设计大奖赛优秀奖

Location: Chongqing
Design: 2006-2007
Completion: 2007
Site Area: 12,677 m^2
GFA: 58,409 m^2
Award:
Excellence Award, Blue Star Cup · The 5th China Weihai International Architectural Design Award & Competition

设计强调建筑与自然的交融、人与人的交融、人与环境的交融，为学校提供一个标志性的方“核”。

交融

以人为本的原则充分考虑使用者的需求，体现从过去以书为本过渡到现代以人为本的时代要求。图文信息中心的使用发展是个动态过程，设计注重灵活可变的建筑空间，实现方便快捷的使用效果和可持续发展的可行性。生态优先的原则注重生态效益，通过自然环境和建筑内部环境的交融，创造出良好的图文信息中心生态环境。

标志

图文信息中心是校园内重要的建筑物，设计需考虑其标志性。所以方案在造型上采用了简洁庄重的体量，以此体现出重庆师范大学庄重大气的校风。同时，设计考虑到尊重校园内部其他建筑的基本尺度和组合手法，采用建筑大小不同体量之间的穿插咬合，以形成舒适宜人的建筑尺度。通过平台台阶及斜面草坡基座的处理，高耸的高层像是从土地蔓延上升一样，增强了建筑的整体感和标志性，使该图文信息中心在感官认知层面上成为校园内的标志建筑。

With great efforts exerted to integrate the architecture with nature, the human with human, and the human with the environment, the campus design intends to offer a representative square "core" for the university.

Integration

The human-oriented principle takes the user demands into full account, and reflects the requirements of the time, i.e. the human-centered concept that has replaced the previously prevailing book-centered concept. The use and future evolution of the Library and Information Center are dynamic process, so great attention is attached to creation of flexible and changeable building spaces, the realization of convenient and rapid uses and feasibility of sustainable development. Following the Ecology First principle that emphasizes the ecological benefits, an attractive environment is created for the Center by integrating the natural environment with the interior built environment.

Iconic Building

As the most important building on the campus, the Center has to present some iconic features. Therefore, a concise and sedate building form is created to represent the generous and sedate temperament of the University. Meanwhile, the building volumes in varied scales are designed to interweave with each other, showing respect for the basic scales and composition of other buildings on the campus and establishing the pleasant and intimate building scale. With the terraces, steps and bases of the slanting grass slope, the high-rise appears to grow and rise elegantly from the earth. This enhances the integrality and iconic feature of the building and makes the Library and Information Center a true icon of the campus in terms of sensory perception.

重庆师范大学大学城校区图文信息中心
LIBRARY AND INFORMATION CENTER OF CHONGQING NORMAL UNIVERSITY (CHONGQING UNIVERSITY TOWN)

国防科技大学图书馆

LIBRARY OF NATIONAL UNIVERSITY OF DEFENSE TECHNOLOGY

项目地点：湖南省长沙市
设计时间：2005 年
竣工时间：2006 年
建筑面积：45,000 m^2

Location: Changsha, Hunan
Design: 2005
Completion: 2006
GFA: 45,000 m^2

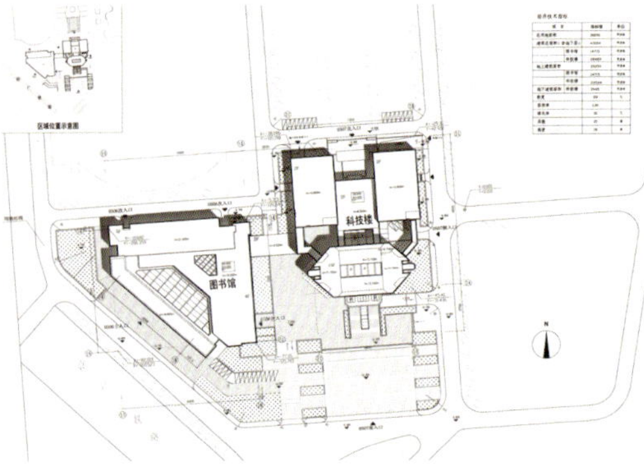

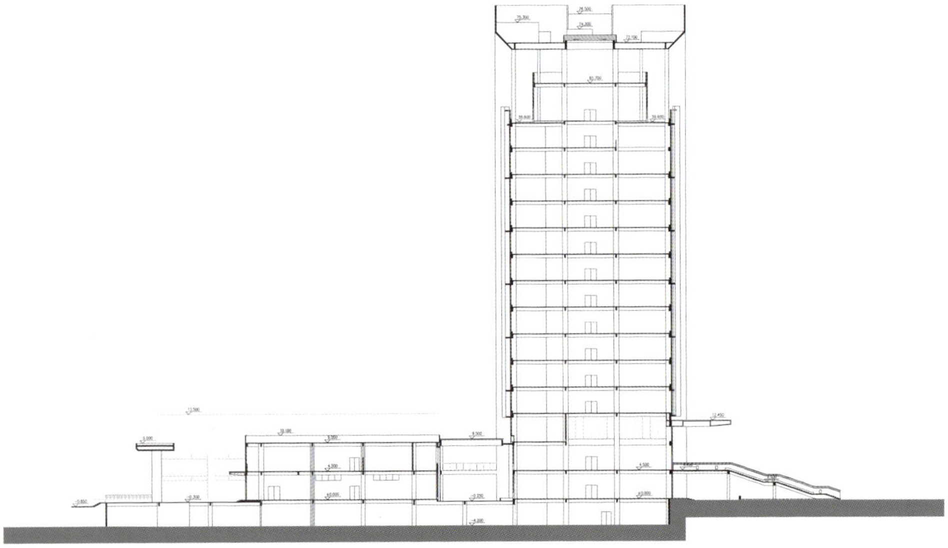

国防科技大学图书馆由科技大楼和图书馆两部分组成，位于校园北区的南端，其中科技大楼位于北门与体育馆所连接中轴线的末端，图书馆位于其西侧的南向轴线上。这样的布局完全符合校园总体规划的要求，使北部校园的建筑空间到此有一个完整的结束，同时又成为南部校园空间转换的起点，使南北校园有机地联系在一起，起到纽带的作用。

两栋楼的主入口均设在南面开阔的广场上，既便于人流疏散，又能突出建筑形象。次要入口（包括疏散出口）则放在北面及东西两侧，这样布局也符合校园整体道路系统的要求。

两栋楼的南面广场，按功能要求设置铺装和绿地，加强景观设计，使得建筑物景观简约实用，又重点突出，成为校园内的一个景观亮点，进一步提升校区的整体环境质量。

The Library of National University of Defense Technology (NUDT), which comprises the technology building and the library, is situated at the southern end of the north area of the campus, with the technology building at the end of the central axis connecting the north gate and the gymnasium and the library on the southward axis to the west of the technology building. Such layout perfectly accords with the requirements of the campus master plan, provides a fulfilling end to the architectural space of the northern campus as well as a transitional starting point to the space of the southern campus. The northern and southern campuses are thus organically connected by the library as a tie therefor.

The main entrances of the two buildings are both arranged facing the open square to the south to facilitate the pedestrian distribution and present a prominent architectural image. The secondary entrances (including evacuation exits) are placed at the north, east and west sides, which also complies with the requirements for the overall road system of the campus.

The square to the south of the two buildings is provided with hard pavement and green spaces as required, which creates the concise and practical landscape for the building without sacrificing any prominent elements; instead, add another highlight on the campus and further improve the overall campus environment.

国防科技大学图书馆

LIBRARY OF NATIONAL UNIVERSITY OF DEFENSE TECHNOLOGY

福建工程学院新校区图书馆
LIBRARY OF FUJIAN UNIVERSITY OF TECHNOLOGY

项目地点：福建省福州市
设计时间：2008 年
竣工时间：2013 年
建筑面积：40,500 m^2

Location: Fuzhou, Fujian
Design: 2008
Completion: 2013
GFA: 40,500 m^2

福建工程学院新校区图书馆是校园的中心建筑，也是福州大学城的最高建筑物。项目具有户外空间和强烈的向心性，考虑到福州温暖湿润的气候特征，通过底层架空层、内院、螺旋上升的空中花园等形成适合当地气候的多层次室外交流场所。建筑裙楼采用半圆形的环廊与地形相呼应，层层退台簇拥高层塔楼，强调了图书馆在校园中的中心地位和向心力。

The new campus library of Fujian University of Technology is the central building of the campus and the tallest structure in Fuzhou University Town. The library has a variety of outdoor spaces, and shows a strong sense of centrality on the new campus. In view of the warm and humid climate characteristics of Fuzhou, we design a number of overhead floors, inner courtyards and spiraling sky gardens for the library, which form a multi-level outdoor communication venue suitable for the local climate. The semi-circular corridor of the podium echoes the topography, while the terraced podium form around the high-rise tower highlights the central position and the centrality of the library.

福建工程学院新校区图书馆
LIBRARY OF FUJIAN UNIVERSITY OF TECHNOLOGY

广西东盟国际职业技术学院图书馆
LIBRARY OF GUANGXI ASEAN INTERNATIONAL VOCATIONAL AND TECHNICAL COLLEGE

项目地点：广西壮族自治区崇左市
设计时间：2017 年
竣工时间：2019 年
建筑面积：257,537.21 m^2

Location: Chongzuo, Guangxi
Design: 2017
Completion: 2019
GFA: 257,537.21 m^2

设计缔造东盟特色，借鉴中国传统合院式空间布局和重檐与架空等东盟建筑特征，以轴线、对称、均衡等手法强化校园的空间序列，以规划、景观、建筑三位一体的整体化校园设计手法，打造壮域学府、东盟之窗。

“一轴”是指校园中心礼仪轴。规划中充分考虑主入口的形象问题，在东面设置校园主入口，并于主入口处设校前广场，两侧的教学楼围合成校园的礼仪广场，并延伸至图书馆，形成一条中心礼仪主轴。“一带”是指沿湖景观带。用地中心设置连续的景观水体，各大功能区环湖而设，有效地串联起园区功能组团，形成一条贯穿南北的沿湖景观带。

The design reflects the characteristics of ASEAN by drawing on the traditional Chinese courtyard-style spatial layout and the characteristics of ASEAN architecture such as double eaves and open-up floors, and strengthens the spatial sequence of the campus by means of axis, symmetry and balance. The campus design is integrated with planning, landscape and architecture to create a college in the region of Zhuang ethnic group and a window of ASEAN.

"One axis" refers to the campus'central ceremonial axis. The presence of the main entrance is fully considered in the planning. The main entrance of the campus is planned on the east where a front square is also provided. The teaching buildings flank the ceremonial square which extends to the library to form a central ceremonial axis. "One belt" refers to the landscape along the lake. Continuous landscaping water elements are provided at the center of the site, while the major functional zones are planned around the lake. By doing so, the functional zones are effectively linked up with each other and a lakefront landscaped belt is established from north to south.

广西东盟国际职业技术学院图书馆
LIBRARY OF GUANGXI ASEAN INTERNATIONAL VOCATIONAL AND TECHNICAL COLLEGE

教学实验楼
TEACHING & LABORATORY BUILDING

华南理工大学 31、32 号楼

NO. 31 AND NO. 32 BUILDINGS, SOUTH CHINA UNIVERSITY OF TECHNOLOGY

项目地点：广东省广州市
设计时间：2001 年
竣工时间：2004 年
建筑面积：46,000 m^2

Location: Guangzhou, Guangdong
Design: 2001
Completion: 2004
GFA: 46,000 m^2

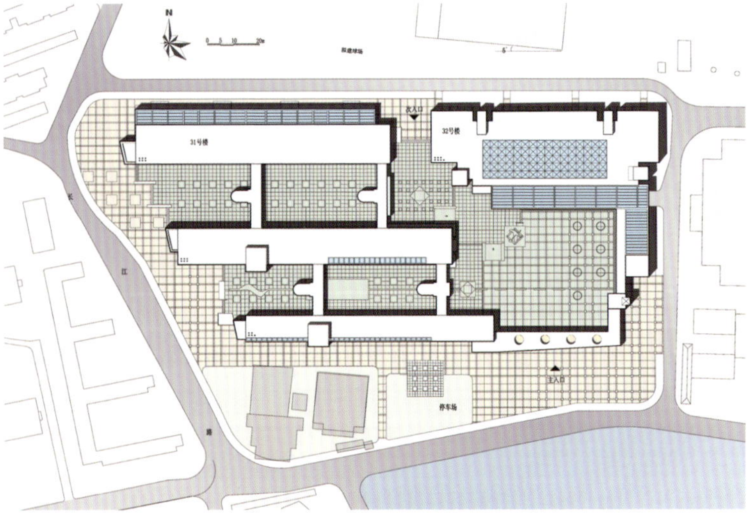

华南理工大学 31、32 号楼
NO. 31 AND NO. 32 BUILDINGS, SOUTH CHINA UNIVERSITY OF TECHNOLOGY

华南理工大学31号、32号教学楼位于华南理工大学教学区内，面向景色怡人的西湖，其总建筑面积46,000 m^2，采取庭院式布局，围绕自身庭院与周围绿化、湖面相掩映，组成了一个优美、亲切、宜人的教学区。华南理工大学31号、32号教学楼创作实践，以适应地域自然与人文环境为出发点，兼容并蓄地吸取古今中外建筑文化的精华，并以现代建筑语言表达岭南新建筑特点——适当的开口、丰富的阴影与充分的通风，形成一种适合岭南地区湿热气候的有韵律的美感，力图塑造具有地域特色、文化内涵与时代气息的岭南校园新建筑。本设计力图在以下几方面有所创新：

· 建筑与环境的和谐共生；

· 富有岭南地域特色的建筑设计策略；

· 场所文化意义表达。

No. 31 and No. 32 Teaching Buildings are located in the academic area of SCUT, facing the scenic West Lake with a gross floor area of 46,000 m^2. They takes a Courtyard layout that interacts with the the surrounding green spaces and the lake to form a beautiful, amicable and agreeable academic area. The design starts with the concept of adapting to the local natural and humanistic environment, then eclectically absorbs the essence of ancient and modern Chinese and foreign architectural culture to portray, with modern architectural language, the new characteristics of Lingnan architecture-that is, appropriate openings, plenty of shadow and sufficient ventilation, which presents a rhythmic aesthetics ideal for the hot and humid climate of Lingnan region-, and eventually create two new campus buildings with regional features, cultural connotations and the tempo of modern times. Some innovation attempts are made for this project, including:

· Harmonious coexistence of buildings and the environment.

· Architectural design strategy full of regional features of Lingnan.

· Representation of the cultural meanings of a place.

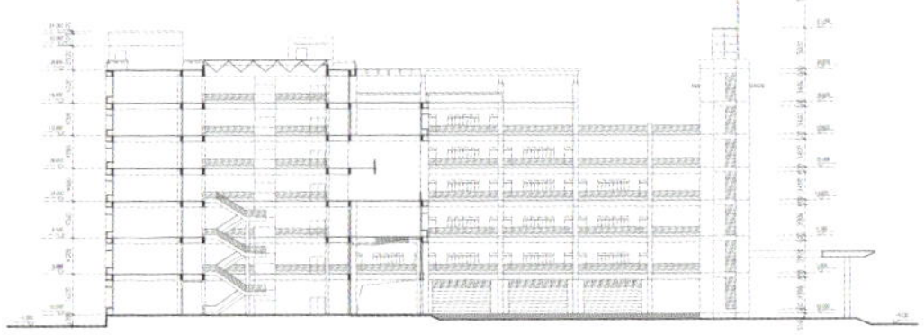

华南理工大学 31、32 号楼
NO. 31 AND NO. 32 BUILDINGS, SOUTH CHINA UNIVERSITY OF TECHNOLOGY

五邑大学教学楼
MAIN TEACHING BUILDING OF WUYI UNIVERSITY

项目地点：广东省江门市
设计时间：1984 年
竣工时间：1986 年
用地面积：46,000 m^2
曾获奖项：建设部优秀建筑工程设计二等奖（1987 年）
教育部全国教育建筑优秀设计奖二等奖（1987 年）

Location: Jiangmen, Guangdong
Design: 1984
Completion: 1986
Site Area: 46,000 m^2
Awards:
The Second Prize for Excellent Construction Engineering Design by the Ministry of Construction (1987)
The Second Prize for National Excellent Architectural Design of Education Building by the Ministry of Education (1987)

五邑大学教学主楼建筑面积 46,000 m^2，设计突出岭南气候特点、大学校园人文氛围和校园环境特征，在新意识、新功能、新技术条件下，创造岭南建筑的新风格，采用“位移”的剖面设计和架空手法，解决遮阳、通风、挡雨和“交往空间”的问题，造型简洁大方。

With a floor area of 46,000 m^2, the main teaching building of Wuyi University responds to the climate characteristics of South China, the cultural atmosphere of a university campus and the distinctive elements on campus in design. Driven by the new vision, new functions and new technologies, it establishes a new architectural style of Lingnan region. The section design of "displacement" and the approach of open-up spaces have successfully provided solutions to the issues regarding sunshading, ventilation, rain canopy and "social spaces" and portrayed a concise and elegant building shape.

五邑大学教学楼

MAIN TEACHING BUILDING OF WUYI UNIVERSITY

四川大学新校区第二基础实验楼
NO. 2 BASIC EXPERIMENT BUILDING OF SICHUAN UNIVERSITY (NEW CAMPUS)

项目地点：四川省成都市
设计时间：2001 年
竣工时间：2003 年
建筑面积：42,380 m^2

Location: Chengdu, Sichuan
Design: 2001
Completion: 2003
GFA: 42,380 m^2

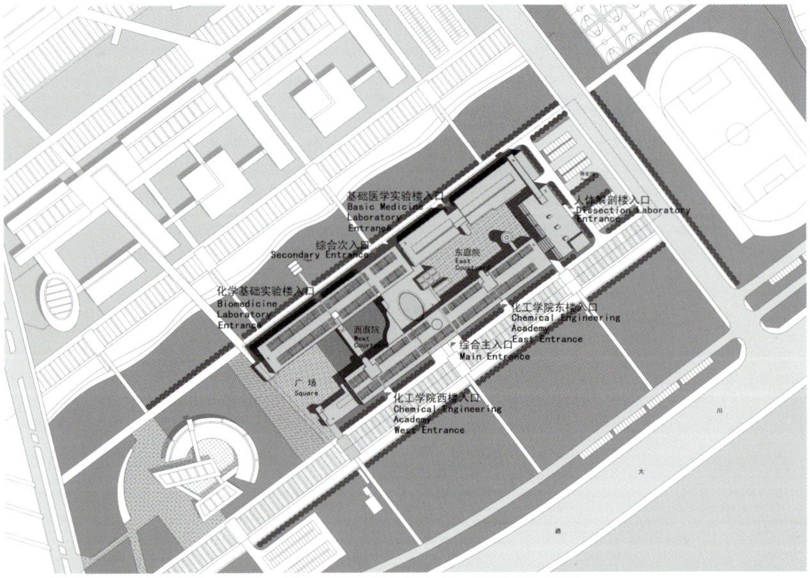

四川大学新校区第二基础实验楼

NO. 2 BASIC EXPERIMENT BUILDING OF SICHUAN UNIVERSITY (NEW CAMPUS)

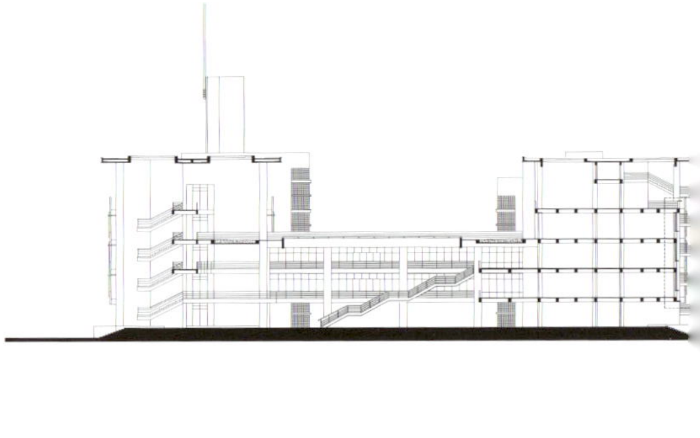

实验楼群位于四川大学新校区的东南角，设化学基础实验（A区）、化工学院（B区）、生物医学基础实验（C区）、人体解剖实验（D区）四个不同的功能区，各功能分区相对独立，设有独立的出入口。在总体布局上通过中庭空间把这些使用功能复杂、性质各异的实验楼清晰地组合成一个有机整体，并围合成两种不同形态的院落空间。

布局上适应实验楼日常教学实验的要求，更为其提供所缺乏的对共享空间和设施的使用机会。为加强内走廊采光与通风效果，并避免狭长感，每 30 m 左右设 10 m 宽开口，并设置阳台，与电梯厅相结合，可供师生休憩。

作为科学实验建筑，设计坚持形式与功能的统一，在表现出严谨与理性的同时，利用建筑语言及其张力体现了灵活性的一面。由于建筑长度超过 240 m，因此在适当的部位设置了虚空间，同时也作为建筑的各入口空间，嵌以鲜色体块加以识别，活跃立面气氛。

在屋面设有排风机技术夹层，排风口上方采用通透的混凝土百叶，保证了建筑群的一体性，同时也产生了丰富的光影。室外挂板为第二立面，挂板不但可以起到遮阳作用，其与外墙之间的间隙可以放置空调室外机。

实验楼虽采用了常规的构造和材料，却创造出了大气精致的立面效果和丰富的室内外空间，有效地结合使用功能，塑造了具有鲜明特性的现代实验建筑。

The cluster of experiment buildings located at the southeast corner of the new campus of Sichuan University is composed of four different functional areas: basic chemical experiment area (Area A), College of Chemical Engineering (Area B), basic biomedical experiment area (Area C) and human anatomy experiment area (Area D), which are separated from one another with independent entrances and exits. In the master plan, an atrium is designed to link together these experiment buildings of complex functions and distinct properties into an organic whole, which gives shape to two different forms of enclosed courtyard space.

The layout not only meets the requirements of the daily teaching experiments but also makes up for the shortage of opportunities for use of shared spaces and facilities. To improve daylighting and ventilation and avoid the lengthy and narrow space in the inner corridor, 10 m wide openings are arranged at intervals of around 30 m and balconies provided in combination with the elevator lobbies for the teachers and students to have a rest.

The design for this scientific experiment building adheres to the unity of form and function, and, while presenting a sober and rational appearance, also offers flexibility via the architectural vocabulary. Since the building is more than 240 m long, some voids are provided at the proper locations as entrance spaces, and finished with bright-colored tiles for identification and for spicing up the facade.

A technical mezzanine is provided on the roof for installation of the exhausters, with open concrete lamella placed on top of the exhaust outlets to ensure the integrity of clustered buildings and create varied shadow and light effects. The exterior hanging panels, as the secondary facade, not only function as sunshade, but also allow the gap between the exterior wall and the panels for installation of the outdoor AC units.

Despite of the conventional structures and materials employed, generous and elegant facades and diverse indoor and outdoor spaces are created in combination with the functional requirements, constituting a modern experiment building with distinctive identity.

河海大学江宁校区核心教学区

CORE TEACHING AREA OF JIANGNING CAMPUS OF HOHAI UNIVERSITY

项目地点：江苏省南京市
设计时间：2000 年
竣工时间：2001 年
用地面积：26,000 m^2
建筑面积：30,000 m^2
曾获奖项：广东省注册建筑师协会第二次优秀建筑提名奖（2003 年）

Location: Nanjing, Jiangsu
Design: 2000
Completion: 2001
Site Area: 26,000 m^2
GFA: 30,000 m^2
Award:
Finalist of 2nd Excellent Architecture Creation Award by Guangdong Chapter of Association of Chinese Registered Architects (ACRAGD) (2003)

河海大学江宁校区核心教学区包括图书馆，第一、第二教学楼，现代教育中心，建筑面积约为 30,000 m^2，位于学校的中轴线上，是整个新校区的核心部分。

核心教学区的总体布局在原来规划的框架中有所发展，实现了彻底的人、车（包括自行车）的分流。教学楼面临环路的底层部分设置半地下的自行车停放场地，以解决学生上课时的自行车停放问题。

中心广场的东面是第一教学楼和现代教育中心，西面是第二教学楼。三栋建筑的山墙面成对称布局，走廊尽端的楼梯间在这里是重要的造型元素，这一相同的元素使得中心广场的界面单纯而富有韵律，突出了中心广场。与中心广场相接的是每栋建筑各有主题的内庭院，它们互为背景，又共同组成丰富整体的核心区室外环境。

教学区建筑群各楼高度均为五层，局部六层，教室均采用外走廊，面向庭院的界面都处理成敞廊，把人的活动从室内延伸到室外。建筑的色调以朴素的青灰和白色为主，点缀以蓝色、红色、黄色的钢构件，沉稳中不失活泼。各栋建筑既是分开设计各有特点，同时也依据一些相同的准则——色彩、材料、建筑高度等，利用相同的建筑元素——造型楼梯间、栏杆、连廊等，始终保持着建筑和环境系统的整体性。

The Core Teaching Area of Jiangning Campus, Hohai University, consists of the library, Teaching Building A, Teaching Building B and Center for Modern Education. With a GFA of about 30,000 sqm, it is located right on the central axis of the campus and forms the core of the entire new campus.

The overall layout of the Core Teaching Area, which has been improved on the original plan, effectively separates pedestrian circulations from vehicular circulations (including bicycle circulations). Semi-underground parking areas are designed in the lower part of the ring road facing the teaching buildings to provide bicycle parking spaces for students.

The Central Square faces Teaching Building A and Center for Modern Education to the east and Teaching Building B to the west. Gable walls of the three buildings form a symmetrical layout. Stairways, located at the end of the corridors, become an important element in building shape. This identical element highlights the Central Square by creating simple yet rhythmic interfaces. Internal courtyards of buildings, each with its own theme, are all connected to the Central Square. They not only act as a background for each other but also make up of a diversified and integral outdoor environment for the Core Teaching Area.

Most buildings within the Core Teaching Area have 5 levels and some have 6 levels aboveground. Classrooms are arranged along the external corridor. Interfaces facing courtyards are designed as open corridors, extending people's activity space from indoor to outdoor space. As for colors, plain grey and white are used in general for buildings, which are combined with blue, red and yellow steel members to create a sedate yet lively style. Each building has its own design and still follows some unified principles in terms of colors, materials and building heights. Identical architectural elements, such as regular stairways, handrails and corridors, consistently help maintain the integrity of the buildings and environment.

河海大学江宁校区核心教学区
CORE TEACHING AREA OF JIANGNING CAMPUS OF HOHAI UNIVERSITY

吉林大学中心校区基础教学园

BASIC EDUCATION PARK OF JILIN UNIVERSITY CENTER CAMPUS

项目地点：吉林省长春市
设计时间：2013 年
用地面积：508,000 m^2
建筑面积：518,000 m^2

Location: Changchun, Jilin
Design: 2013
Site Area: 508,000 m^2
GFA: 518,000 m^2

建筑布局庄严肃穆，稳重大气，沿轴线向周边舒展对称，整体氛围符合吉林大学校园基调。校园环境布局呼应老校区，景观区及中心绿带张弛有度，适度变化，与自然环境形成相互渗透、气韵流动的整体形态。建筑形态借鉴中国古典城市，形成围合院落式。建筑功能立足于现代高等教育的教学与科研需求，结合长春本地的建筑文化与吉林大学的悠久历史，将时代性、文化性、地域性融于一体。

The layout of the building is solemn and stable, and it is symmetrical along the axis. The overall atmosphere conforms to the tone of the campus of Jilin University. The layout of the campus environment echoes the old campus. The landscape area and the center green belt are relaxed and moderately changed, forming an overall form of mutual penetration and air flow with the natural environment. The architectural form draws on the classical Chinese city and forms a courtyard. Based on the teaching and research needs of modern higher education, the building function combines the local architectural culture of Changchun with the long history of Jilin University to blend the era, culture and regionality.

武汉大学文科区
LIBERAL ARTS AREA OF WUHAN UNIVERSITY

项目地点：湖北省武汉市
设计时间：2002 年
竣工时间：2004 年
用地面积：50,000 m^2
建筑面积：80,000 m^2

Location: Wuhan, Hubei
Design: 2002
Completion: 2004
Site Area: 50,000 m^2
GFA: 80,000 m^2

武汉大学文科区由法学大楼、商学大楼和外语大楼组成，建设用地位于武汉大学内校园东区，基地坐拥珞珈山，东望东湖，地势蜿蜒起伏，错落有致，绿树成荫。基地西侧山顶为校园标志建筑之一——人文博物馆。

文科区建筑群通过空间序列的组织切入原有校园环境中，形成具有特色的规划语言。整个规划通过自由轴线的贯穿，围合广场的点缀及对位关系的形成，充分体现了文科建筑群其理性与感性相结合的专业特性。建筑采用多层院落式布局手法，通过高低错落的坡屋顶的做法，弱化了建筑庞大体量并有效地保护了原有绿化环境。

The Liberal Arts Area of Wuhan University consisting of Law Building, Commerce Building and Foreign Language Building is located in the east of Wuhan University. With superior views of the Luojia Mountain as well as the eastern Donghu Lake, the site features winding and undulating landforms and the shades of luxuriant trees. On mountaintop in the west of the site is one of the landmarks of the campus, namely, the Museum of Humanities.

The building complex of Liberal Arts Area is integrated into the original campus environment through the organization of space sequence, and forms the distinctively featured planning language. The planning solution fully reflects the specialty characteristic of liberal arts complex, i.e., combination of sense and sensibility through the free-flowing axis penetrating through the site, the plazas enclosed by buildings, as well as the symmetrical composition. The building layout features the multi-level courtyards, while the sloping roofs at varied vertical levels mitigate the huge building volumes and effectively preserve the original green environment.

肇庆学院艺术教学大楼
ZHAOQING COLLEGE ARTS BUILDING

项目位置：广东省肇庆市
设计时间：2011 年
竣工时间：2016 年
建筑规模：19,880 m^2

Location: Zhaoqing, Guangdong
Design: 2011
Completion: 2016
GFA: 19,880 m^2

一体化的设计理念是艺术教学大楼方案设计的指导思想，同时，艺术教学大楼作为肇庆学院新的标志性建筑，对其艺术文化理念的演绎也是本案的重点。艺术教学大楼外形采用飘带作为母题，墙面上水平向的韵律变化，像跳动的音符，暗示其深厚的艺术文化积淀和活跃的空间氛围。在视觉上，不同的色彩塑造着不同的空间氛围，基于不同功能用房的空间性格，赋予不同的空间色彩，能够形成活跃的视觉焦点，为艺术教学大楼带来充满生机活力的空间感受。

An integrated design approach is adopted to guide the design of the arts building. Meanwhile, the interpretation of the artistic and cultural connotation of the building is also a focus of this project, a new landmark planned for the college. The building form resembles a ribbon, while the horizontal rhythmic changes on the facade, just like the beating notes, implying the profound artistic and cultural connotation and dynamic atmosphere of the spaces. Visually, different colors foster different spatial atmospheres. Different colors are applied in view of the spatial characteristics of different functional rooms, creating lively visual focus and dynamic spaces in the building.

中国石油大学（北京）实验办公综合楼
LAB AND OFFICE COMPLEX OF CHINA UNIVERSITY OF PETROLEUM (BEIJING)

项目位置：北京市
设计时间：2014 年
竣工时间：2015 年
建筑规模：72,000 m^2

Location: Beijing
Design: 2014
Completion: 2015
GFA: 72,000 m^2

原有的校园规划遵循着两套轴线系统。其一是以图书馆为中心的 45° 轴线，统领校园的整体秩序；另一套是正南北朝向，与周边的城市形态呼应，两套轴线系统互相交错。受到以上因素的综合制约，综合楼布局的形态决定其融入校园秩序的成败。考虑到建设规模的巨大以及 60 m 的高度限制，设计决定采用周边式布局。东南面设置四层裙楼，很好地与城市交叉口四周的建筑高度、形态呼应，其容纳对外办公服务功能，减少高层部分的面积。两座高层塔楼则通过错位布置，保证景观视线的畅通，也很好地呼应两套轴线系统，创造和谐共存的校园秩序。

The original campus plan follows two sets of interwoven axis systems. The first is a library centered 45° grid that leads the spatial order of the whole campus. The second one is in due north-south to echo with the urban context. Given the aforesaid constraints, how to locate the complex becomes key to its successful integration into the campus order. Considering the huge building scale and the 60-meter height limit, we decided to place the building along the perimeter of the site. A four-storey podium in the southeast perfectly responds to the heights and forms of the buildings around the intersection with the city. Planned as offices serving external visitors, the podium sees reduced floor area on higher floors. The two towers are staggered to ensure unblocked views, respond to the two sets of axis systems and create a harmonious campus order.

校园特色建筑
CAMPUS CHARACTERISTIC BUILDING

华南理工大学逸夫人文馆

SIR RUN RUN SHAW BUILDING OF HUMANITIES, SOUTH CHINA UNIVERSITY OF TECHNOLOGY

项目地点：广东省广州市
设计时间：2001—2002 年
竣工时间：2002 年
用地面积：8,805 m^2
建筑面积：6,398 m^2
曾获奖项：2005 年教育部优秀勘察设计一等奖
2005 年建设部优秀勘察设计一等奖
第三届广东省注册建筑师优秀建筑创作奖
第三届中国建筑学会建筑创作奖（佳作奖）
获 2006 年度全国优秀工程设计金奖

Location: Guangzhou, Guangdong
Design: 2001-2002
Completion: 2002
Site Area: 8,805 m^2
GFA: 6,398 m^2
Awards:
The First Prize for Excellent Exploration and Design by the Ministry of Education (2005)
The First Prize for Excellent Exploration and Design by the Ministry of Construction (2005)
The 3rd Excellent Architectural Creation Award by Guangdong Chapter of Association of Chinese Registered Architects
Honorable Mention of the 3rd ASC Architectural Creation Award
Gold Award for National Excellent Engineering Design (2006)

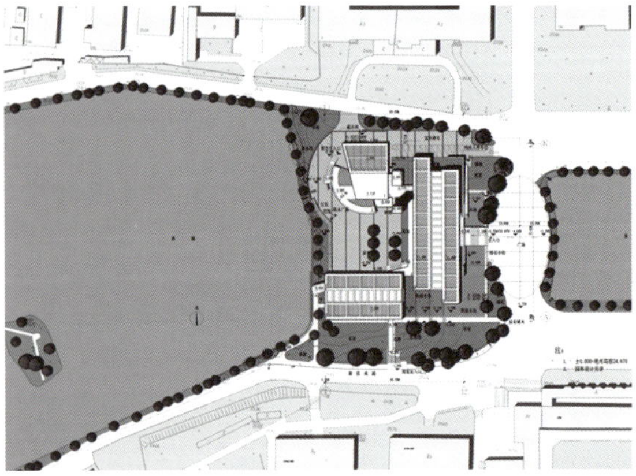

华南理工大学逸夫人文馆
SIR RUN RUN SHAW BUILDING OF HUMANITIES, SOUTH CHINA UNIVERSITY OF TECHNOLOGY

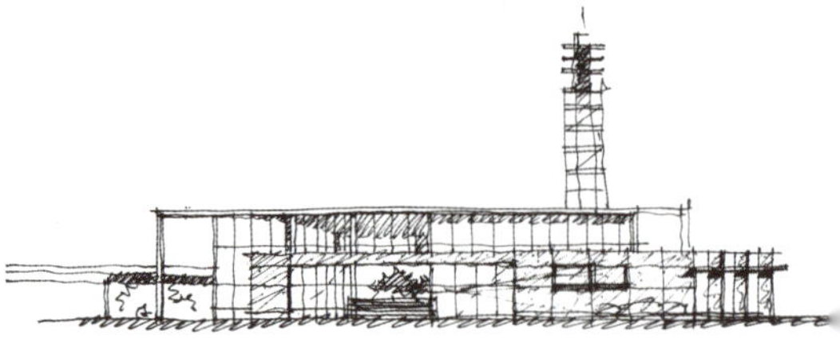

该方案为内部竞赛中标方案。方案延续以院落为中心的空间格局，保留人们心中"庭院深深""绿树成荫"的美好记忆，创造出空灵通透、步移景异的新岭南建筑。在设计时以"少一些、透一些"为原则，积极回应南方建筑特有的通风、采光、遮阳问题。平面为三组建筑围合而成，中间穿插以院落，建筑高 2 ~ 3 层。

This bid-winning design scheme continues the courtyard-centered spatial layout, maintaining the fond memory about the deep yard sheltered by trees and creating the new Lingnan architecture characterized by the light and transparent spaces and the changing views Following the principle of being less and more transparent, this scheme proactively responds to issues peculiar to the architectures in south China, such as ventilation, lighting and sun-shading. In terms of the planar layout, the project is enclosed by three groups of architectures with courtyard interwoven therein from time to time. Buildings are two to three stories.

华南理工大学逸夫人文馆

SIR RUN RUN SHAW BUILDING OF HUMANITIES, SOUTH CHINA UNIVERSITY OF TECHNOLOGY

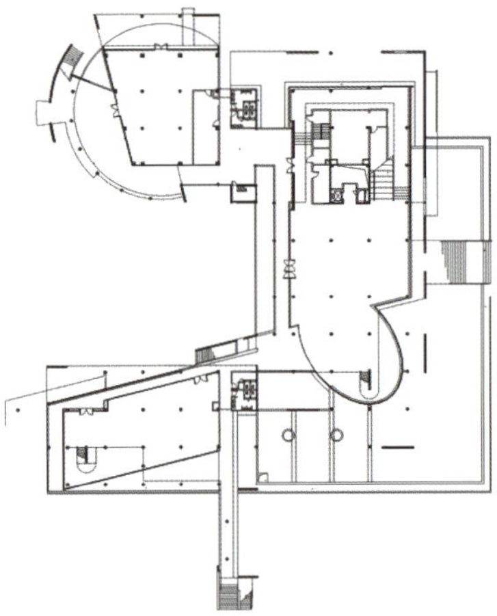

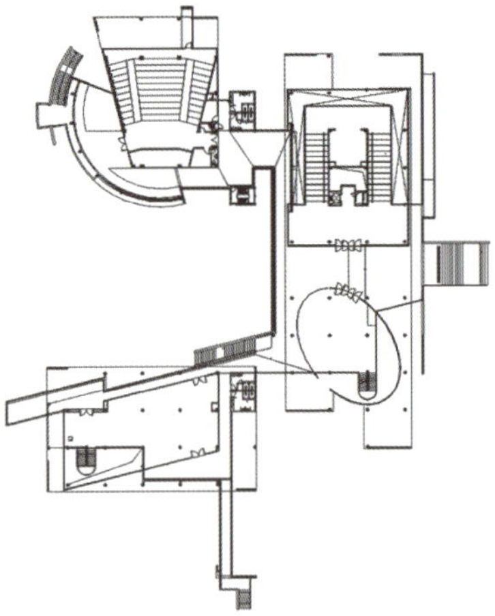

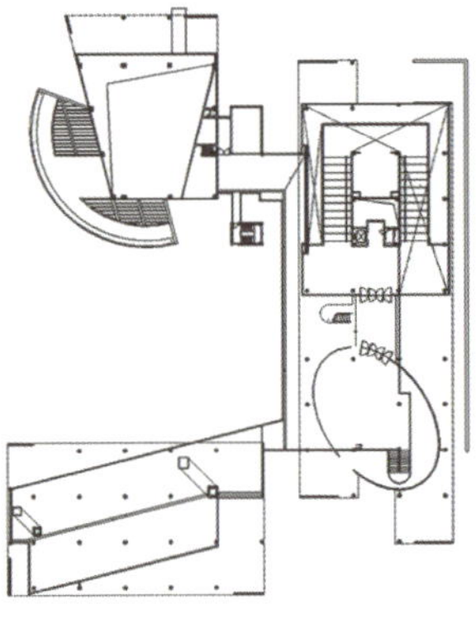

华南理工大学逸夫人文馆
SIR RUN RUN SHAW BUILDING OF HUMANITIES, SOUTH CHINA UNIVERSITY OF TECHNOLOGY

延续校园生态走廊——华工大逸夫人文馆创作随笔

华工大逸夫人文馆是华南理工大学校庆 50 周年的重点工程。校方的意见是将其建成一个“窗口”，展示华工大的人文历史及现代风貌，同时为师生提供交往活动的场所。人文馆位于华工大东湖、西湖生态带的中心点，东西皆景；同时也是华工大南、北二区的连接中枢，地理位置得天独厚。用地原址为教工俱乐部，是一个文化及生活交流的场所。其优美的环境、深深的庭院曾带给华工大师生许多美好的回忆，是华工大校园文脉的重要组成部分。新的人文馆如何与这个特有的环境相互沟通，特别是与东湖、西湖景观沟通，它能否延续华工大师生对原地址的固有情结，成为摆在设计者面前的首要问题。

每个基地从某种概念上说都是独一无二的，是自然和社会活动相互作用的结果。建筑师有责任使设计同先前存在的场所保持某种连续性。东西走向的校园生态走廊由景致优美的东、西湖组成。东湖为一个矩形水面，是华工大校园规划中轴线的主要组成部分，其水面开阔，四岸浓荫，气势不凡。校园教学区许多建筑如 2 号楼、27 号楼、逸夫科学馆、设计院等均沿东湖周围整齐排列，给人一种方整、严肃的感觉。西湖则为一个自由水面风景湖，湖水曲折，杨柳垂岸，气象万千。其四周为校园的生活区，研一、专家楼、华工宾馆星星点点撒落其间，显得格外自然、亲切。针对上述情况，人文馆之布局顺应东、西湖的特点：在东湖边布置一条南北走向的展厅，以期对矩形湖面形成围合之势，保持东湖现有方整的格局。而西面则采用较自由的平面构成，以较小的建筑体量结合园林、亲水设计与环境融为一体。同时在用地南北两侧留出适当的“空白”做休闲绿化用地，强调了一种退让的感觉，减少建筑对南北两侧道路的压迫，这样一来也贯通了东、西湖湖滨路的景观视线，使两湖在空间上更好地融为一体。在总体规划上，面向东湖一侧的展厅亦退入 12 m 做景观水池，用建筑手法延伸了东湖水的格局，拓宽了入口处的视野。一桥飞跨水池，穿过开放式的围墙，进入宽敞的架空门廊，透过内庭院的白玉兰树，这时人的视线豁然开朗，望向远处波光粼粼的西湖，可以真正感受到一个激动人心的校园空间！

根据现有场地的特殊位置及校园生态的空间设计要求，我们确定了建筑的设计思想为——少一些、空一些、透一些、低一些，以强调场所精神和整体效果。首先考虑的是其整体尺度不应过大，其次是建筑空间应有较大的“弹性”。在设计上，建筑组合采用了化整为零的手法进行处理，在整体框架内加进了方形、平行四边形、椭圆等活跃元素，刻意强调了空间、光线的转换。整体结构也结合南方气候进行遮阳设计，使建筑光影在一天中的不同时间里随太阳的移动而改变，突出了空间、场所在视觉上的感染力。建筑的平、剖面设计和大片玻璃的运用，也突显了建筑的通透性。建筑高度控制在 2—3 层，尽量体现“低一些”的设计精神，使建筑掩映在绿树丛中。在材料上，通过选用水色透明玻璃，浅米色大理石及浅灰色铝板进行组合，使建筑基面处理更加简单、透明，同时强调虚实对比，使人文馆具备了内敛明快的气质。

功能分区是定义场所秩序的最有效手段。人文馆功能分为三个部分——展厅、阅览室及报告厅、咖啡厅，分别布置在了东、南、北三个方向，由连廊将各功能区联系在一起。它们共同围合成了一个面向西湖的半开放庭院，延续了原教工俱乐部庭院空间布局。同时很好地解决了各功能区采光通风的问题，体现了“空一些，透一些”的设计思想。展厅是一个三层的建筑，由一个方形和一个椭圆形平面构成。方形的展厅为平坡式的展廊，坡道围绕展墙旋转而上，展厅四周均设计成透明的，人们在观看展览的同时也能欣赏到诗一般的东、西湖美景。椭圆形的展厅以平面布展为主，以满足不同展览的需要。展厅除展墙外，其余均采用大面积透明玻璃，强调内外情景交融。阅览室为一个二层空间，沿南北向设置，与展厅成斜角布局，从而拓宽内庭院的开口空间。人文馆的北侧一层为咖啡厅，二层是报告厅，在其西南角用一弧形的架空廊弱化其实体感，并将人的视线从内院延伸至开阔的西湖。在弧线的尽端位置设立了钟塔，钟塔高为 40 m，使宽广的校园中心区有了一个空间上的视觉制高点。此外，我们希望在建筑组合上为学校与师生之间建立一个自由进出的交流空间。原建筑围合出来的院落及院落之间穿行的经历，深深印在每个华工大师生的脑海中，充满文脉气息的人文馆，理应将这一记忆及人文延续和发展下去，因此在方案中充分尊重原有的院落空间布局，保留了基地内树木，以新的建筑形式扩大、围合、限定，并通过空间渗透将两个气氛不同的院落空间联系起来，成为一个整体、通透、开敞的绿色空间。结合新设的咖啡厅，令人在此驻足，观赏美景，品味人生，也拉近了新建筑与华工大师生的“距离”。人文馆水榭小品位于其东广场水边，是一个简之又简的作品。由人文馆斜线延续过来的折线框架与 6 m × 6 m 的正方形水榭的几何组合表达出对空间的一种限制和暗示，其造型并没有直接的功能作用，但却是空间秩序极其重要的组成部分，它与西湖小亭遥遥相对，也是将来师生摄影留念的好地方。

在建筑地域性问题上，除了利用庭院、连廊进行通风组织外，还从建筑物理方面针对岭南气候特征做了进一步探讨和设计，如在屋顶设可调节百叶，通过变换百叶板角度进行有效遮阳组织；利用连廊及独立的造型墙体对西晒进行积极的遮蔽。另外，采用 Low—Ⅰ 玻璃及浅色墙面减少太阳光辐射作用。这些措施提高了建筑的适应能力，为南方建筑的未来发展迈出了试验性的一步。这组建筑不仅在于它充分考虑了与校园环境的组合、延续了校园的生态走廊，还在于它的功能赋予其人文性，是学校 70 年历史文化展览的缩影，从而极大地提高了校园的文化品位，比单纯的环境改造有了更为丰富的文化内涵。

作者：何镜堂、倪 阳

文章出处：本文曾发表于《世界建筑》2007 年 11 月

Extended Campus Ecological Corridor-An Essay on the Design of Building of Humanities of SCUT

The Building of Humanities of South China University of Technology (SCUT) is the key project for the 50th anniversary of SCUT. The owner's vision is to create a window to display the humanistic history and modern look of SCUT and to provide teachers and students with a place for communication. The building of humanities is located in the center of ecological strip mainly consists of the east lake and the west lake, with scenic attractions on both east and west sides. The site is also the connection hub of south and north parts of SCUT. The geographic location is unique. The site used to be the faculty club, a place for cultural and recreational communications. Its beautiful environment and spacious courtyard used to be fond memories of SCUT teachers and students and one of the most important components of SCUT's humanistic spirit. The first and foremost issues to the designers are how the new Building of Humanities communicate with this unique environment, especially with the lake scenes, and whether it can carry on the inherent complex attached to the original site.

Each site is unique in certain sense and it is the result of the interaction between natural and social activities. The responsibility of a designer is to retain certain continuity between the design and the original site. The campus ecological corridor in an east-west direction consists of beautiful east lake and west lake. The east lake is a rectangular water surface, and a major component of the axis of SCUT's campus planning. The open water is surrounded by tall trees on four banks, with a unique momentum. Many teaching buildings, such as the 2nd teaching building, 27th teaching building, Sir Run Run Shaw Science Building, the Design Institute are neatly arranged around the east lake to give it a square and solemn feeling. The west lake, on the other hand, is a scenic lake without particular shape. The lake scene is spectacular with water flowing freely and willows drooping over the water. Surrounding the west lake, it is the living quarter. No.1 graduate dormitory, expert building, SCUT Hotel scattered here and there, creating a pretty natural and cordial atmosphere. In consideration of the environmental factors, the layout of the Building of Humanities shall be in consistence with characteristics of the two lakes. An exhibition hall oriented north/south is arranged along the east lake to enclose the rectangular lake surface and to maintain the current square layout of the east lake. On the west side, comparatively free elevations and small building volume are adopted to allow the building to be integrated into the garden and water environment. At the same time, certain blanks are left out on the south and north side of the site for greenery, leaving a feeling of concession to relieve the pressure of the building on roads along south and north sides. By doing this, the two lakes are somehow connected when they are viewed from roads along banks and are better blended with each other in space. In the master plan, the exhibition hall along the east lake concedes for 12m for a landscape pool. This architectural design technique helps extend the layout of the east lake and expand the horizon from the entrance. Walking across a bridge over the pool, through the open wall and a spacious overhead porch, visitors are suddenly greeted by the shimmering water surface of the west lake in distance, appearing through the magnolia tree in the inner courtyard. An exciting campus space reveals itself just in front of them.

According to the specific position of the site and the spatial design requirements of campus ecology, we decided the architectural design concepts to be with less building mass, more transparency and lower height, to emphasize the spirit of the place and the overall effect. The first consideration is the whole size shall not be too large, and the second is the architectural space shall be with more flexibility. The building structure is taken into parts in design and squares, parallelograms, ovals and other lively factors are added into the overall framework to deliberately emphasize the transition of space and light. The climate of southern China is considered in shading design to allow lights and shadow of the building change along the position of the sun during the daytime and to improve the visual appeal of the space and the place. The building plan and profile design and the usage of large glasses help increase the transparency of the building. In compliance with the design concept of being lower, the whole building is of 2-3 stories and can be shaded by trees. In terms of material, the combination of water-color transparent glass, beige granite and light grey aluminium panel makes the building base simpler and more transparent, while the comparison of transparent and solid materials brings out the lively yet restrained temperament of the Building.

Functional zoning is the most effective way to define the order of a place. The Building of Humanities consists of three functional zones: the exhibition halls, the library and lecture hall and cafeteria, which are planned in east, south and north of the building and connected with corridors. Together they enclose a semi-open courtyard facing the west lake. The courtyard space layout is reserved from the original faculty club. The layout also solves the problem of lighting and ventilation for each functional zone and is in compliance with the design concept of more transparency and lower height. The exhibition hall is a three-storey building structure and consists of a square and an oval plan. The square exhibition hall is a flat sloping gallery and the slope spirals up around the display wall. The whole exhibition hall is designed transparent in four directions and visitors could admire the idyllic lake scene. The oval exhibition hall mainly supports horizontal display and meets the need of different exhibitions. Only except the display wall, large-scale transparent glasses are adopted for all the enclosing walls to allow the integration of exterior and interior. The library is a two-storey space along the south-north direction, forming a bevel together with the exhibition hall and allowing more open space for the interior courtyard. The ground floor of the north side of the Building is a cafeteria while the second floor is a lecture hall. A curved overhead porch on the southwest corner reduces the heaviness of volume from the building and leads the eyesight to the open west lake from the interior courtyard. At the end of the curve, a bell tower is designed with a height of 40m to provide a visual high ground to the spacious campus center. In addition, we hope to build a free exchange space for teachers and students with the combination of building structures. The original enclosed courtyard and the experience of walking through the courtyard have been the fond memory of every teacher and students of SCUT. The Building of Humanities, which is full with humanistic spirit, shall carry on and develop such memory. Therefore, the design scheme reserves the original courtyard space layout and the trees on the site, while new building structures enlarge, enclose and redefine the space and connect the two different courtyards through spatial penetration into one holistic, transparent and open green space. The newly added cafeteria gives visitors a moment to stay, to enjoy and to ponder, and the distance between the new building and the teachers and students of SCUT is shortened. An accessorial pavilion is located by the water of the eastern square of the Building and it is a work of simplism. the combination of the bevel framework extended from the Building and the square pavilion of 6m×6m forms a confinement and implication of space. The shape of the pavilion is not functional but it is a very significant part of the spatial order. It echoes with the small pavilion in the west lake and will be a nice place to take a shot.

In terms of regional characters of architecture, we not only organized ventilation through courtyard and corridors, but also applied architectural physics to the design in consideration of Lingnan climate. Adjustable blinds are adopted on the roof and the angle of blinds can be changed to improve the efficiency of shading. Corridors and independent decorative walls are used to reduce sun exposure on the west wall. Low-E glass and light hue is used on the walls to reduce sun radiation. These measures help improve the adaptability of the Building and started an experimental step toward the future development of buildings in south China. This Building is significant not only because of the thorough consideration of its integration with the campus environment and the extension of campus ecological corridor, but also because of its humanistic spirit articulated by its functions. It is a miniature of the 70-year historical and cultural heritage of SCUT. It greatly improves the taste of campus culture and conveys richer cultural connotations than pure environment renovation.

By He Jingtang, Ni Yang

Source: World Architecture, Nov. 2007

华南理工大学松花江路 14、18、20、30 ~ 37 号历史建筑保护更新

RENEWAL OF HISTORIC BUILDINGS AT NO. 14, 18, 20, 30 ~ 37, SONGHUAJIANG ROAD, SOUTH CHINA UNIVERSITY OF TECHNOLOGY

项目地点：广东省广州市
设计时间：2004 年
竣工时间：2011 年
用地面积：5,100 m^2
建筑面积：2,600 m^2
曾获奖项：首届岭南特色建筑设计奖

Location: Guangzhou, Guangdong
Design: 2004
Completion: 2011
Site Area: 5,100 m^2
GFA: 2,600 m^2
Award:
The First Lingnan-style Architectural Design Award

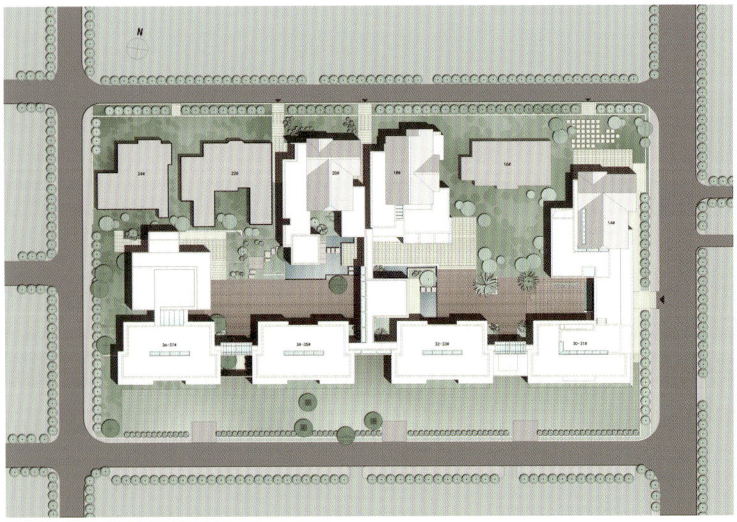

华南理工大学松花江路 14、18、20、30 ~ 37 号历史建筑保护更新

RENEWAL OF HISTORIC BUILDINGS AT NO. 14, 18, 20, 30 ~ 37, SONGHUAJIANG ROAD, SOUTH CHINA UNIVERSITY OF TECHNOLOGY

华南理工大学松花江路 14、18、20、30 ~ 37 号，原为 20 世纪 30 年代中山大学教授的居住区，现已被列为历史保护建筑。在该居住区内，北面一列是 5 栋 30 年代建成的坡屋顶别墅，南面一列是 4 栋 60 年代建成的独立式住宅。由于年久失修，这些建筑已破败，更有部分已成危房。面对这些在城市高速发展中被遗忘的历史建筑，我们从 2004 年起至今，经过三次渐进式的更新改造，采用园林化、机能更新、社区融入、生态节能等设计策略，将这组破败的历史建筑逐渐转变为一个独具岭南地域特色的、充满朝气活力的建筑师工作室，为校园创造了一个富有文化气息的创新基地，为社区创造了一个自然、人性化的公共活动场所。

Buildings at No. 14, 18, 20, 30~37, Songhuajiang Road on the campus of South China University of Technology (SCUT) were once the residences for the professors working with the former Sun Yat-sen University in the 1930s and are now listed as the historic buildings. In this residential block, the north part is occupied by five slope-roofed houses built in the 1930s, while four detached residential buildings built in the 1960s stand in the south. These buildings have fallen into disrepair, and some have been judged as dilapidated house. From 2004 until now, three rounds of renewal and renovations have been conducted step by step, and these run-down historic buildings forgotten in the rapidly growing city have been transformed into a vibrant architect studio with unique Lingnan features. The strategies employed thereof include the gardening, function renewal, community integration and ecology and energy efficiency. The renewal practices not only create an innovation base with cultural atmosphere on SCUT campus, but also offer a natural and human-oriented public activity place for the community.

华南理工大学松花江路 14、18、20、30 ~ 37 号历史建筑保护更新

RENEWAL OF HISTORIC BUILDINGS AT NO. 14, 18, 20, 30 ~ 37, SONGHUAJIANG ROAD, SOUTH CHINA UNIVERSITY OF TECHNOLOGY

中山大学科技综合楼

SCIENCE AND TECHNOLOGY COMPLEX, SUN YAT-SEN UNIVERSITY

项目地点：广东省广州市
设计时间：2007 年
竣工时间：2012 年
建筑面积：36,000 m^2
曾获奖项：2013 年度全国工程建设项目优秀设计成果三等奖
2013 年广东省优秀工程勘察设计三等奖
2014 年广东省注册建筑师协会优秀建筑佳作奖

Location: Guangzhou, Guangdong
Design: 2007
Completion: 2012
GFA: 36,000 m^2
Awards:
The Third Prize for Excellent Design of National Engineering Construction Project (2013)
The Third Prize for Excellent Engineering Exploration and Design of Guangdong Province (2013)
Honorable Mention of Excellent Architectural Creation Award by Guangdong Chapter of Association of Chinese Registered Architects (2014)

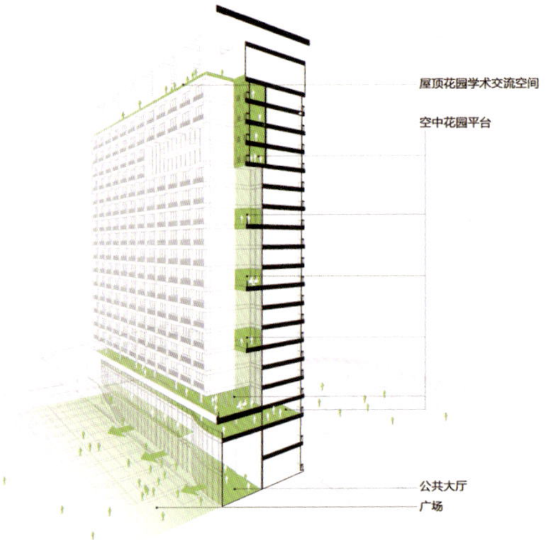

空中架空花园、办公楼层的园林电梯厅，营造科研创新空间中的非正式交往场所，起到休闲放松、激发创意的作用。空中花园结合绿化环境在改善环境的同时也加强了建筑物的通风散热效果，以适宜的节能技术实现生态型办公环境。

The elevated sky garden and the garden-like elevator lobbies on the office floors together create the informal social places in the building mainly for scientific research and innovation, which help people relax and inspire their creativity. The sky garden, with its green environment, not only improves ventilation and heat dissipation effect in the building but also puts into reality an ecological office environment with suitable energy efficient technologies.

中山大学科技文化交流中心

SCIENCE AND CULTURE EXCHANGE CENTER OF SUN YAT-SEN UNIVERSITY

项目地点：广东省广州市
设计时间：2007 年
竣工时间：2014 年
建筑面积：38,640 m^2

Location: Guangzhou, Guangdong
Design: 2007
Completion: 2014
GFA: 38,640 m^2

项目集接待、会议、餐饮、办公、住宿于一体，依托北面珠江城市景观和东面中大北湖校园景观，把餐饮和住宿沿基地东北两侧展开布置。裙楼的架空层花园及塔楼东面的空中花园和退台空中绿化，增加了建筑的观景平台，丰富客人的公共活动空间，体现岭南建筑的地域特征。建筑造型稳重大气，既彰显了中大校园形象，也丰富了珠江沿岸的城市界面，成为中大校园的城市名片。

The project integrates reception, conference, F&B, office and accommodation into one complex. F&B and accommodation facilities unfold along the east and north sides of the site, taking advantage of the cityscape of the Pearl River to the north and the North Lake campus view of the University to the east. Elevated garden of the podium, coupled with the sky garden and terraced sky greening east of the tower, provides additional building look-out and varied public spaces while reflecting the regional characteristics of Lingnan buildings. The calm and generous architectural form of the project, as the icon of the campus, enhances the presence of the University while diversifying the urban interface along the Pearl River.

临沂大学艺、音、美综合体
ARTS COMPLEX OF LINYI UNIVERSITY

项目地点：山东省临沂市
设计时间：2006 年
竣工时间：2011 年
用地面积：88,410 m^2
建筑面积：47,009 m^2

Location: Linyi, Shandong
Design: 2006
Completion: 2011
Site Area: 88,410 m^2
GFA: 47,009 m^2

“自由与秩序恰当结合是人们的永恒任务。没有自由，就无法发展；没有秩序，就无法持续发展。”

艺、音、美建筑综合体以一条流动的共享步行走廊把艺术中心、音乐学院和美术学院串联起来，脉络清晰有序。建筑整体是在无序中寻求有序，流动的空间形体在有序的背景下，增添了无序的艺术特质。以此为脉络，琴房、室外剧场、室外展场、临水跌落平台等由特殊要求的使用功能和设施配套，均找到了适合自身的合理位置。这种有序与无序辩证结合的布局方式，既延续了艺术特有的气质，也为将来建筑群的按需扩建提供了很有利的前提。多变的空间组合与简单的色彩，让未来的新建部分可以更为容易地融入整体建筑群之中，做到生长型的可持续发展。

“The proper combination of freedom and order is the eternal task of people. Without freedom, there can be no development. Without order, there can be no sustainable development.”

The complex connects the art center, the conservatory of music and the academy of fine arts via a flowing and shared walking corridor, showing a clear and orderly sequence. The building as a whole seeks order out of disorder. The flowing spatial form adds disordered yet artistic characteristics against an orderly background. Following this principle, the facilities of specific uses and requirements, such as the piano rooms, outdoor theater, outdoor exhibition halls, and waterfront cascading platform, etc. are all properly located. This layout approach combines order and disorder dialectically. It not only continues the unique artistic temperament, but also facilitates the future building expansion. The varied spaces and minimal colors enable the newly-built parts to better integrate with the building ensemble x, thus achieving the growth-oriented sustainable development.

武汉光电国家研究中心
WUHAN NATIONAL LABORATORY FOR OPTOELECTRONICS

项目位置：湖北省武汉市
设计时间：2012 年
竣工时间：2018 年
建筑规模：118,891 m^2

Location: Wuhan, Hubei
Design: 2012
Completion: 2018
GFA: 118,891 m^2

武汉光电国家研究中心位于华中科技大学校内，是全国六大国家研究中心之一，功能包括专业实验室、科研平台、行车大厅、会议中心等，为一座教学科研综合体。设计以“光电律动，绿韵华中”为设计概念，建筑通过水平与垂直两个维度的叠加、错动，形成一系列有机连续的共享空间，同时，上部连续空间与底层地景空间相互融合，组合出的架空灰空间成为汇聚各种活动的核心场所，建筑力求从多方面达到建筑与科技、艺术、生态、人性化的完美交汇融合。

Located on the campus of Huazhong University of Science and Technology, Wuhan National Laboratory for Optoelectronics is one of the six national research centers in China. As a teaching and scientific research complex, it includes functions of laboratories, research platforms, driving halls, and conference centers, etc. Following the concept of “a dynamic photoelectric facility in the green campus” , the building features a series of continuous organic shared spaces by overlapping and staggering the horizontal and vertical spaces. Meanwhile, the continuous spaces on upper floors integrate with the landscaped spaces on the ground level. The open-up floor thus formed provides gray spaces that become core places for various activities. The building strives to integrate architecture with technology, art, ecology and humanization from various aspects.

华南理工大学逸夫科学馆
SIR RUN RUN SHAW SCIENCE BUILDING OF SOUTH CHINA UNIVERSITY OF TECHNOLOGY

项目地点：广东省广州市
设计时间：1992 年
竣工时间：1993 年
建筑面积：7,353 m^2
曾获奖项：1995 年国家教委建筑设计一等奖第一名
1995 年建设部优秀设计二等奖
全国第四批逸夫捐款工程一等奖
中国建筑学会优秀建筑创作提名奖

Location: Guangzhou, Guangdong
Design: 1992
Completion: 1993
GFA: 7,353 m^2
Awards:
The First Place of the First Prize of Excellent Architectural Design Award by the State Education Commission of the PRC (1995)
The Second Prize for Excellent Design by the Ministry of Construction (1995)
The First Prize for the Fourth Batch of Chinese Aid Projects Donated by Sir Run Run Shaw
Nominee of ASC Excellent Architectural Creation Award

华南理工大学逸夫科学馆由教学科研和学术交流两大部分组成，总的设计构思既考虑与校园总体规划协调，保持校园文脉的延续，又着眼于现代功能的使用和室内外文化气氛的营造，在建筑艺术上突出时代和科技特色。

Sir Run Run Shaw Science Building on SCUT campus is composed of two main parts respectively for teaching & research and academic exchange. The design concept on one hand coordinates with the campus' master plan to pass on the cultural heritage, on the other hand, focuses on the modern functionality and interior/exterior cultural atmospheres to highlight the characteristics of times and technology.

华南理工大学逸夫科学馆
SIR RUN RUN SHAW SCIENCE BUILDING OF SOUTH CHINA UNIVERSITY OF TECHNOLOGY

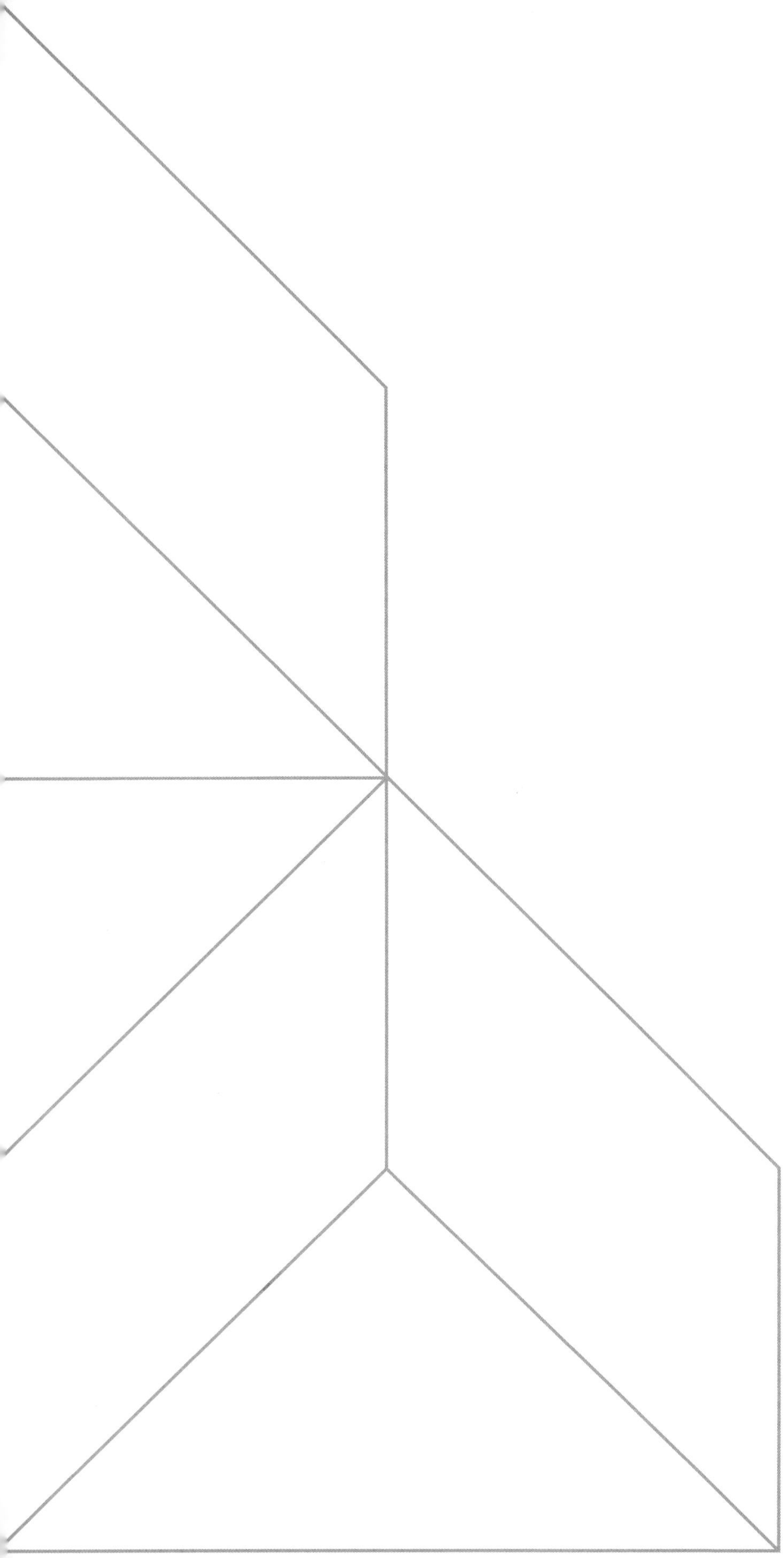

体育馆
SPORTS VENUE

2008 北京奥运会摔跤馆
WRESTLING ARENA FOR BEIJING 2008 OLYMPIC GAMES

项目地点：北京市
设计时间：2004 年
竣工时间：2007 年
用地面积：30,000 m^2
建筑面积：23,950 m^2
曾获奖项：2008 年北京奥运会摔跤比赛馆国际建筑设计方案竞赛第一名（2004 年）
中国建筑学会中华人民共和国成立 60 周年建筑创作大奖（2009 年）
中国建筑学会建筑创作奖：佳作奖（2008 年）
中国建筑学会蓝星杯第五届中国威海国际建筑设计大奖优秀奖（2009 年）
教育部优秀建筑设计奖一等奖（2009 年）

Location: Beijing
Design: 2004
Completion: 2007
Site Area: 30,000 m^2
GFA: 23,950 m^2
Awards:
The First Place of International Architectural Design Competition for Wrestling Arena for Beijing 2008 Olympic Games (2004)
ASC Grand Architectural Creation Award for the 60th Founding Anniversary of PRC (2009)
Honorable Mention of ASC Architectural Creation Award (2008)
Excellence Award, Blue Star Cup · The 5th China Weihai International Architectural Design Award & Competition (2009)
The First Prize of Excellent Architectural Design Award by the Ministry of Education (2009)

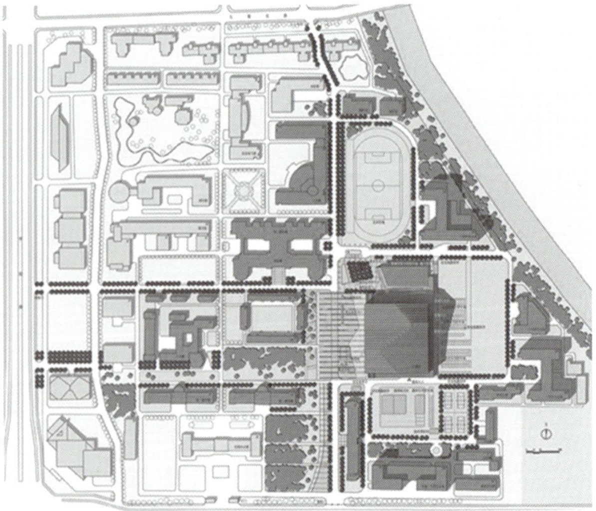

2008 北京奥运会摔跤馆

WRESTLING ARENA FOR BEIJING 2008 OLYMPIC GAMES

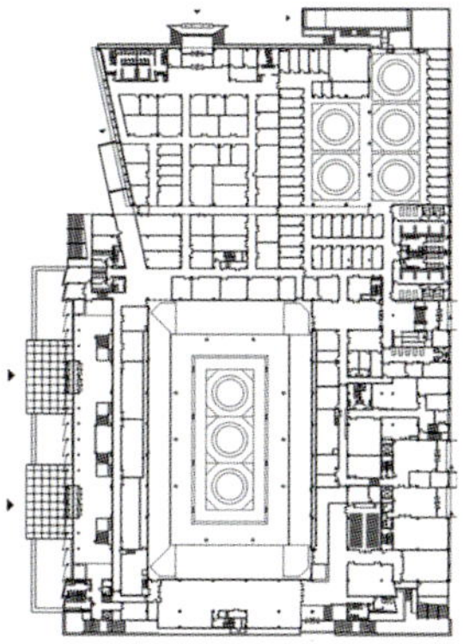

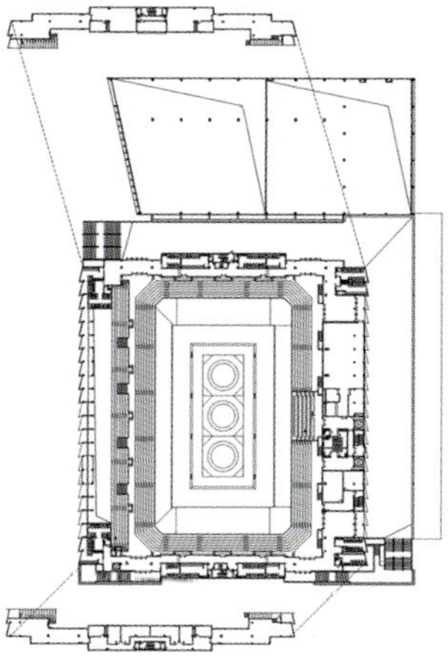

奥运摔跤馆位于中国农业大学东校区，北京 2008 年奥运会将其作为摔跤比赛用馆及残奥会的坐式排球比赛用馆。奥运会后经改造后包括：比赛大厅、标准篮球训练馆及游泳馆。在保证继续承接各类体育赛事的同时，满足体育教学、文艺演出、集会及学生社团使用。本工程很好地解决了校园环境中大型体育场馆的设计难题，建筑体量平实，功能配置紧凑，使赛时赛后的良性转换成为可能。

奥运摔跤馆于 2004 年 3 月经国际招标中标实施。2007 年 8 月首次对外开放，媒体对摔跤馆造型的“内敛精巧”（科技日报）与“整体节能”（人民网）表现出浓厚的兴趣，出自不同角度的报道繁多。

The Wrestling Arena in the east campus of China Agricultural University was designed for both the wrestling and Paralympics sitting volleyball during Beijing 2008 Olympic Games. The post-game renovations include the competition hall, basketball training center and natatorium, so that it can not only accommodate the various sports events but also the sports teaching, art performances, assemblies and student unions. This project sets up a very good sample for large gymnasium in campus environment. The building features plain and practical form and compact functional configurations, allowing for the positive renovation during and after the Games.

The Wrestling Arena was a successful implementation through an international bidding since March, 2004. It was thrown open to the public in August, 2007. The media showed a keen interest in reports from many different angles on the Wrestling Arena, in particular on the "restrained delicacy" (Science and Technology Daily) and "the total energy conservation" (www.people.com.cn).

回归基本点：体育建筑设计的理性原则

伴随北京奥运建设，体育建筑也进入建设的高峰期。奥运、亚运、大学生运动会、全运会、省级体育中心的升级换代及高等院校、公司组织各种各样的需求蓬勃发展，目睹百样翻新的体育建筑外表，在建筑创作繁荣的华丽外表之下隐含的却是对体育建筑基本原则的屡屡违背。通过奥运摔跤馆的设计，我们反思和重温体育建筑设计的理性原则，针对体育建筑特殊性提出以下几点与大家探讨。

一、内外双修——基于城市的体育建筑设计理念

从类型建筑的角度，体育建筑的复杂性、不确定性名列榜首。长期以来体育建筑复杂的功能组织与大跨结构选型，使设计师首先面对的是建筑自身问题。“建筑设计从功能出发，建筑形式是内部功能的忠实反映”，作为现代建筑运动提出的基本原则，曾经被奉为天条。回顾体育建筑的历史，我们可以发现，在理性主义的设计理念之下，出现过众多的大师与杰作，奈尔维的罗马小体育馆、丹下的东京代代木体育馆都是发人深省的隽永之作。

出于对狭隘功能主义的反思，国际上近 20 年来对体育设施的相关研究已扩大到城市设计研究的范畴，体育场馆建设不仅与大型体育赛事相关，甚至与城市更新改造相呼应，规划设计研究中特别重视体育设施对城市的影响。在审慎的城市设计研究之后，出现了许多优秀的实例。体育设施一改以往坐落于郊区的庞然大物形象，越来越多尺度亲切、功能配置合理的各种体育设施成为城市中有意义的公共活动场所。其中最为著名的实例是美国克里夫兰的体育中心，体育建筑的策划、选址与旧城复兴计划相关，甚至体量的确定都遵从了城市设计的空间组织。1996 年亚特兰大奥运会主体育场，赛时被某些媒体认为形象不佳的体育场，却是预先进行了潜伏设计，在会后部分拆卸组合成为新的棒球场，建设投资全部由开发商支付。这样的建设决策反映了不先入为主、以城市需要为目标的规划思想。

可以看出，现代体育建筑的设计早已突破以往局限于从内到外的单项思维。关注城市整体环境、城市生活需求，从理性、实际的城市设计分析入手，已成为体育建筑设计重要的理性原则。

奥运摔跤馆坐落的中国农业大学东校区，是一座典型的中国 20 世纪 50 年代大学校园，逻辑严整的校园建筑布局、亲切的毛主席塑像留住了那些并非久远却在快速逝去的历史。其中独具一格的是校园内几栋旧的砖混教学建筑，虽然造型与 50 年代的教学建筑一样普通，材料也是质量一般的红砖。然而，建筑师将砖体按照规律略有嵌出，改变了墙面质感，几栋主要教学建筑虽细节有不同，均采用了类似的手法，加上养护良好的树木绿化，顿时使校园形成独特的氛围。

在如此独特的校园环境之下，我们对体育建筑的构思就开始于对城市空间环境所进行的严谨的图底关系分析。最终外在的逻辑分析确定了以矩形体量为主，尽量减少建筑高度的构思。结合内部功能的分析，我们将建筑的主次功能分别处理，使游泳馆、热身馆与主馆空间分开处理，便于功能灵活处理。这样从外而内、内外兼顾、理性分析的方法为摔跤馆设计的成功奠定了基础。在成为 3 家优秀方案入围后，经过历时半年的业主比选和奥运设施瘦身优化过程最终胜出。

二、精致得体——体育建筑的生命所在

今天，建筑的理念与原则新颖多变。由于不加区别的主观代用，先入为主、只重外表的设计手法使体育建筑创作越来越多地陷入歧途。在将建筑创作退化为美丽叙事的氛围之下，表皮建筑泛滥正深刻影响着体育建筑的健康发展。忽略体育建筑的功能内涵，将体育建筑创作退化为“表皮 + 基本几何形体”的操作过程，导致雷同方案频繁出现。

多年来，我们在公共建筑设计特别是大空间公共建筑上坚持理性原则，如：平面安排忌大空间重叠覆盖小空间，竖向空间安排忌讳小空间在大空间上面等。这些本来属于设计原理中必须遵守的基本原则，却被许多建筑师特别是国外建筑师以创新的名义抛弃，直接导致大空间公共建筑普遍存在跨度浪费、荷载分布畸形的弊端，也成为体育场馆造价不断上涨的根源。

体育建筑的主体空间构成是大跨度、大空间，虽为一至二层却不同于一般民用建筑，高度超过 24 m 也不属高层建筑。因此，对建筑空间处理应遵守体育建筑的基本要求，对大跨度的“斤斤计较”和大空间的“量体裁衣”是应该始终坚持的设计理念，其重要性在体育投资不断增加的新时期特别具有意义。

摔跤馆独特造型的产生和优化并没有牺牲理性的设计原则，相反在优化过程中不断精致，更加合体，减少了空间体积，丰富了造型。由于空间体积控制得当，摔跤馆节省了声学处理材料，没有作特殊的吸音处理，经过“世界青年摔跤锦标赛”运行测试使用，效果符合要求。同时，摔跤馆设计注意空间的集约，在有限的体积内尽力完成最大灵活性的功能转换。赛后在体积不变，主馆仍然能够满足国际单项赛事要求的情况下，馆内还可出现一个供学生使用的具有一个标准游泳池的设施完善的游泳馆。

三、物为我用——结构技术与材料工艺作为建筑创作的手段

作为建筑物构成的重要组成部分，建筑结构和材料是不可或缺的营造手段。对于大空间公共建筑而言，大跨度结构技术尤其重要，往往成为结构技术创新的里程碑。建筑材料对体育建筑而言同样十分重要，新材料的出现为建筑创作提供着不断更新的可能。然而，技术的进步，材料的更新其目的不是为了求异，而在于更好地服务于建造的本质目的——满足人的需求。

近年来，国内的结构技术和材料选择运用与国际接轨日渐迅速，新结构体系和材料的创造性运用也为中国设计师掌握。然而对于体育建筑来说，应该引起注意的现象是，由于“表皮建筑”在体育建筑上的泛滥，许多设计为了在效果上先声夺人又将注意力集中于表皮材料的新奇，致使不符合国情、超标准、超常规的材料蜂拥而至，体育建筑的建筑材料畸形使用情况普遍。更有甚者，将大跨建筑结构曲解为表皮元素的构成手段，使许多体育建筑的结构设计先天缺陷明显，用钢量等经济技术指标节节攀升，体育建筑造价水涨船高。一些打着高科技旗号的材料，由于造价、寿命、维护等原因，还将使体育建筑的维护成本大幅增加，成为“可持续的贻害”。

成熟结构体系的选用是设计师的基本素养与职业要求，普通材料的创新运用也是建筑师面临的挑战。体育建筑的赛后灵活使用要求存在着相当大的不确定性，屋盖在预留荷载与灵活悬吊方面对结构形式的选用具有制约性。摔跤馆没有追求结构技术的先进性，在满足采光和确保灵活使用上给予更多关注，采用技术成熟的门式钢架结构，保证了较低的用钢量，使 其成为北京奥运新建场馆中造价最低的场馆。

四、和谐永续——节能降耗是体育建筑的永恒主题

今天，体育场馆的保养与运营已受到广泛关注，“赛后运营”“以馆养馆”甚至成为管理决策者、管理者和设计者的口头禅。然而，我国的体育产业发展尚在初级阶段，体育职业联赛的社会基础薄弱，无法形成规模市场；文艺演出的市场同样不乐观，文化场所互相竞争，进入体育场馆的演出数量有限；商业、会展也同样面临专业场所的竞争。实事求是地说，目前我国的社会发展根本无法解决体育场馆真正意义上的商业运营和养馆问题。短时期内，政府补贴与支持仍将是体育场馆的主要经费来源，这一状况也决定了体育场馆应以公益服务为主的地位。另一方面，场馆使用费用多、维护成本高又客观上造成体育场馆公共服务的强度与质量下降。其中，由于建筑设计原因造成的建造与使用成本高企也不断出现。探讨体育建筑的可持续设计策略已成为当务之急。

作为大空间公共建筑，体育场馆的采光与空调一直是运行成本的大户。20 世纪 50 年代中国兴建的第一批体育馆大多考虑了比赛大厅的天然采光，但由于设计与材料、工艺的原因，天窗大多封盖掉，没有起到应有的作用。天然采光的被弃造成其后兴建的大批体育场馆成为黑盒子。如：首都体育馆、上海体育馆及 70 年代修建的许多省级场馆。80 年代开始，天窗采光得到部分设计师的运用。吉林冰球馆是当时采光面积较大的场馆。但是，时至今日，还有相当多的体育场馆无视这样的需求。

摔跤馆赛后将以学生使用为主，节能降耗、减少维护成本就成为确保体育场馆真正为学生服务的关键。我们经过艰苦努力，在设计中将自然采光、通风的可能性作为十分重要的原则来遵守，使建筑造型与自然通风、采光很好地结合起来。层层错开的屋面与外墙便于引入自然光，也便于利用主导风向组织通风。

五、结语

作为公益事业的体育建筑，是以长期服务于普通大众为其建设目的。只要建筑师坚持理性的设计理念，健康、清新的体育建筑形象是能够实现的。

作者：孙一民

文章出处：《建筑学报》2007 年第十二期 P26—31

Back to the Basic: Principle of Rationality in Sport Building Design

Along with the development for Beijing Olympics, the construction of sport buildings reached a peak. Sport buildings have been built, upgraded and reconstructed for major games like Beijing 2008 Olympics, Guangzhou 2010 Asian Games, Universiade Shenzhen 2011 and 2013 National Games. Moreover, the demand for various sport activities by universities, colleges and companies has also greatly promoted the development of sport buildings. However, underneath the fancy and ever-changing appearances of the buildings and behind the flourisher of architectural creation are cryptic violations of basic design principles of sport buildings. We have reviewed and reflected on the principle of rationality in sport building design and would like to share some of our thinking on the uniqueness of sport buildings as below.

Ⅰ. Emphasis on Both the Interior and the Exterior-A City-based Design Concept for Sport Buildings

Sport buildings have topped the ranking in terms of complexity and uncertainty among all building typologies. For a long time, the complicated functional organization and the large structural span of a sport building has been what an architect had to deal with first in design. The fundamental principle put forth during the Modern Architectural Movement that architectural design was oriented to satisfy functional needs and architectural form was a truthful reflection of the internal functions of a building, was once seen as a dogma. Looking back to the history of sport buildings, we can see that under the influence of the design concept of rationalism, there have been many grandmasters and masterpieces, like Pier Luigi Nervi and Palazzeto Dellospori of Rome, KenzoTange and Yoyogi National Gymnasium, which are meaningful and intriguing works that set people thinking.

Based on reflection on the narrowly defined functionalism, studies on sport facilities conducted in the world in the last two decades have been extended to the field of urban design. The construction of a sport venue not only is related to large games but also responds to urban renewal and reconstruction. Therefore, special attention has been paid to the impact of sport facilities on a city in studies on planning and design. Many excellent precedents have emerged as result of careful studies on urban design. Sport facilities are no longer huge structures located in suburban areas. Instead, their scales are becoming friendlier and various sport facilities with reasonable functional arrangements have turned into meaningful places for public activities in cities. Among them, the most well-known precedent would be the Sports Center in Cleveland, U.S.A., planning and site selection of which was part of the urban regeneration initiative. Even the volume of the complex was subject to the spatial organization in the urban design of Cleveland. As the main stadium of Atlanta 1996 Olympics, it was criticized by some media for its image. However, with the approach of hidden design, the stadium was partially demolished after the Olympics and re-organized into a new baseball field and the construction investment was completely made by the developer. The decision made on construction of the stadium revealed the planning idea that was oriented to satisfy the demand of the city instead of creating a great first impression.

It can be seen that breakthroughs have long been made in modern sport building design and the unilateral thinking that only addressed the interior and the exterior aspects has become outdated. Attention paid to both environment and urban living needs and urban design analysis that is rational and practical and used as a design entry point have formed the principle of rationality that is essential in design of sport buildings nowadays.

The wrestling venue for Beijing Olympics is located in East Campus of China Agricultural University, which is a typical Chinese campus completed in the 1950s. A logically rigorous campus layout and the statue of Chairman Mao remind people of the moments that happened not long ago but could be easily forgotten. The most distinctive feature of the campus is the old brick-concrete teaching buildings. Although their shapes are similar to other teaching buildings completed in the 1950s and they are built with the same ordinary red bricks, the architect changes the wall texture by having the bricks slightly protrude following certain patterns. Despite of the differences of the details, similar approaches are adopted in the design of the main teaching buildings. Similarity of buildings and trees and greenery that are well conserved make up a unique atmosphere on campus.

As the stadium is embedded in such an unusual environment, the design of the building starts with a precise analysis on the base drawing effect of the urban space. At last, the concept is finalized to be a rectangular volume of minimal building height following the logical analysis on the external elements. Then based on analysis on the internal functions, the primary and secondary functions of the stadium are placed into separate spaces, so that the natatorium, the warm-up venue and the main hall are independent to each other and can be put into use flexibly. Such an approach which starts from external elements and ends up at the internal elements, while giving equal emphasis to the both, is based on rational analysis and lays a solid foundation for the success of the project. Our design scheme was among the three shortlisted ones, and, six months later, eventually won the bid after the client had carefully compared the schemes and Olympic facilities had gone through a process of downsizing and optimization.

Ⅱ. Exquisiteness and Appropriateness-The Life of Sport Buildings

Today, architectural concepts and principles have been novel and changing. As a result of those design approaches which advocate subjective substitution without differentiation, first impression creation and emphasis on mere appearance, architectural design of sport buildings is going towards a wrong direction. When architectural creation is degraded to nothing but aesthetic expression, excessive buildings that only stress building skins have brought a profound impact on the sound development of sport buildings. The neglect of functional connotations of sport buildings and the design process that has simplified architectural creation of sport buildings to combinations of "skin + basic geometry" have led to common occurrence of similar designs.

For years, we have been adhering to the principle of rationality in design of public buildings, particularly large-space public buildings. For instance, we avoid having small spaces inside a large space in floor plan, or putting small spaces on top of a large space in vertical layout. These should have been basic principles that are strictly adhered to in design; however, they have been forgotten by many architects, especially foreign architects, under the disguise of innovation. As a result, large-space public buildings are commonly found with the problems of excessive spans and abnormal load distributions. Moreover, it is a cause of the continuously rising construction cost of sport buildings.

The main space of a sport building is usually featured with a large space and a large span. Different from ordinary civil buildings, a sport building that exceeds 24 meters in height cannot be defined as a high-rise structure even though it has only one floor or two. Therefore, some basic requirements should be satisfied in spatial arrangement. And the design concepts that carefully plan the large span and appropriate dimensions of the large space should be adhered to all along, as they are particularly meaningful at a time when investments made in sport industry keep growing.

The design principle of rationality was not compromised in the creation and optimization of the unique shape of the Wresting Stadium. On the contrary, it was continuously refined and improved in the optimization process and finally became a stadium with an exquisite and proper shape, a smaller volume and a diverse appearance. Due to the right control on the space and volume, the stadium was spared from acoustic materials and special sound absorption measures. Test results of World Youth Wrestling Championship showed that the stadium was up to the requirements. On the other hand, the strategy of compact space and intensive use was employed allowed for the most flexible functional transformation within a limited volume. After the Olympics, the main hall was added with a students' natatorium comprised of a standard pool and complete facilities while its volume remained unchanged and it could still host international single-sport events.

Ⅲ. Making the Best out of Everything-Structural Technology and Material Processing as Means of Architectural Creation

As important components of a building, both structure and material are indispensible means of creation. For a large-space public building, large-span structural technologies are extremely essential and are often seen as milestones of structural technology innovation. Building materials are of equal significance. The emergence of new materials provides more possibilities to architectural creation. However, the purpose of technology advancement and material upgrade is not for seeking differentiation. Instead, it is to better serve and fulfill the nature of construction, i.e. to satisfy the needs of people.

In recent years, structural technology and material selection by Chinese architects have quickly kept up with international practice. And Chinese designers have become more familiar with creative uses of new structural systems and materials. However, as far as sport buildings are concerned, we need to notice that many designers focus on the novelty of skin materials in order to create an overwhelming first impression at a time when there are excessive skin-oriented sport buildings being completed. As a result, new materials those are unconventional, unsuitable to Chinese market and beyond the standard range come in great numbers. Abnormal and wrong use of materials on sport buildings has become common. It is even worse that some large-span structures are mistaken as composition means of building skins, which become an inherent defect in the structural design of many sport buildings. Consequently, economic and technical indicators, including the quantity of steel, keep increasing and construction costs are higher and higher. Some materials that are claimed to contain high technologies lead to dramatic increases in maintenance expenditure of sport buildings for their costs, life cycles and maintenance needs and eventually become "a sustainable trouble".

Selecting a mature structural system is a basic quality of and a professional requirement on a designer. Innovative uses of conventional materials can also be a challenge architects are faced with. Flexible uses of a sport building after major games pose great uncertainties to design. Reserved load capacity and flexible suspensions of a roof are constraints on selection of structural form. Instead of the advanced nature in terms of structural technology, the design of the Wrestling Stadium paid more attention to daylighting and flexible uses. The steel portal frame structure, as a mature technology, was used to ensure a lower quantity of steel, making it the one with the lowest construction cost among all newly built sport venues for Beijing Olympics.

Ⅳ. Harmony and Sustainability-Energy Efficiency and Consumption Reduction Being the Permanent Theme of Sport Buildings

Today, maintenance and operation of a sport venue has drawn attention of the public and even words like "post-game operation" and "self-sufficiency running" have become pet phrases of decision-makers, operators and designers of sport buildings. However, the development of sport industry in China is still at an early stage and the social base for professional league matches is too weak to form a market of scale. As cultural venues are competing with each other, the market of artistic performances is not optimistic either and only a small number of shows are hosted in stadiums. Retail spaces and exhibition & convention centers are also faced with the threat posed by professional venues. As a matter of fact, with the social development level of China, it is impossible to truly realize commercial operations and self-sufficiency of sport venues. In the short term, government subsidies and supports will remain the main financial source of sport venues, which determines that they should be oriented to provide public services. On the other hand, high running expenditures and high maintenance costs make the quality of public services of sport venues less satisfactory. When the construction and operation costs of sport buildings are getting higher as a result of improper architectural design, it is urgent to discuss the sustainable design strategies for sport buildings.

Lighting and A/C have always contributed a lot to the operating costs of a sport venue that is a large-space public building in most cases. Most of the first batch of stadiums completed in the 1950s in China used daylighting for the competition halls. However, due to causes of design, material and workmanship, most skylights have been sealed up and are no longer in use. The less satisfactory experience with the use of daylighting changed the later designs of sport venues and made them into "black boxes". For example, Capital Indoor Stadium, Shanghai Indoor Stadium and many other provincial stadiums completed in 1970s fit into this category. Since the 1980s, some designers started to use skylights for daylighting again. Jilin Ice Hockey Stadium is a venue with a relatively large daylighting area built back then. However, such need is still being overlooked in the design of quite a few stadiums.

The Wrestling Stadium is planned to be mainly used by students after the Olympics. Therefore, energy efficiency, consumption reduction and maintenance cost reduction are the keys to ensure that it could really serve the desired purpose. With tremendous efforts, the natural ventilation and daylighting are successfully integrated into the building shape by adhering to the essential design principles like daylighting and natural ventilation. The staggering configuration of the roof and the external walls help bring in daylight and facilitate ventilation with the prevailing wind.

Ⅴ. Conclusion

Sport buildings, as a non-profit undertaking, are constructed to serve the public in the long run. When an architect adheres to the design principle of rationality, it is achievable to create a sound and fresh image for a sport building.

By Sun Yimin

Source: Architectural Journal, 2007 Issue 12, P26-31

2008 北京奥运会羽毛球馆
BADMINTON GYMNASIUM FOR BEIJING 2008 OLYMPIC GAMES

项目地点：北京市
设计时间：2004 年
竣工时间：2007 年
用地面积：66,000 m^2
建筑面积：24,383 m^2
曾获奖项：2008 年北京奥运会羽毛球馆国际建筑设计方案竞赛第一名（2004 年）
第八届詹天佑土木工程大奖（2008 年）
中国建筑学会蓝星杯第五届中国威海国际建筑设计大奖优秀奖（2009 年）
广东省优秀工程勘察奖一等奖（2009 年）
广东省注册建筑师协会优秀建筑创作奖提名奖（2005 年）

Location: Beijing
Design: 2004
Completion: 2007
Site Area: 66,000 m^2
GFA: 24,383 m^2
Awards:
The First Place of International Architectural Design Competition for Badminton Gymnasium for Beijing 2008 Olympic Games (2004)
The 8th Tien-yow Jeme Civil Engineering Prize (2008)
Excellence Award, Blue Star Cup · The 6th China Weihai International Architectural Design Award & Competition (2009)
The First Prize of Excellent Engineering Exploration Award of Guangdong Province (2009)
Finalist of Excellent Architecture Creation Award by Guangdong Chapter of Association of Chinese Registered Architects (2005)

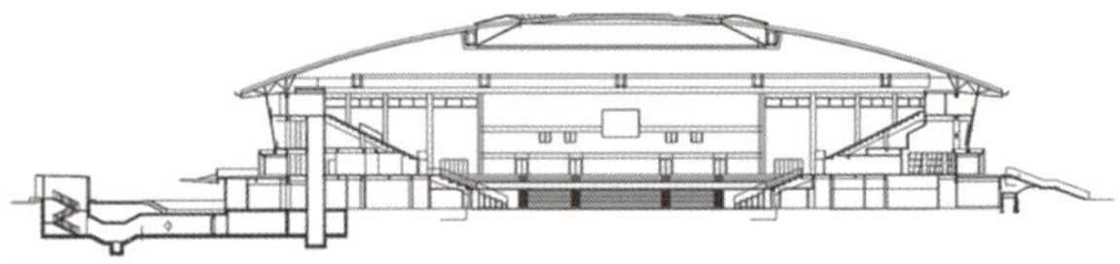

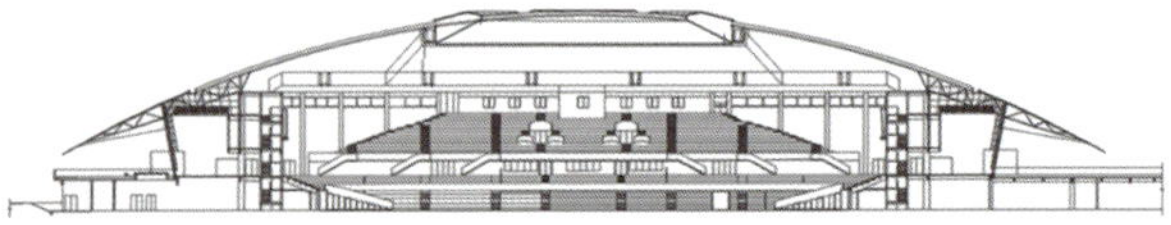

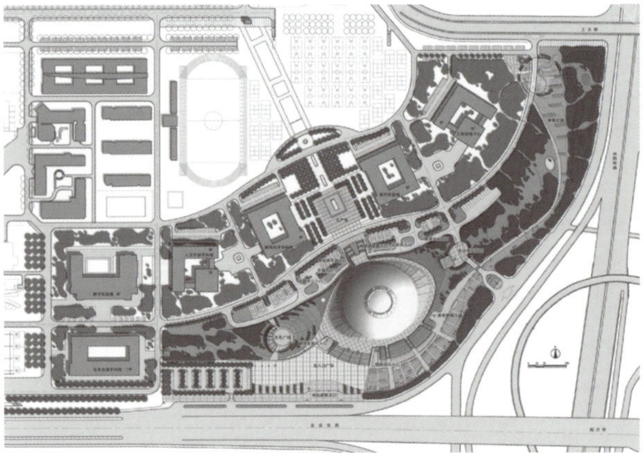

2008 北京奥运会羽毛球馆

BADMINTON GYMNASIUM FOR BEIJING 2008 OLYMPIC GAMES

好运北京
111 区
SECTION

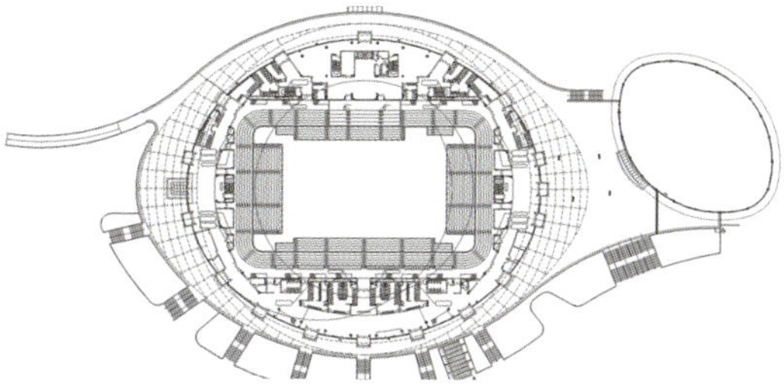

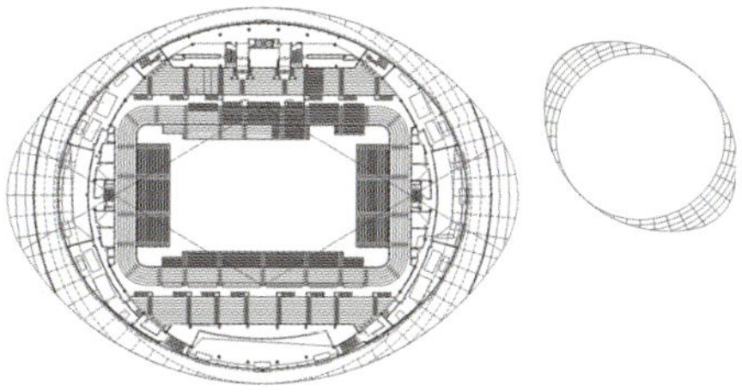

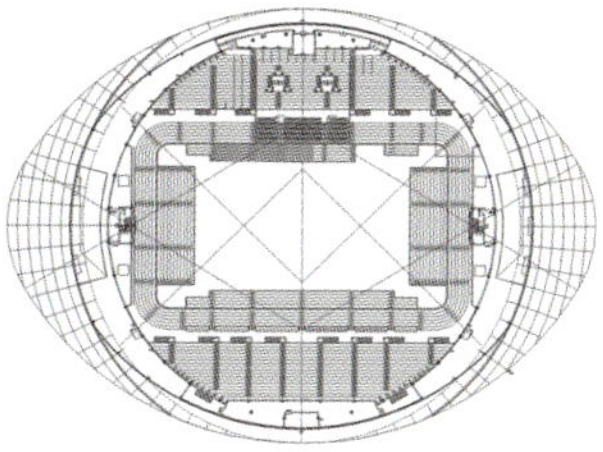

奥运羽毛球馆位于北京工业大学校区，是北京 2008 年奥运会羽毛球和艺术体操比赛用馆，奥运会后在保证继续承接各类体育赛事的同时，也满足了体育教学、文艺演出、集会及学生社团使用并作为国家羽毛球队的训练基地。

体育馆创造性地解决了校园空间与城市景观的需要，结构技术国际领先，空调、灯光等多项技术协同良好，充分满足羽毛球和艺术体操复杂苛刻的功能要求。

奥运羽毛球馆 2004 年 3 月通过国际招标中标实施。2007 年 9 月举办了“好运北京”奥运测试赛，被国际羽毛球联合会主席誉为“世界上最好的羽毛球馆”，得到了中国羽毛球队中众多世界冠军的肯定。

The Olympic Badminton Gymnasium, located in Beijing University of Technology, serves as gymnasium of badminton and rhythmic gymnastics competitions during Beijing 2008 Olympic Games. While it continues to host various types of sporting events after the Games, the gymnasium also needs to accommodate the uses like physical education, art performances, assemblies, activities of student organizations, and training of the national badminton teams.

The gymnasium is a creative solution to the needs of campus space and urban landscape. It embodies the international leading structural technology and the synergy of air-conditioning, lighting and other technical systems, hence is able to meet the complex functional requirements of badminton and rhythmic gymnastics.

The Olympic Badminton Gymnasium was implemented through an international competition in March 2004 and hosted the “Good Luck Beijing” Olympic test in September 2007. It was acclaimed by the president of International Badminton Federation as “the world’s best badminton gymnasium”, and praised by many of the world champions from the Chinese badminton team.

体育场馆适应性研究

作为大型公共建筑代表的体育建筑，投资巨大，运行费用高，建设决策的科学与否不仅关系着重大公共投资的效益评价，对体育建筑全寿命过程的低能耗、高效率运行也有着深厚的影响。因此，体育建筑的设计过程就不仅是对“形”的设计过程，更是参与建设决策的过程。分析今天十分活跃的体育建筑创作成果，广泛存在着忽视研究积累、片面迎合、错误导引的倾向。许多花费高昂代价的体育建筑将由于缺乏适应性而使业主和经营者背负长期的负担。

强调体育建筑的适应性，其意义在于：在对体育运动要求与体育产业发展充分关注和研究的基础上，基于适宜的建筑技术手段，对建筑功能及其发展变化做出具有前瞻性的解决策略。在日益丰富、变化迅速的我国现代社会条件下，一方面对体育建筑的需求不断增加，另一方面，体育产业发展尚在萌芽阶段，缺乏必要的积累，体育建筑的适应性就显得尤为重要，应该成为重大体育建筑项目评价与决策的重要基准。在过去的体育建筑研究与设计实践中，我们一直坚持这样的理念，特别是在奥运工程的投标竞争、设计深化与建设过程中，获益匪浅。在此将心得托出，求教于前辈与同行。

一、总图规划与体量组合的适应性

随着体育建筑的发展，对体育场馆多功能使用和赛后运营的要求已被广泛接受，业主要求的功能逐渐丰富，建筑面积也逐渐增多。在这种背景下，体育场馆满足比赛观赏的主空间及满足多种使用要求的副空间为建筑体量组合提出了新的要求。集中与分散成为两种不同的处理手法。

近年来，由于建筑理念的变幻，在以体育馆为代表的大型公共创作中，以往空间组合尊重功能空间、外形反映空间本质的理性设计思想被颠覆，如国家大剧院、水立方等集中处理不同空间的公共建筑设计作品的实施，更加推动了注重表皮、淡化空间组合设计手法的流行。

体育建筑的核心空间是大跨度的公共空间，最为引人注目也最为影响造价。因此，无论集中与分散布局，还是空间组合的基本单元都应该是按照功能空间划分。以此为原则，不仅有利于减少建筑跨度，也有利于适应城市空间环境。我们在羽毛球馆和摔跤馆两个奥运场馆的设计中均坚持了这一原则。

北京奥运羽毛球馆，建设于北京工业大学校内，是唯一兴建于北京东南部的奥运场馆。羽毛球馆的招标要求主要包括 3 部分的内容：10000 个座位的主比赛馆、作为羽毛球训练基地的训练馆和赛时热身馆。我们在分析地形与研究功能使用后，确定了 3 部分分别形成体量，以一大带两小为体量组合的基本策略。在国际竞赛的初评阶段，我们的方案与集中布置的方案共同入围。随后而来的奥运场馆优化、瘦身过程中，体育馆规模首先进行了调整，规模从万人馆减少到 8000 席，训练中心也取消了，由于我们的设计中三个体量单独处理，每个体量的取消与缩减都比较容易。甚至在后期，规划变更，羽毛球馆的建设用地西移、用地规模减小的重大变更出现时，我们的设计都没有受到太大影响，原方案的创意一直保持，最终实施完成。而集中式的布局方案则在瘦身阶段就出现极不适应的问题，最终落选。

二、功能策划与参数配置的适应性

体育建筑的功能配置包括了较为复杂的策划工作，科学合理的策划与配置需要长期的研究积累。在配置过程中，有许多使用要求的不确定性和发展需要，灵活适应性就成为重要的基本原则。这里，仅就体育馆比赛场地的选型，特别是高校体育馆的场地选型提出我们的观点。关于体育馆的比赛场地选型，经过了一个发展变化的过程，其原因一方面是由于篮球等运动项目本身的发展。另一方面，也代表了对体育场馆灵活适应性的不断深入与发展的思考。从 20 世纪 50 年代开始，国内体育馆的场地主要以篮球场地为基准，在 70 年代后期篮球场地从 14 m x 26 m 扩大到 15 m x 28 m 的过程中，许多国内体育馆都承受了痛苦的改造。在 80 年代初，梅季魁教授在国内率先开展体育馆多功能场地的研究，提出（34 m—36 m）x（44 m—46 m）的多功能场地类型，促进了场地选型的科学发展。2003 年由马国馨院士主持完成的我国第一部《体育建筑规范》则比较全面地综合了相关的研究成果。

在高校体育馆方面，由于兼顾比赛和教学、课余活动，场地的适应性尤为重要。1988 年，笔者在梅季魁先生的指导下，完成了关于高校体育馆的硕士论文，根据调研和分析提出 34 m x 50 m 的高校体育馆场地选型方案（哈尔滨建筑工程学院硕士论文《高校多功能厅堂设计研究》学生：孙一民，导师：梅季魁，1988）。并于 1990 年在哈工大体育馆首次运用。

进入 21 世纪，国际体操比赛场地要求发生变化，40 m x 70 m 的轮廓尺寸使大多数兴建于 20 世纪的体育馆无法满足国际体操比赛使用要求。2002 年我们提出以 40 m x 70 m 或 48 m x 70 m 作为场地选型的建议。（华南理工大学硕士论文《体育馆多功能设计研究》学生：李玲，导师：孙一民，2002）2002 年，我们在华中科技大学要求体育馆的设计中采用 40 m x 70 m，使其成为武汉第一个满足国际体操比赛的场馆。北京工业大学体育馆作为奥运羽毛球馆，场地的确定较为简单。但考虑到作为大学体育馆及赛后多种利用的要求，我们以确保体育场馆最大的灵活性、适应性为原则，确定了 40 m x 70 m 的比赛场地，以便在赛后满足包括国际体操在内的各种比赛要求。在同为高校体育馆的奥运摔跤馆中也采用了相同的选型。

通过奥运羽毛球和艺术体操测试赛的考察，场地的尺寸是适应不同比赛场地及各种仪式活动的，而对于教学训练使用，排球场地布置数量达到 5 个，羽毛球场地达到 18 个，乒乓球场地 25 个以上，可以适应高校的多种使用要求。

三、屋盖形式与结构选型的适应性

结构选型是体育建筑创作的重要环节。合理的结构选型是优秀体育建筑产生的必要途径。但同时应该看到，结构技术只能是建筑表达的手段而不应成为建筑表达的目的。作为手段的选择，其灵活性、适应性就十分重要，结构选型要针对技术要求、施工条件、工期要求、造价投资而具备多项选择，即在结构构思上要充分考虑适应性。

以奥运羽毛球馆为例，根据规模和奥运设计大纲的要求，我们确定了圆形的建筑基本体量，并努力形成飘逸轻盈的外观。结构选型就以积极配合建筑构思为目的了。作为由高校投资建设的奥运场馆，造价的控制极其严格，因此羽毛球馆方案在投标阶段确定了采用球网壳的结构形式。

为了表达建筑构思，在力学性能良好的球网壳结构上，经过切割，产生了流畅的曲线。不仅满足了建筑功能的要求，同时利用网壳结构的灵活性，创造出流畅的曲线造型。为了满足低视点的视觉效果，网壳在两端沿球面外延伸展，在网壳的边缘再加以曲线型的玻璃雨棚，从而突出结构本身的美感和韵律感。

在方案深化阶段，业主特别强调结构技术的先进性，提出了采用预应力钢结构的设想。由于我们的屋盖形式具有极强的适应性，这一要求完全可以满足。在符合建筑室内外空间形式原创构思的前提下，初步设计阶段提出了三种结构方案，并向业主提出了不同用钢量和经济指标的结构方案比选建议。最终在业主的坚持下，完成了预应力张悬结构方案，使羽毛球馆屋盖结构成为 2008 北京奥运场馆中最为先进的结构形式。但由于复杂性的相应增加，工期有所延长，张悬结构本身对屋顶设备悬吊有所限制，灵活性受到制约。通过实践，我们认为结构技术的先进性、适用性与易建造性之间存在着辩证关系，不同场馆应该实事求是地分析选用，而强化适应性则应该是基本的原则。

以上是通过奥运羽毛球馆的实践，对研究中几个方面问题的分析与思考。

（北京工业大学体育馆“2008 年奥运会羽毛球及艺术体操比赛馆”项目设计团队由何镜堂院士亲自负责，方案设计阶段研究生申永刚、吴翰斌、邓芳、陈伟志、杜卫华、郑海砾等参与了工作。）

作者：孙一民

文章出处：《建筑学报》2008 年第一期 P94—97

Study on Adaptability of Sport Venue

A sport venue, a typical type of structure among large public buildings, always involves a large investment and high operating costs. Whether a decision made on construction is scientific not only concerns the cost-benefit evaluation results of a major public investment but also has a serious impact on the low energy consumption and efficient operation during the entire life cycle of a sport venue. Therefore, the design process of a sport building is more than a simple design process of its "appearance". It is a process that involves construction decision-making. Today, looking at the seemingly very productive design of modern sports buildings, we see less emphasis on research accumulation but more pandering and wrong directions. As a result, many heavily-invested sports buildings will end up as long-term burdens to owners and tenants due to lack of adaptability.

The significance of putting emphasis on the adaptability of sport buildings lies in the forward-looking solutions and strategies for building functions and their development and changes, which are based on full attention to and studies on sport demands and sport industry development and realized with appropriate architectural and technological approaches. In China where things are becoming more diverse and changing rapidly, the demand for sport buildings keeps increasing; on the other hand, the sport industry is still in its infancy and lacks necessary experiences. Consequently, the adaptability of sport buildings is critical and should be regarded as an important criterion in the evaluation and decision-making process of major sport building projects. In studies and design practice of sport buildings, we have been holding onto such idea, especially in bid, design detailing and construction of Olympic construction projects and we have benefited a lot from this. Now, we would like to share the experiences with others and take the opportunity to learn from our predecessors and peers.

Ⅰ. Adaptability of Master Planning and Combination of Building Volumes

With the development of sport buildings, the demands for the multi-purpose uses and post-game operation for a sport venue have become common. A client's demands for function are increasing, resulting in an increase of floor area. Under this circumstance, the building volume of the primary space for game watching and that of the others for supplementary uses need to be combined in a better way. There are normally two design approaches to this, centralization and de-centralization.

In recent years, as a result of the changing architectural ideas, the creation of large public facilities, mainly the sports venues, has completely diverted from the previous rational design philosophy which advocates that the spatial combination is always subject to functional spaces and building appearance match with building nature. Along with the implementation of public projects like Grand National Theatre and National Swimming Center where various spaces are handled in a centralized manner, the approach that emphasizes building skin with less attention to the spatial combination has become more and more popular.

The core space of a sport building is usually a public space with a large span which is the most noticeable and costly part. Therefore, the basic units of spatial combination should be the functional spaces, regardless of which architectural layout, the concentrated one or the distributed one, is selected. Adhering to this principle, the design not only helps reduce building span but also fits the building into its urban context, especially for the two Olympic venues, respectively the Badminton Stadium and the Wrestling Stadium.

The 2008 Olympic Badminton Stadium, built in Beijing University of Technology, is the only one Olympic stadium constructed in the southeast of Beijing. As required by the competition brief, the project is comprised of three main parts, the 10,000-seat main stadium, the training venue that could be used as a badminton training base and a warm-up hall. After our analysis on the topography and functionality, we decided to create the building volumes respectively for these three parts and eventually form a spatial combination comprising one large building volume and two small ones. At the preliminary review stage of the international design competition, our design proposal and the others featuring centralized layout were shortlisted. Later, when the Olympic venues were being optimized and downsized, the scale of the Badminton Stadium was first reduced from 10,000 seats to 8,000 seats. And the training center was cancelled as well. As the three building volumes in our design were rather independent and could be dealt with separately, it was easy to delete and reduce any one of them. Still, our design was not seriously affected even when the construction site of the badminton stadium was relocated westwards and the site area was reduced due to changes with the planning. The creativity of the original scheme was preserved all along till the completion of the project. However, the other design scheme with a centralized layout failed to adapt to the change at the downsizing stage and was phased out.

Ⅱ. Adaptability of Functional Planning and Parameter Configuration

The functional configuration of a sport building involves planning work that is rather complicated. Scientific and reasonable planning and configuration require long-time studies and experiences. In the configuration process, a designer will see many uncertainties of use and different development demands. Consequently, flexibility and adaptability become the fundamental principle. Here we would like to share our opinion regarding types of competition areas, particularly that in a university or college. Typology of competition areas has developed and changed, which was partially caused by the evolvement of some games like basketball. It was also the result of continuous exploration in the adaptability of sport venues. Since the 1950s, the competition area of a sport venue in China had usually been based on basketball courts. When the size of the basketball court increased to 15 m x 28 m from 14 m x 26 m in the late 1970s, many stadiums in China had to go through painful reconstruction. In the early 1980s, Professor Mei Jikui took the lead to conduct studies on the multifunctional spaces of sport venues in China and proposed the size range of (34-36) m x (44-46). His efforts had pushed forward the scientific development of typology of competition areas. The Design Code for Sport Buildings completed by the team led by Academician Ma Guoxing in 2003, the first of its kind in China, has summarized study findings in this area comprehensively.

As for sport venues in university or college, the adaptability of the venue is extremely essential as the venue is for competition, teaching and after-school activity. In 1988, under the guidance of Professor Mei Jikui, the author completed his master's degree thesis which was on sport venue construction in university. The size of 34 m x 50 m was proposed in the thesis based on investigation and analysis. (See Studies on Design of Multifunctional Venues in University, a master's degree thesis of Sun Yimin from Harbin Civil Engineering and Architecture Institute. The thesis was supervised by Mei Jikui and written in 1988.) The size (34 m x 54 m) was first adopted in the construction of the stadium of Harbin Institute of Technology in 1990.

Since the 21st century, the requirements on spaces for international gymnastics competitions have changed. The size of 40 m x 70 m made it hardly possible for most sport venues constructed in the last century to be put into use in international gymnastics competitions. In 2002, we recommended the sizes of 40 m x 70 m and 48 m x 70 m for competition areas. (See Studies on Multifunctional Design of Sport Venues written by Li Ling and Supervised by Sun Yimin, 2002) In 2002, the size of 40 m x 70 m was employed in the design of the sport venue of Huazhong University of Science and Technology, making it the first venue in Wuhan that allowed for international gymnastics competition. As for the Olympic Badminton Stadium in Beijing University of Technology, the decision made on its size was rather straightforward. Yet given that the stadium would be used for many purposes after the games as a facility in the university, we decided to make it the most flexible and adaptable venue by selecting the size of 40 m x 70 m. This way it would be able to host various games including international gymnastics competitions after Beijing Olympics. The same size was used in the Wrestling Stadium that was also a facility in the other university.

Both the Olympic badminton matches and gymnastics rhythmic test competitions show that the size of the venue is suitable for various games, ceremonies and activities. On the other hand, in order to make a sport venue available for teaching and training and other uses in a university, the numbers of volleyball courts, badminton courts and table tennis courts should at least be 5, 18 and 25 respectively.

Ⅲ. Adaptability of Roof Shape and Structural Type

Selection of structural type is an important step in sport building design. A rational structure is an indispensible feature of an outstanding sport building. However, we should understand that structural technology serves only as a means, instead of a purpose, of architectural expression. Therefore, flexibility and adaptability become very important when it comes to the selection of means. A structural type should satisfy the requirements of technology, construction, project period and cost and investment. Yet, it should provide multiple choices. In other words, full consideration should be given to adaptability in structural conception.

Take Olympic Badminton Stadium in Beijing University of Technology as an example. In view of its scale and the requirements of the Olympic design brief, we decided to select the rounded shape for the building and tried to give it a graceful and light appearance. Therefore, when selecting a suitable structural type, we aimed to find one that could fit into the design conception. Because it was an Olympic venue invested and constructed by the university, the control on cost was extremely tight. Therefore, we determined to use the spherical shell structure at the tendering stage.

In order to present the design conception, the spherical shell structure with good mechanical performances was cut to form flowing curves. This design not only satisfied the requirements on building functions but also created a smooth and curvy shape by making use of the flexibility of the structure. In order to realize a low sightline between the view and the stadium, the two edges of the shell were extended along the spherical surface. Curvy glazed canopies were added at the edge of the shell to articulate the beauty and the rhythmical feature of the structure itself.

At the design detailing stage, the client emphasized the advanced nature of the structural technology and recommended the pre-stressed steel structure. As the roof we selected was extremely adaptable, this request was accommodated. We proposed three structures at the preliminary stage which could fit into the interior/exterior spatial forms we conceived. Also, we compared the steel quantities and economic and technical indicators of the three proposals and provided our suggestions to the client. Eventually, we completed the design scheme using the pre-stressed suspension structure as insisted by the client, making the roof structure of the Badminton Stadium the most up-to-date structure among all sport venues of Beijing 2008 Olympics. However, due to the higher complexity level of the structure, the construction period was extended. The suspension structure had some constraints on the hanging of equipment under the roof, thus it became less flexible. We have learned about the dialectical relation among structural and technical advancement, practicability and construction easiness in practice. Venues, regardless of their types, should be properly designed with consideration given to their actual conditions through analysis. However, it should become a fundamental principle to emphasize the adaptability of building in design.

The above are our analysis and thoughts on some noticeable issues in the design of the Olympic Badminton Stadium.

(The design team for the project of Badminton and Gymnastics Rhythmic Stadium for Beijing 2008 Olympics in Beijing University of Technology was led by Academician He Jingtang. Graduate students Shen Yonggang, Wu Hanbin, Deng Fang, Chen Weizhi, Du Weihua and Zheng Haili participated in the schematic design stage.)

By Sun Yimin

Source: Architectural Journal, 2008 Issue 1, P94-97

广州大学城建设项目华南理工大学体育馆

GYMNASIUM OF SOUTH CHINA UNIVERSITY OF TECHNOLOGY, GUANGZHOU HIGHER EDUCATION MEGA CENTER

项目地点：广东省广州市
设计时间：2005—2006 年
竣工时间：2007 年
用地面积：19,779 m^2
建筑面积：12,783 m^2

Location: Guangzhou, Guangdong
Design: 2005-2006
Completion: 2007
Site Area: 19,779 m^2
GFA: 12,783 m^2

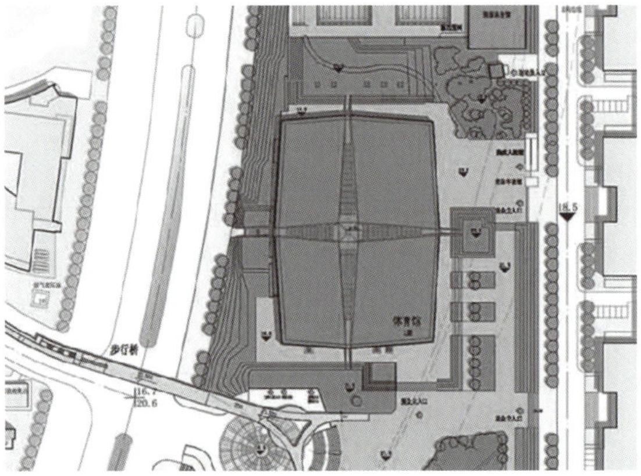

大学城华南理工大学体育馆是规模为 5000 个座席的校园体育建筑，曾作为 2007 年中国第 8 届大学生运动会的乒乓球比赛用场地及 2010 年亚运会的柔道、摔跤比赛场馆。

华工体育馆规划布局利用基地原有高差的地形特点，建筑设计为半覆土，不仅减小了体量，同时通过立体交通对不同人员进行分流。

建筑向四周翘起的屋面及出挑深远的檐口，与华工北校区历史悠久的岭南建筑在神韵上有几分相似；屋面结构形式成熟而又新颖：由 4 片非对称的扭壳（厚度为 130 毫米）组合而成，屋盖的平面投影达到了长轴 99.8 m，短轴 70 m 的大跨度。

体育馆的场地选型为 40 m X 70 m，适应高校体育场馆在满足学校正常教学要求的基础上，兼顾大型运动会的比赛要求。

建筑采用机械辅助浮力通风系统，半覆土为浮力通风创造了底层温度较低的空气，组合扭壳结构形成了由四边向中部升起的室内大空间造型，比赛场地与屋盖顶部的高差达 32 m，为浮力通风创造了优良的气流高差条件，在过渡季节和冬季能够有效地改善场地中心的热状况。

比赛大厅通过四个梯形的天窗及东西屋檐下的高侧窗获取自然光照明。天窗的 Z 形遮阳板与支撑结构的连接件结合于一体，并根据模拟太阳的运行轨迹确定四个朝向的遮阳板尺寸及遮阳角度。

体育馆造型优雅独特，成为华工南校区的标志性建筑之一，首次建设的投资额仅约为 8000 万元，建筑每平方米造价约为 6300 元，经济节约。大学城华工体育馆体现了我们在体育建筑设计上运用可持续设计策略的创作理念。

SCUT Gymnasium in GHEMC is a 5,000-seat campus sport building. It hosted the table tennis games during the 8th Universiade of China in 2007 and the judo and wrestling competitions of the 2010 Asian Games.

In the planning layout of the gymnasium, buildings are designed to be semi-earth sheltered by making use of the elevation differences of the landform. This not only reduces building volumes but also separate different pedestrian flows through a multi-level traffic system.

The turnup roofs and the protruding eaves share some resemblance to the long-existed Lingnan buildings in the SCUT North Campus. Comprising four pieces of asymmetrical twisted shells (130 mm in thickness), the roof features a mature yet novel structural form, with its planar projection covering a large span that is 99.8 m in long axis and 70 m in short axis.

The competition fields measures 40 m x 70 m in size to accommodate both the general teaching requirements for a university sports building but also those of the large games.

The mechanical buoyancy-driven ventilation system is employed, while the semi-earth sheltering structure cools down the air in the base for buoyancy-driven ventilation. The combined twisted shell structure forms a large indoor space of which the four sides rise towards the center. The height difference between the competition ground and the roof top is as many as 32 meters, facilitating buoyancy-driven ventilation with an ideal height difference between air flows. It also effectively improves the thermal conditions of the gymnasium in transitional seasons and winters.

Four wedged skylights and high side windows under the east and west eaves bring daylight into the competition hall. The Z-shaped sunshade panels of the skylights are integrated into the fastenings of the support structures. The dimensions and angles of the panels on four directions are determined as per the simulated sun movement.

Thanks to its distinctive and elegant form and appearance, the gymnasium becomes one of the landmark buildings on SCUT South Campus. It is highly cost effective with the investment of initial development at RMB 80 million and the per square meter construction cost at merely RMB 6, 300, The SCUT gymnasium in GZHEMC embodies the sustainable strategies in creation and conception of sport buildings.

广州大学城建设项目华南理工大学体育馆

GYMNASIUM OF SOUTH CHINA UNIVERSITY OF TECHNOLOGY, GUANGZHOU HIGHER EDUCATION MEGA CENTER

南京工程学院文体综合馆

SPORTS AND CULTURE COMPLEX OF NANJING INSTITUTE OF TECHNOLOGY

项目位置：江苏省南京市
设计时间：2012 年
竣工时间：2014 年
建筑规模：11,445 m^2

Location：Nanjing, Jiangsu
Design：2012
Completion：2014
GFA：11,445 m^2

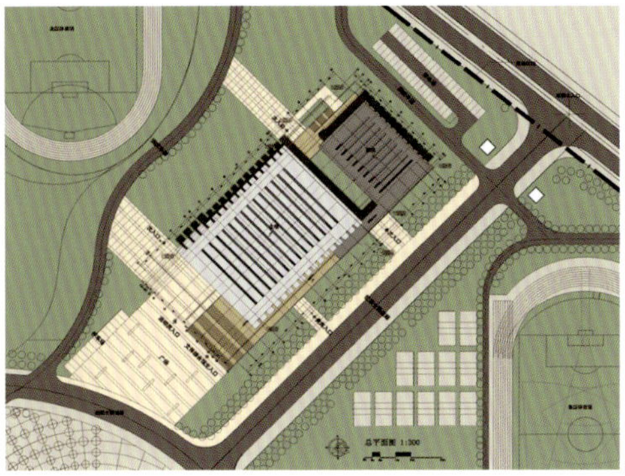

南京工程学院文体综合馆的设计概念来自“更高、更快、更强”的体育奋斗精神，表达了“团结，动感，力量”的设计理念，美好的立意与造型使体育馆具有了独一无二的个性。

综合馆的基本造型可简化为一组流畅灵动的舒展平台翻转成训练馆，其上叠加主馆方正造型的组合。两者一动一静、一灰一白形成鲜明对比，建筑的天际轮廓线充满了灵动的韵律，上下起伏，宛如虬龙，又如波涛，成为凝固的音乐，给人以汹涌澎湃、充满动感与力量的感受。在有限的资金投入之下，两个馆采用简单的结构形式和低廉的立面材料，通过体量的对比和巧妙的建筑设计形成完美的组合，动感而不失庄重，流畅而不失凝练，并且表达了团结拼搏的竞技精神。

将主馆和副馆拉开，留出 15 m 宽的双层平台通道，既加强了左右 2 个体育区域的联系，也极大地解决了主副馆的通风采光问题。

Inspired by the Olympic motto of “higher, faster and stronger”, the design concept of the complex highlights the sportsmanship and the theme of “unity, dynamics and strength”. The inspiring idea and building form make a sports facility of unique identity.

The basic form of the complex can be simplified into a group of smoothly and flexibly extending platforms that are turned into training halls, above which the combined square volume of the main hall are placed. The two types of elements form sharp contrast between the static and the dynamic, and between the colors of gray and white. The vividly rhythmic skyline of the building waves elegantly. The whole building is like solidified music, portraying a dynamic and energetic image with sweeping lines. Due to limited investment, the two facilities employ concise structures and low-cost facade materials. Yet they are perfectly combined with each other through the contrast of building volumes and the ingenious architectural design. The dynamic and flowing building form are also elegant and concise, celebrating the sportsmanship of unity and hard work.

The main hall is separated from the auxiliary hall by a 15-meter-wide double-deck platform passage, which not only enhances the connection between the two sports areas, but also greatly improves the ventilation and daylight of the two sports facilities.

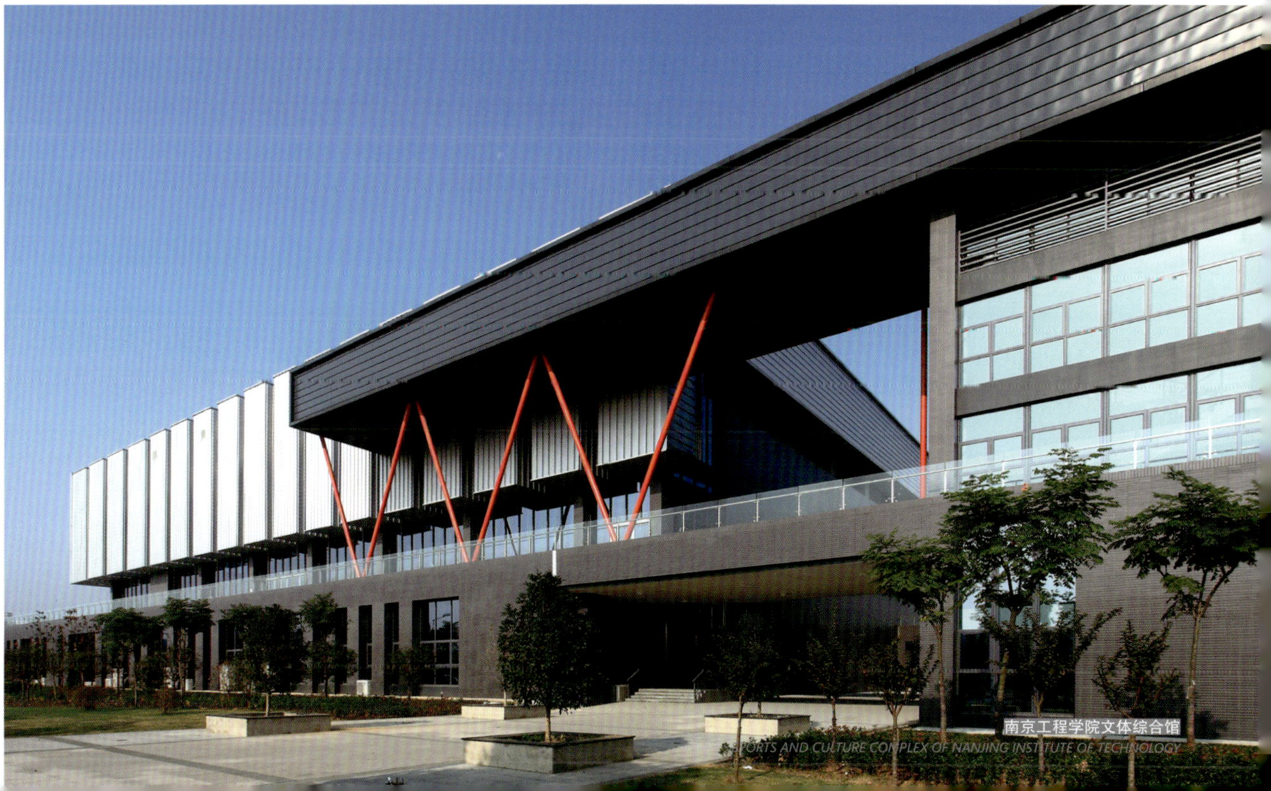

南京工程学院文体综合馆
SPORTS AND CULTURE COMPLEX OF NANJING INSTITUTE OF TECHNOLOGY

华南农业大学体育馆

GYMNASIUM OF SOUTH CHINA AGRICULTURAL UNIVERSITY

项目地点：广东省广州市
设计时间：2019 年
用地面积：39,039.9 m^2
建筑面积：52,450 m^2

Location: Guangzhou, Guangdong
Design: 2019
Site Area: 39,039.9 m^2
GFA: 52,450 m^2

该项目的规划布局采用紧凑集约的立体分区，顺应场地与周边道路，从西到东布置游泳馆、主场馆、训练馆，同时赋予复合的功能，创造丰富多变的空间体验。利用场地原有高差在不同的竖向层面布置功能：游泳馆采用半下沉的方式，尽可能地埋地以减少其对校门周围开敞空间的影响，同时减少对主馆的视线遮挡；主馆及训练馆下沉一层，分别作为地下车库及球类场馆，充分利用了场地的地下空间。场地北侧设置校园交往带，体量的错动形成了大小不一的空间，通过商业的引入、交往设施的置入、绿植的融入，使之成为校园交往的纽带，打破单调乏味的线性空间感受；场地南侧通过平台串联的方式，将各类室外空间活动如滑板、攀岩等联系起来，打造校园活力运动带；场地中央规划路较为开阔，置入伞阵广场，形成半室外灰空间，汇集活动，积聚人气，成为沟通场地东西侧的核心互动轴。

The Project features a compact and intensive vertical zoning. The natatorium, main gymnasium hall and training hall are placed from west to east based on existing site fabric and surrounding roads. Compound functions enable diverse and varied space experience. These functions are placed on different levels to make full use of the existing elevation difference of the site. The natatorium is semi-sunken to minimize impact on the open space around the main gate and avoid obstructing view into the main gymnasium hall. The main gymnasium hall and the training hall are sunken by one floor to provide underground carpark and venue for ball sports, making full use of the underground spaces. A campus communication belt comprising spaces of varied sizes as a result of staggered volumes is provided on the north of the site. Integrating commercial and communication facilities as well as green plants, it comes as a vibrant link for campus communication and avoiding the monotony of linear space. In the south of the site, various outdoor activity spaces, including those for skateboarding and rock climbing, are linked up to form a dynamic campus sports belt. The generous planned road at the center of the site is embedded with a square featuring umbrella matrix. This square serves as a semi-outdoor gray space to gain popularity and a central interactive axis to connect the east and west of the site.

华南农业大学体育馆
GYMNASIUM OF SOUTH CHINA AGRICULTURAL UNIVERSITY

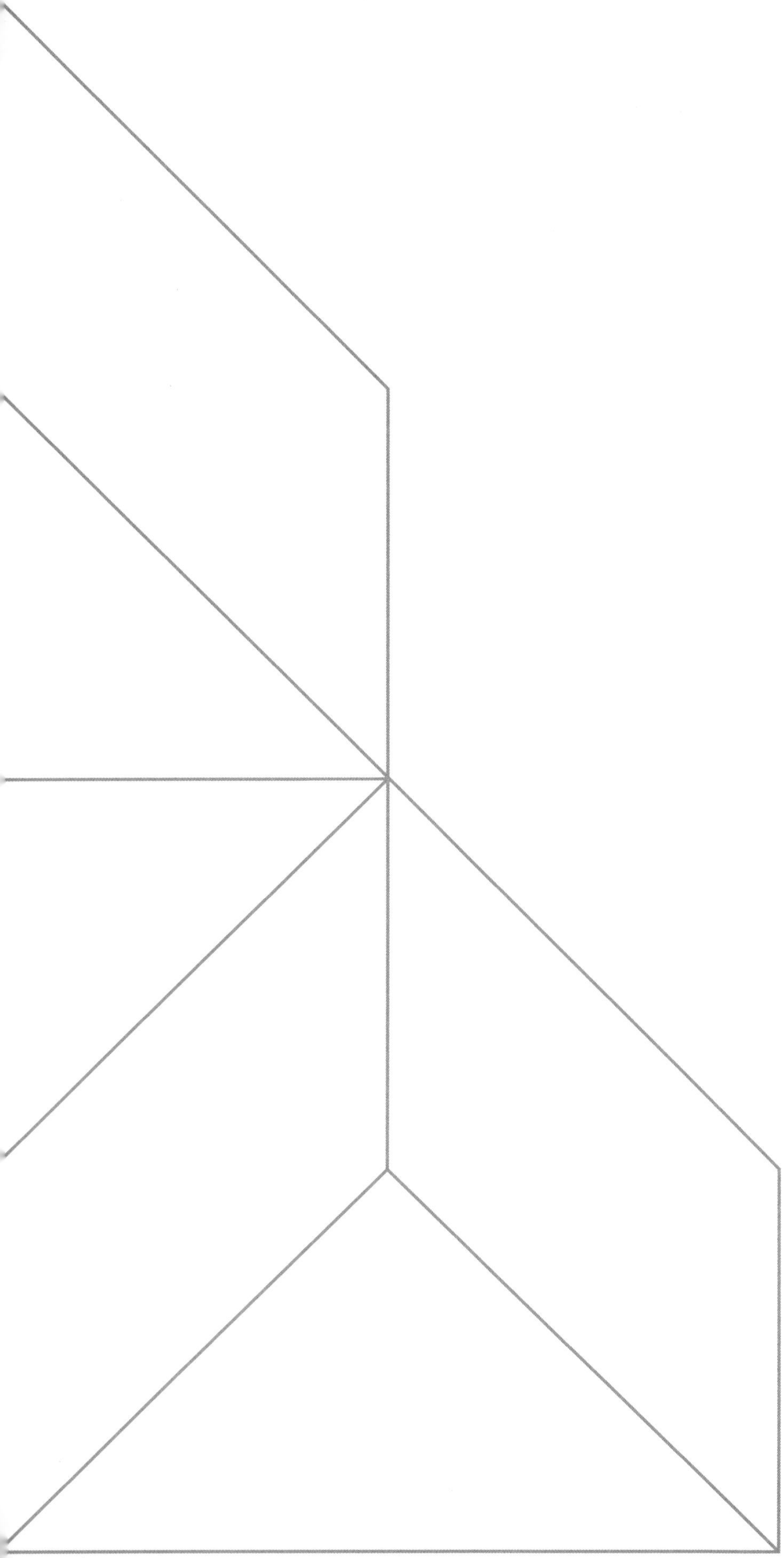

校园总体规划
CAMPUS MASTER PLANNING

烟台汽车工程职业学院
YANTAI AUTOMOBILE ENGINEERING PROFESSIONAL COLLEGE

项目地点：山东省烟台市
设计时间：2005 年
用地面积：400,000 m²
建筑面积：270,000 m²
曾获奖项：山东省优秀城市规划一等奖（2009 年）
全国优秀城市规划表扬奖（2009 年）

Location: Yantai, Shandong
Design: 2005
Site Area: 400,000 m²
GFA: 270,000 m²
Awards:
The First Prize for Excellent Urban Planning Works of Shandong Province (2009)
Honorable Mention for National Excellent Urban Planning Works (2009)

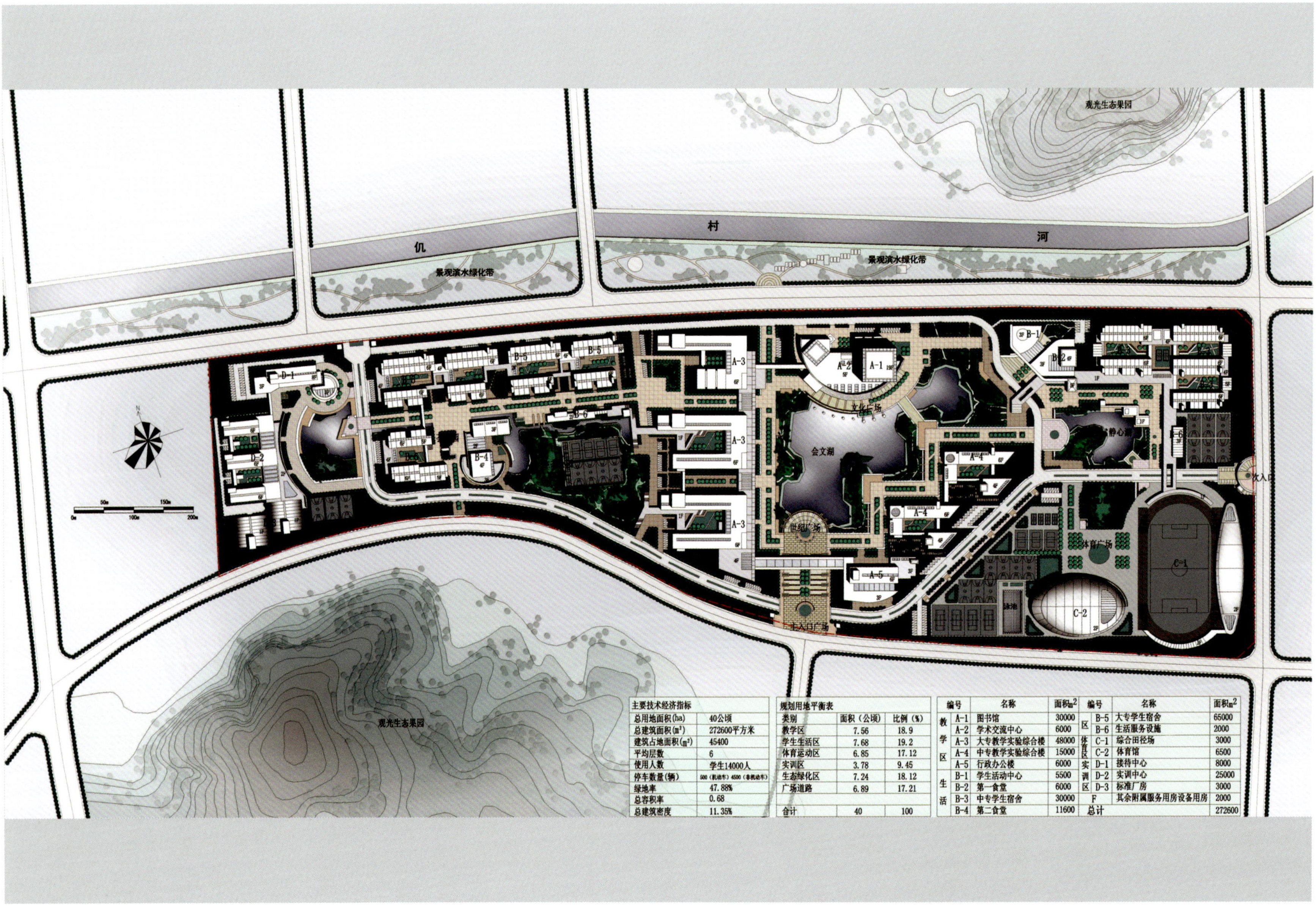

主要技术经济指标	
总用地面积(ha)	40公顷
总建筑面积(m²)	272600平方米
建筑占地面积(m²)	45400
平均层数	6
使用人数	学生14000人
停车数量(辆)	500（机动车）4500（非机动车）
绿地率	47.88%
总容积率	0.68
总建筑密度	11.35%

规划用地平衡表

类别	面积（公顷）	比例（%）
教学区	7.56	18.9
学生生活区	7.68	19.2
体育运动区	6.85	17.12
实训区	3.78	9.45
生态绿化区	7.24	18.12
广场道路	6.89	17.21
合计	40	100

编号		名称	面积m²	编号		名称	面积m²
教学区	A-1	图书馆	30000	区	B-5	大专学生宿舍	65000
	A-2	学术交流中心	6000		B-6	生活服务设施	2000
	A-3	大专教学实验综合楼	48000	体育区	C-1	综合田径场	3000
	A-4	中专教学实验综合楼	15000		C-2	体育馆	6500
	A-5	行政办公楼	6000	实训区	D-1	接待中心	8000
生活	B-1	学生活动中心	5500		D-2	实训中心	25000
	B-2	第一食堂	6000		D-3	标准厂房	3000
	B-3	中专学生宿舍	30000	F		其余附属服务用房设备用房	2000
	B-4	第二食堂	11600	总计			272600

天津国际医学城
TIANJIN INTERNATIONAL MEDICAL CITY

项目地点：天津市
设计时间：2010 年
用地面积：2,750,666 m^2
建筑面积：1,460,734 m^2

Location: Tianjin
Design: 2010
Site Area: 2,750,666 m^2
GFA: 1,460,734 m^2

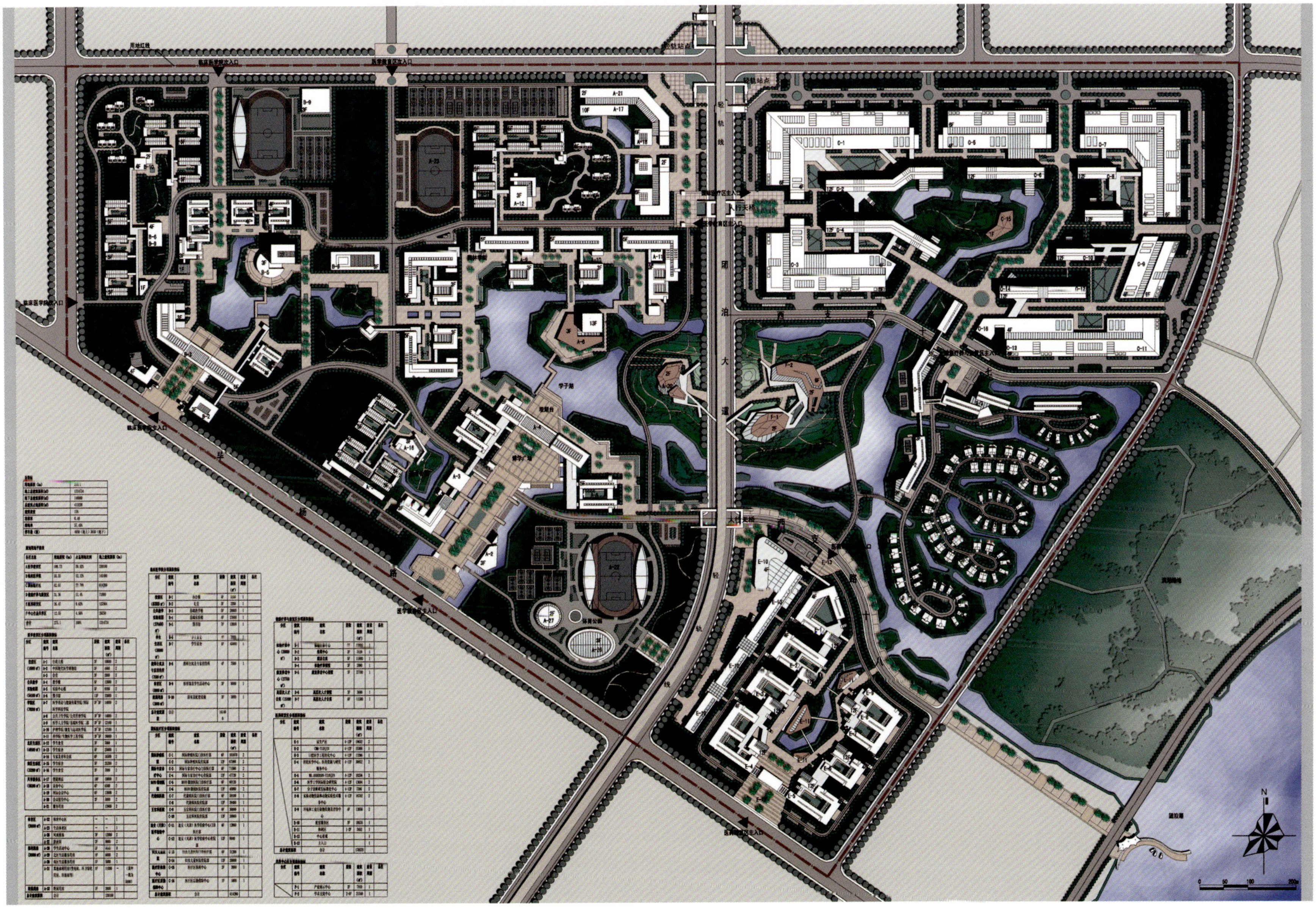

中国传媒大学南广学院
COMMUNICATION UNIVERSITY OF CHINA, NANJING

项目地点：江苏省南京市
设计时间：2004 年
用地面积：888,000 m^2
建筑面积：321,320 m^2

Location: Nanjing, Jiangsu
Design: 2004
Site Area: 888,000 m^2
GFA: 321,320 m^2

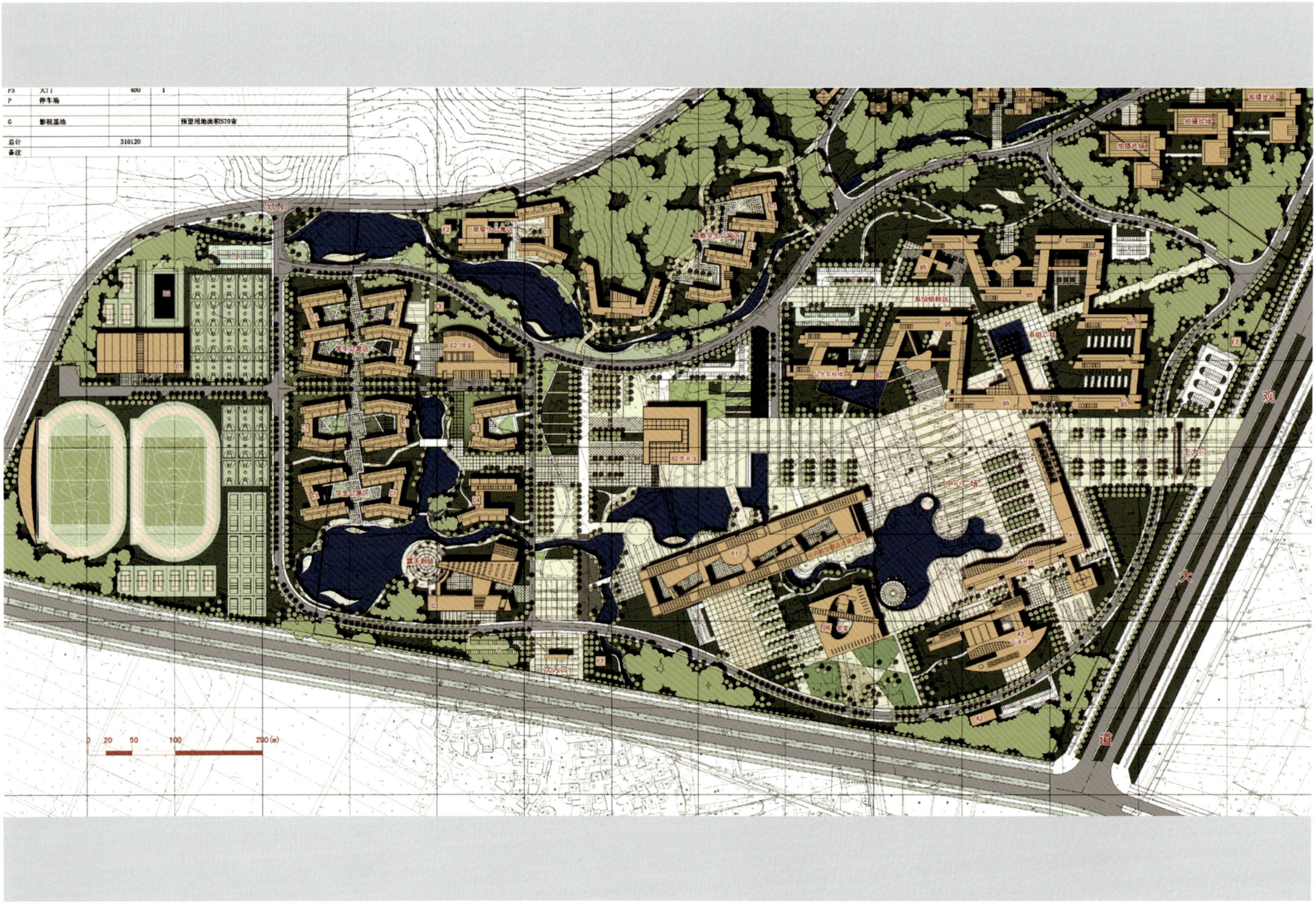

西安电子科技大学
XIDIAN UNIVERSITY

项目地点：陕西省西安市
设计时间：2003 年
用地面积：2,000,000 m²
建筑面积：865,500 m²
曾获奖项：教育部优秀规划设计三等奖（2005 年）

Location: Xi'an, Shaanxi
Design: 2003
Site Area: 2,000,000 m^2
GFA: 865,500 m^2
Award:
The Third Prize of Excellent Architectural Design Award by the Ministry of Education (2005)

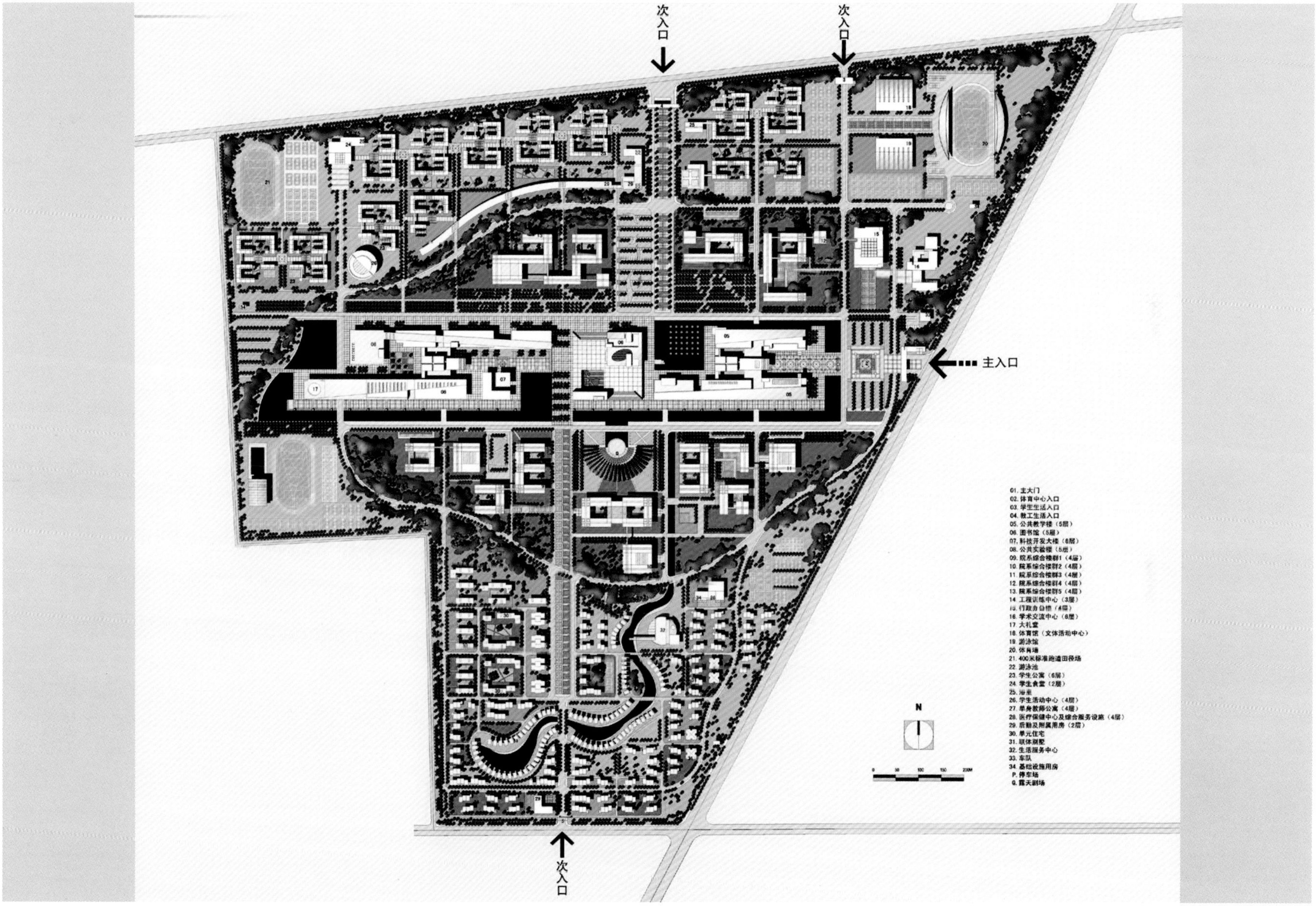

太原大学新校区
NEW CAMPUS OF TAIYUAN UNIVERSITY

项目地点：山西省太原市
设计时间：2007—2009 年
竣工时间：2011 年
用地面积：1,250,900 m^2
建筑面积：652,000 m^2
曾获奖项：新校区规划设计投标一等奖（2007 年）
教育部优秀勘察设计评选规划设计三等奖（2009 年）

Location: Taiyuan, Shanxi
Design: 2007-2009
Completion: 2011
Site Area: 1,250,900 m^2
GFA: 652,000 m^2
Awards:
The First Prize for the Planning and Design Competition for New Campus (2007)
The Third Prize for Planning and Design of Excellent Exploration and Design Evaluation by the Ministry of Education (2009)

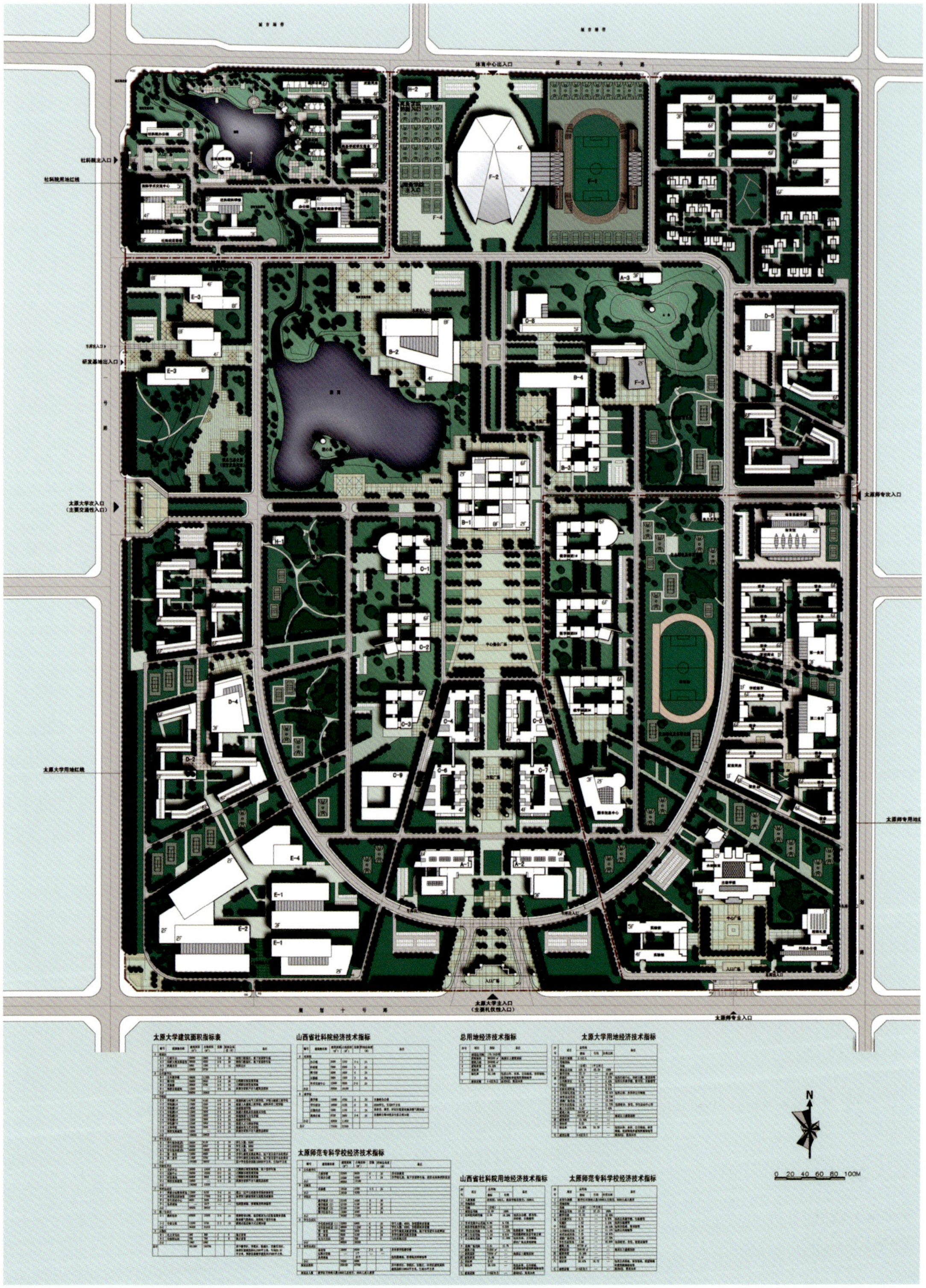

湖南工业大学新校区
NEW CAMPUS OF HUNAN UNIVERSITY OF TECHNOLOGY

项目地点：湖南省株洲市
设计时间：2004—2005 年
用地面积：2,326,400 m^2
建筑面积：803,000 m^2
曾获奖项：新校区规划设计国际竞赛一等奖（2003 年）
教育部优秀勘察设计评选规划设计三等奖（2009 年）

Location: Zhuzhou, Hunan
Design: 2004-2005
Site Area: 2,326,400 m^2
GFA: 803,000 m^2
Awards:
The First Place of the International Planning and Design Competition for New Campus (2003)
The Third Prize for Planning and Design of Excellent Exploration and Design Evaluation by the Ministry of Education (2009)

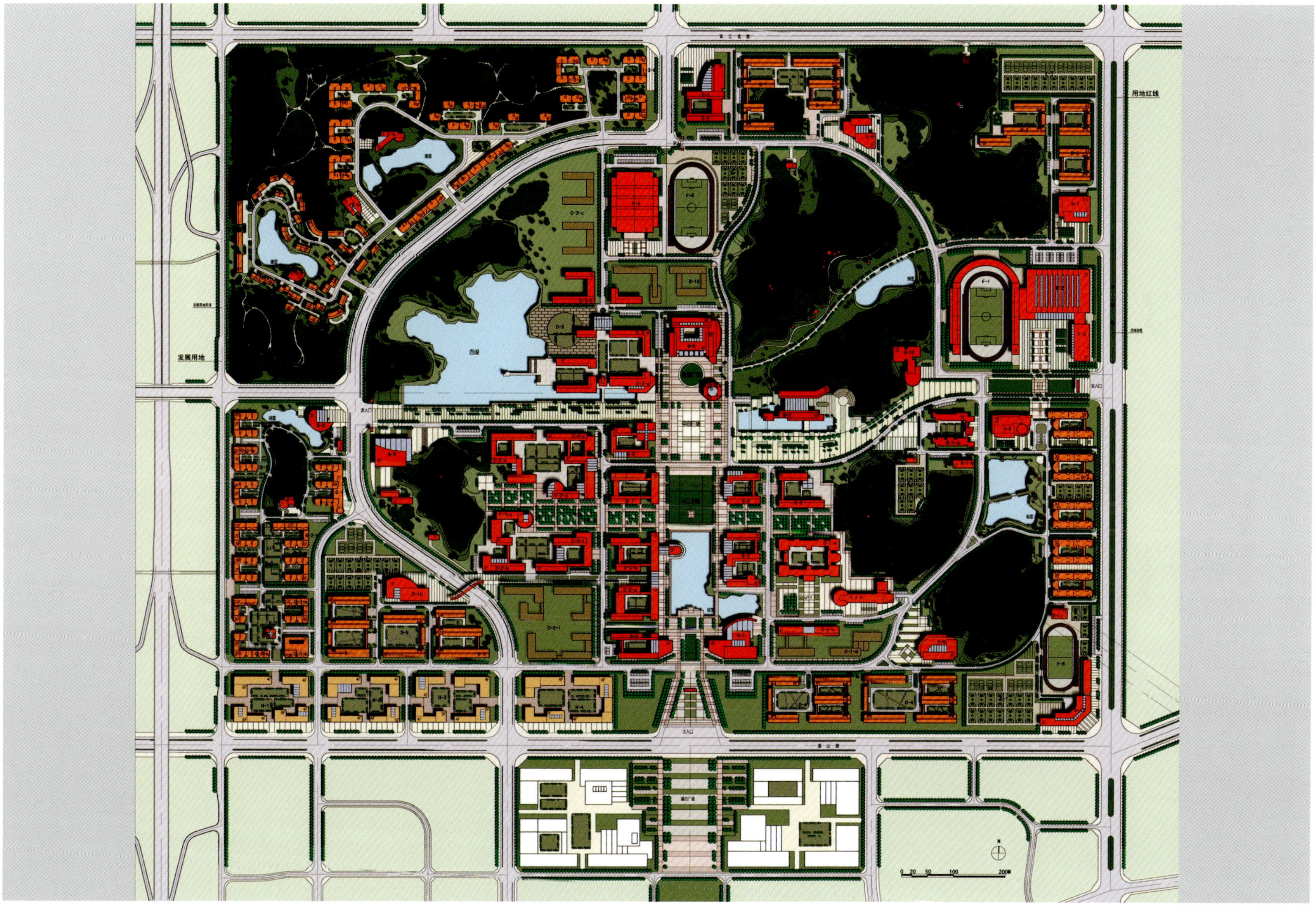

北京航空航天大学
BEIHANG UNIVERSITY

项目地点：北京市
设计时间：2003—2004 年
竣工时间：2005 年
用地面积：约 980,000 m^2
建筑面积：约 600,000 m^2
曾获奖项：国际概念规划竞标第一名

Location: Beijing
Design: 2003-2004
Completion: 2005
Site Area: Approx 980,000 m^2
GFA: Approx 600,000 m^2
Award:
The First Place in the International Conceptual Planning Competition

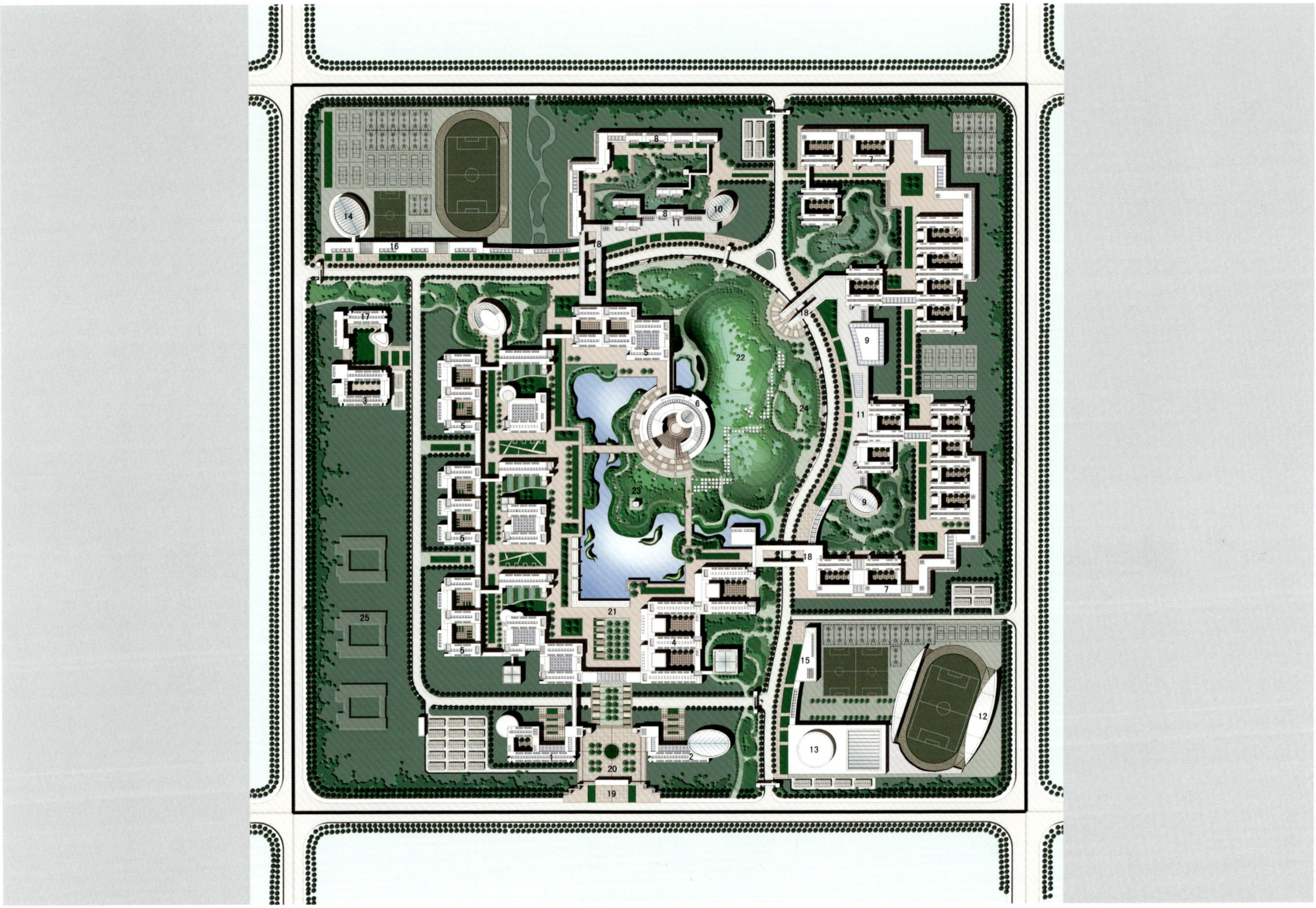

大连海洋大学新校园

NEW CAMPUS OF DALIAN OCEAN UNIVERSITY

项目地点：辽宁省大连市
设计时间：2012 年
用地面积：1,700,000 m^2
建筑面积：520,000 m^2

Location: Dalian, Liaoning
Design: 2012
Site Area: 1,700,000 m^2
GFA: 520,000 m^2

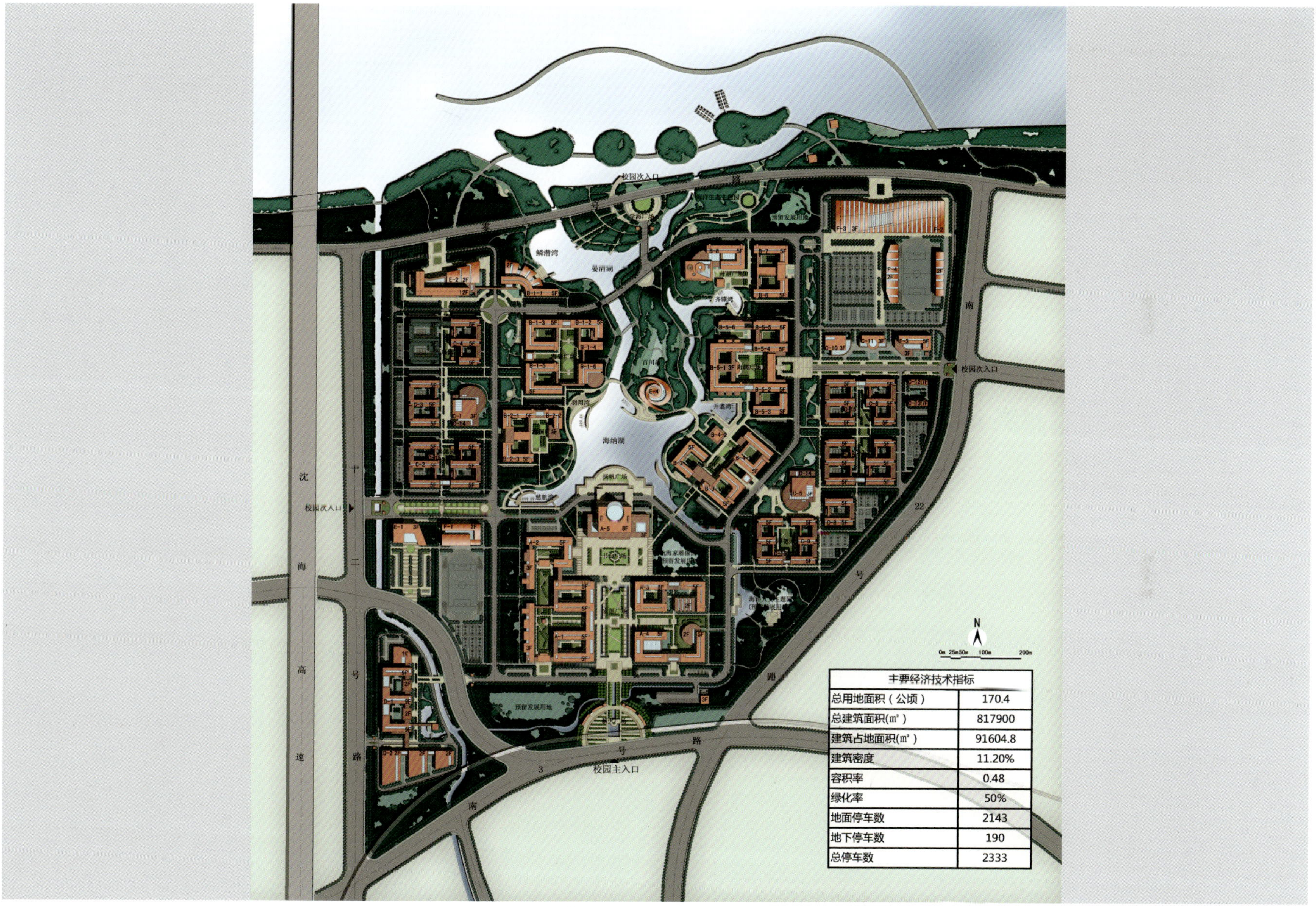

主要经济技术指标	
总用地面积（公顷）	170.4
总建筑面积(㎡)	817900
建筑占地面积(㎡)	91604.8
建筑密度	11.20%
容积率	0.48
绿化率	50%
地面停车数	2143
地下停车数	190
总停车数	2333

安徽中医学院新校区 *

NEW CAMPUS OF ANHUI COLLEGE OF CHINESE MEDICINE*

项目地点：安徽省合肥市
设计时间：2011 年
用地面积：663,333 m^2
建筑面积：715,400 m^2

Location: Hefei, Anhui
Design: 2011
Site Area: 663,333 m^2
GFA: 715,400 m^2

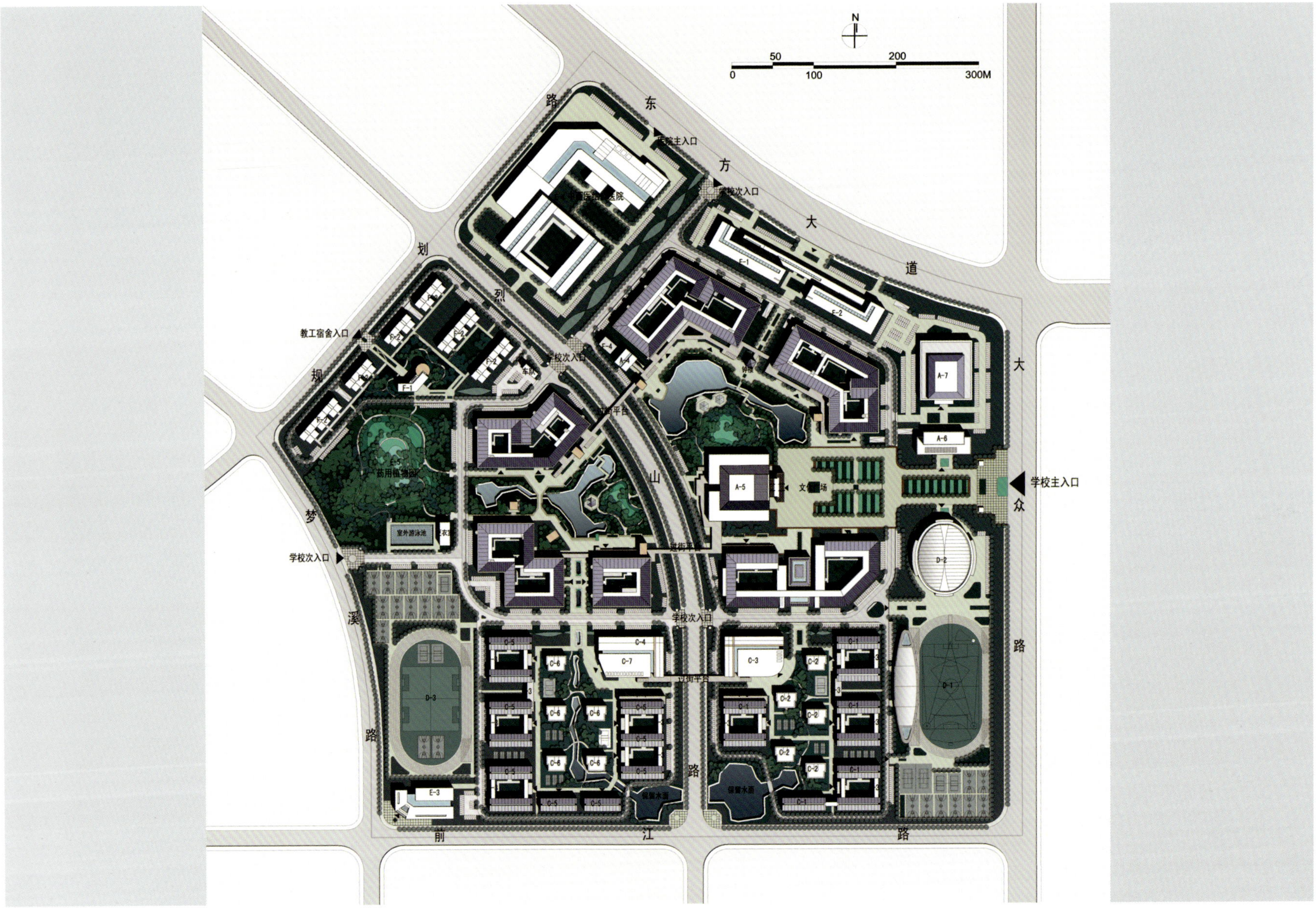

* 安徽中医学院于 2013 年更名为安徽中医药大学
* Anhui College of Chinese Medicine was renamed to Anhui University of Chinese Medicine in 2013

南华大学新校区

NEW CAMPUS OF UNIVERSITY OF SOUTH CHINA

项目地点：湖南省衡阳市
设计时间：2010 年
用地面积：1,083,700 m^2
建筑面积：500,000 m^2

Location: Hengyang, Hunan
Design: 2010
Site Area: 1,083,700 m^2
GFA: 500,000 m^2

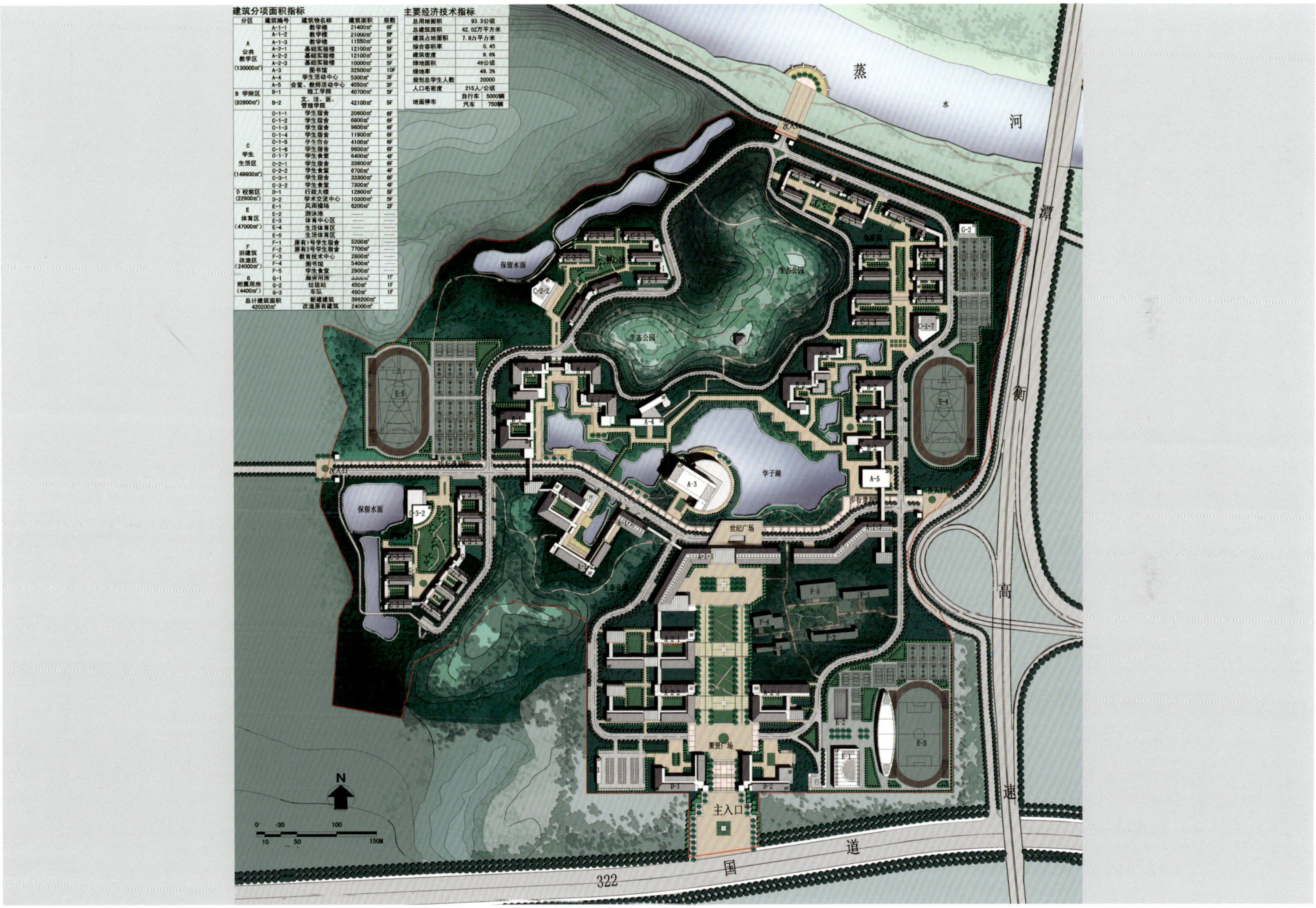

建筑分项面积指标

分区	建筑编号	建筑物名称	建筑面积	层数
A 公共教学区 (130000㎡)	A-1-1	教学楼	21400㎡	6F
	A-1-2	教学楼	21000㎡	5F
	A-1-3	教学楼	11550㎡	6F
	A-2-1	基础实验楼	12100㎡	5F
	A-2-2	基础实验楼	12100㎡	5F
	A-2-3	基础实验楼	10000㎡	5F
	A-3	图书馆	32500㎡	10F
	A-4	学生活动中心	5300㎡	3F
	A-5	会堂、教师活动中心	4050㎡	3F
B 学院区 (82800㎡)	B-1	理工学院	40700㎡	5F
	B-2	文、法、医、管理学院	42100㎡	5F
C 学生生活区 (149900㎡)	C-1-1	学生宿舍	20600㎡	6F
	C-1-2	学生宿舍	6800㎡	6F
	C-1-3	学生宿舍	9600㎡	6F
	C-1-4	学生宿舍	11900㎡	6F
	C-1-5	学生宿舍	4100㎡	6F
	C-1-6	学生宿舍	9600㎡	6F
	C-1-7	学生食堂	6400㎡	4F
	C-2-1	学生宿舍	33600㎡	6F
	C-2-2	学生食堂	6700㎡	4F
	C-3-1	学生宿舍	33300㎡	6F
	C-3-2	学生食堂	7300㎡	4F
D 校前区 (22900㎡)	D-1	行政大楼	12600㎡	5F
	D-2	学术交流中心	10300㎡	5F
E 体育区 (47000㎡)	E-1	风雨操场	6200㎡	2F
	E-2	游泳池	——	——
	E-3	体育中心区	——	——
	E-4	生活体育区	——	——
	E-5	生活体育区	——	——
F 旧建筑改造区 (24000㎡)	F-1	原有1号学生宿舍	5200㎡	——
	F-2	原有2号学生宿舍	7700㎡	——
	F-3	教育技术中心	2800㎡	——
	F-4	图书馆	5400㎡	——
	F-5	学生食堂	2900㎡	——
G 附属用房 (4400㎡)	G-1	服务用房	3500㎡	1F
	G-2	垃圾站	450㎡	1F
	G-3	车队	450㎡	1F
总计建筑面积 420200㎡		新建建筑	396200㎡	——
		改造原有建筑	24000㎡	

主要经济技术指标

总用地面积	93.3公顷	
总建筑面积	42.02万平方米	
建筑占地面积	7.9万平方米	
综合容积率	0.45	
建筑密度	8.6%	
绿地面积	46公顷	
绿地率	49.3%	
规划总学生人数	20000	
人口毛密度	215人/公顷	
地面停车	自行车	5000辆
	汽车	750辆

山东大学青岛校区

QINGDAO CAMPUS OF SHANDONG UNIVERSITY

项目地点：山东省青岛市
设计时间：2010 年
用地面积：2,027,333 m^2
建筑面积：1,000,000 m^2

Location: Qingdao, Shandong
Design: 2010
Site Area: 2,027,333 m^2
GFA: 1,000,000 m^2

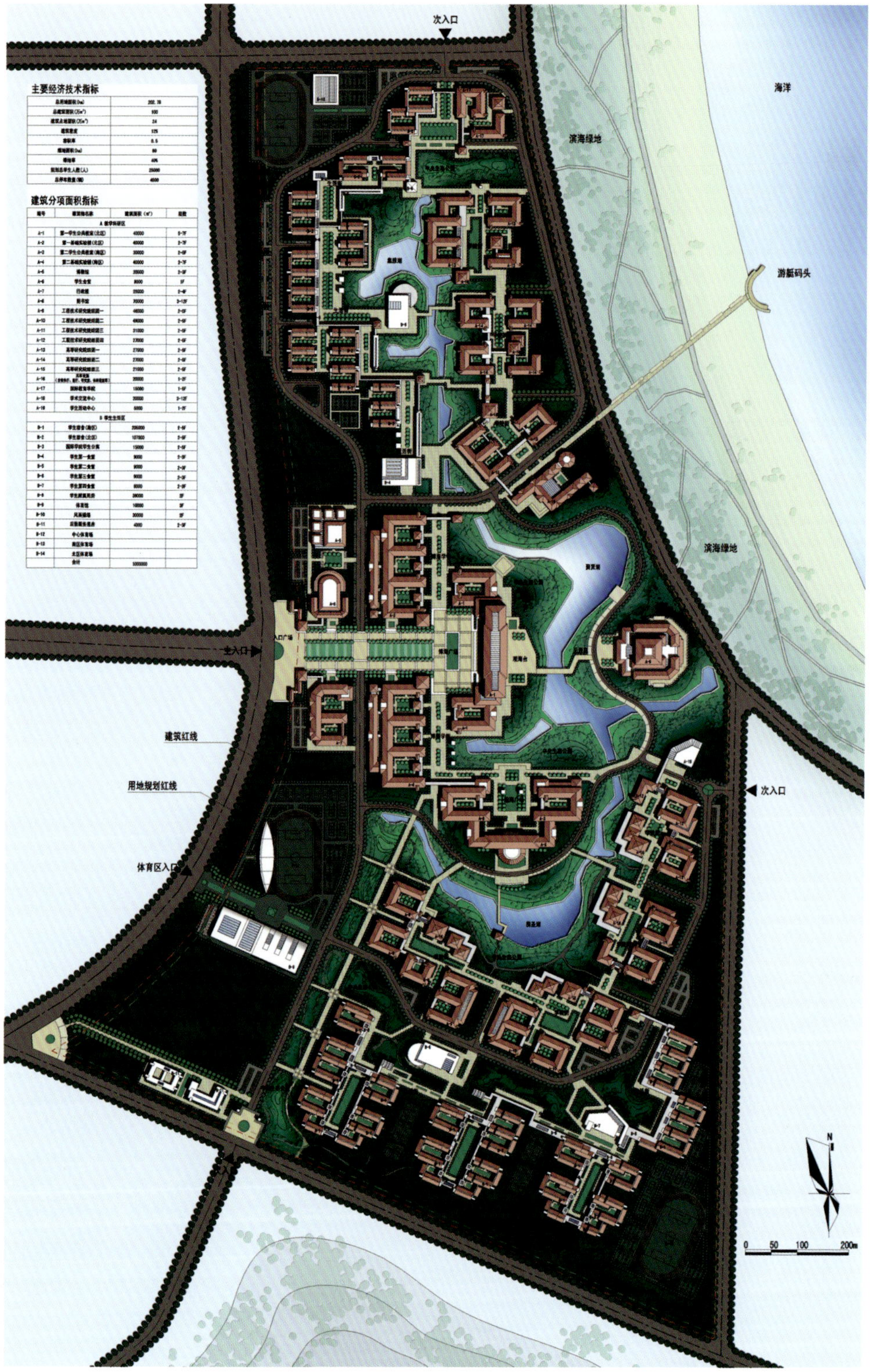

浙江大学紫金港校区西区概念规划（2005 年）

CONCEPTUAL PLANNING FOR ZIJINGANG CAMPUS (WEST) OF ZHEJIANG UNIVERSITY (2005)

项目地点：浙江省杭州市
设计时间：2005 年
用地面积：5,333,333 m^2
建筑面积：2,600,000 m^2
曾获奖项：国际设计竞赛评选第二名

Location: Hangzhou, Zhejiang
Design: 2005
Site Area: 5,333,333 m^2
GFA: 2,600,000 m^2
Award: The Second Place of the International Design Competition

浙江大学紫金港校区西区概念规划（2009 年）

CONCEPTUAL PLANNING FOR ZIJINGANG CAMPUS (WEST) OF ZHEJIANG UNIVERSITY (2009)

项目地点：浙江省杭州市
设计时间：2009 年
用地面积：5,333,333 m^2
建筑面积：2,600,000 m^2
曾获奖项：国际设计竞赛评选第二名

Location: Hangzhou, Zhejiang
Design: 2009
Site Area: 5,333,333 m^2
GFA: 2,600,000m^2
Award: The Second Place of the International Competition

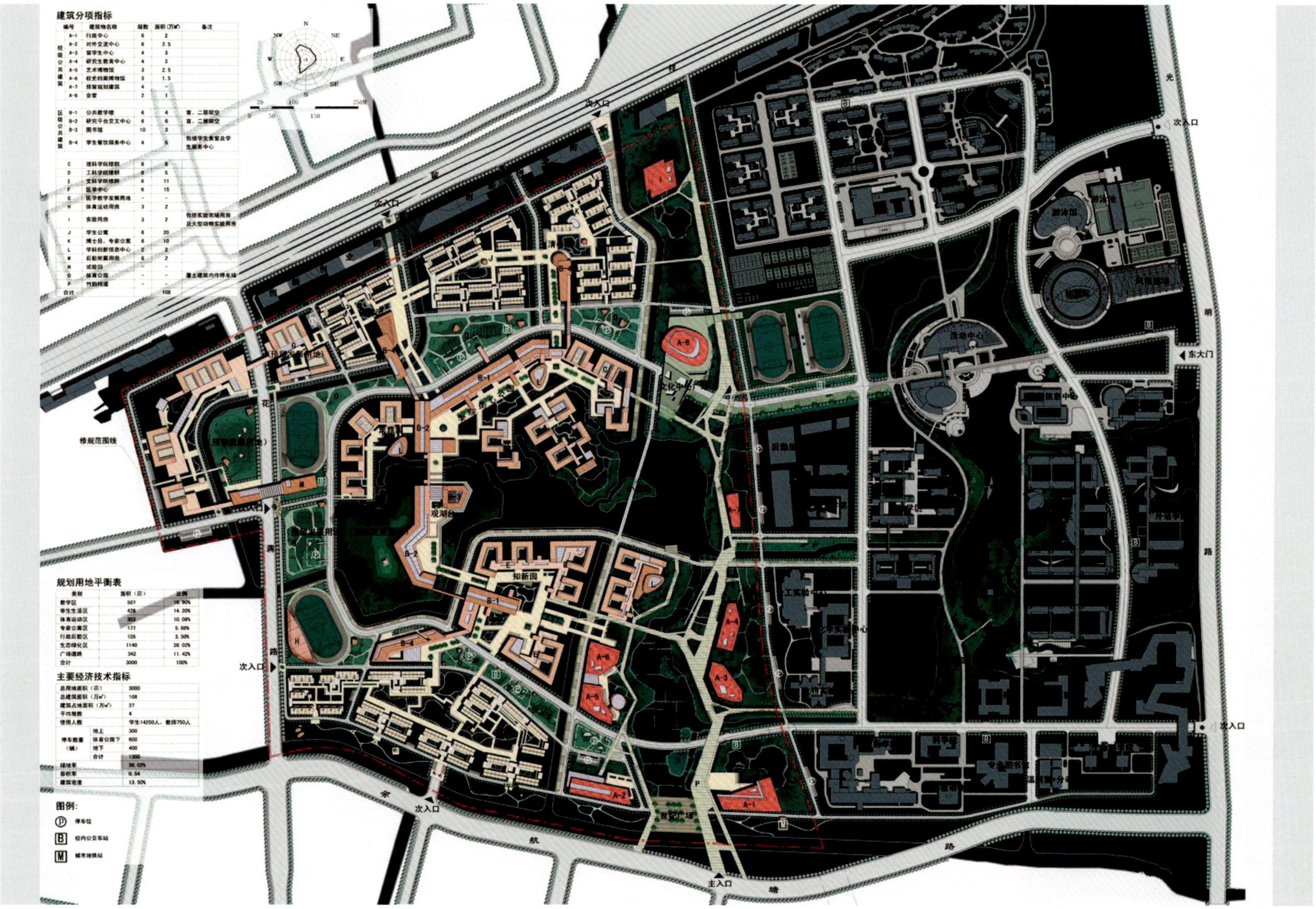

建筑分项指标

编号		建筑物名称	层数	面积(万㎡)	备注
校级公共建筑	A-1	行政中心	6	2	
	A-2	对外交流中心	6	2.5	
	A-3	留学生中心	4	3	
	A-4	研究生教育中心	4	2	
	A-5	艺术博物馆	3	2.5	
	A-6	校史档案博物馆	3	1.5	
	A-7	预留规划建筑	4	-	
	A-8	会堂	2	1	
区级公共建筑	B-1	公共教学楼	6	4	首、二层架空
	B-2	研究平台交叉中心	6	6	首、二层架空
	B-3	图书馆	10	3	
	B-4	学生餐饮服务中心	4	5	包括学生食堂及学生服务中心
	C	理科学院楼群	6	8	
	D	工科学院楼群	6	5	
	E	文科学院楼群	6	11	
	F	医学中心	6	15	
	G	医学教学发展用地	-	-	
	H	体育运动用房	3	2	
	I	实验用房	3	2	包括实验农场用房及大型动物实验用房
	J	学生公寓	6	20	
	K	博士后、专家公寓	6	10	
	L	学科创新信息中心	2	2	
	M	后勤保障用房	6	2	
	N	试验田	-	-	
	O	体育公园	-	-	覆土建筑内作停车场
	P	竹韵栈道	-	-	
合计				108	

规划用地平衡表

类别	面积（亩）	比例
教学区	507	16.90%
学生生活区	426	14.20%
体育运动区	303	10.08%
专家公寓区	177	5.88%
行政后勤区	105	3.50%
生态绿化区	1140	38.02%
广场道路	342	11.42%
合计	3000	100%

主要经济技术指标

总用地面积（亩）		3000
总建筑面积（万㎡）		108
建筑占地面积（万㎡）		27
平均层数		4
使用人数		学生14250人，教师750人
停车数量（辆）	地上	300
	体育公园下	600
	地下	400
	合计	1300
绿地率		38.02%
容积率		0.54
建筑密度		13.50%

莆田学院新校区修建性详细规划

CONSTRUCTIVE DETAILED PLANNING OF THE NEW CAMPUS OF PUTIAN COLLEGE

项目位置：福建省莆田市
设计时间：2014—2017 年
竣工时间：2017 年
建筑规模：1,987,500 m^2

Location: Putian, Fujian
Design: 2014-2017
Completion: 2017
GFA: 1,987,500 m^2

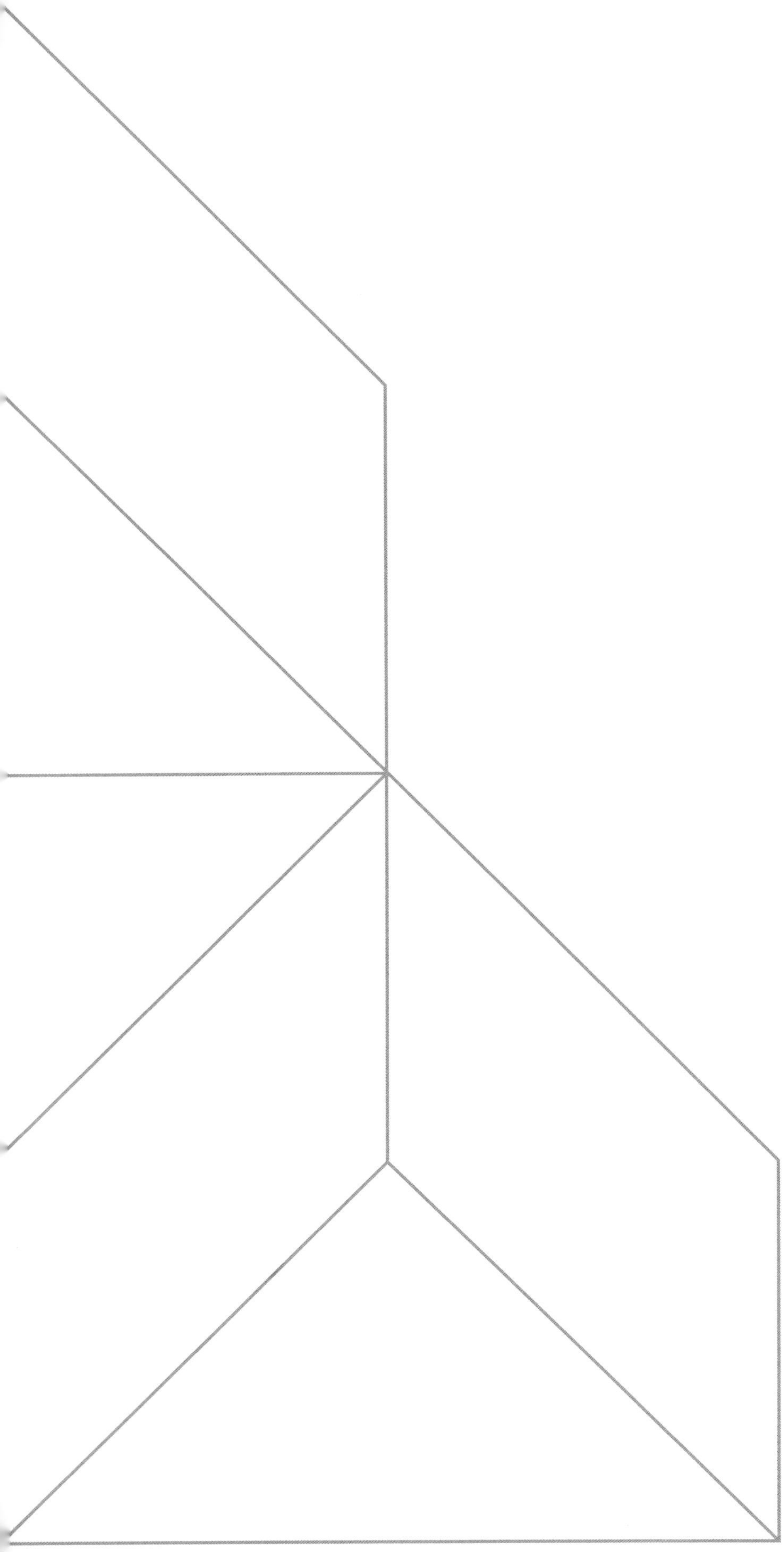

作品概览

SELECTED WORKS

浙江大学紫金港校区东教学组团
East Teaching Building Cluster, Zijingang Campus, Zhejiang University

华南师范大学南海学院
Nanhai College of South China Normal University

重庆工学院花溪校区
Huaxi Campus of Chongqing Institute of Technology

广州大学城华南理工大学教学区
The Teaching Area of South China University of Technology, Guangzhou Higher Education Mega Center

广州大学城广东药学院教学区
Teaching Area of Guangdong Pharmaceutical University, Guangzhou Higher Education Mega Center

南京审计学院
Nanjing Audit Institute

上海大学校本部东区
East Campus of Shanghai University

郑州大学新校区
New Campus of Zhengzhou University

南京工程学院
Nanjing Institute of Technology

江南大学
Jiangnan University

重庆大学虎溪校区
Huxi Campus of Chonging University

南京工业大学
Nanjing Tech University

中国矿业大学南湖校区
Nanhu Campus of China University of Mining & Technology

东华大学松江校区
Songjiang Campus of Donghua University

北京工业大学本部总体规划调整
Master Planning Adjustment for main Campus of Beijing University of Technology

福州大学图书馆
Library of Fuzhou University

钱学森图书馆
Qian Xuesen Library

国防科技大学图书馆
Library of National University of Defense Technology

重庆师范大学大学城校区图文信息中心
Library and Information Center of Chongqing Normal University (Chongqing University Town)

李政道图书馆
Li Zhengdao Library

华南理工大学 31、32 号楼
No. 31 and No. 32 Buildings, South China University of Technology

河海大学江宁校区核心教学区
Core Teaching Area of Jiangning Campus of Hohai University

四川大学新校区第二基础实验楼
No. 2 Basic Experiment Building of Sichuan University (New Campus)

武汉大学文科区
Liberal Arts Area of Wuhan University

华南理工大学逸夫人文馆
Sir Run Run Shaw Building of Humanities, South China University of Technology

华南理工大学松花江路 14、18、20、30 ~ 37 号历史建筑保护更新
Renewal of Historic Buildings at No. 14, 18, 20, 30 ~ 37, Songhuajiang Road, South China University of Technology

中山大学科技综合楼
Science and Technology Complex, Sun Yat-sen University

临沂大学艺、音、美综合体
Arts Complex of Linyi University

华南理工大学逸夫科学馆
Sir Run Run Shaw Science Building of South China University of Technology

五邑大学教学楼
Main Teaching Building of Wuyi University

2008 北京奥运会摔跤馆
Wrestling Arena for Beijing 2008 Olympic Games

2008 北京奥运会羽毛球馆
Badminton Gymnasium of Beijing 2008 Olympic Games

广州大学城建设项目华南理工大学体育馆
Gymnasium of South China University of Technology, Guangzhou Higher Education Mega Center

澳门大学横琴岛新校区
Hengqin Island New Campus of University of Macau

资本市场学院
China Capital Market Institute

天津科技大学泰达校区规划设计
Planning and Design for TEDA Campus of Tianjin University of Science & Technology

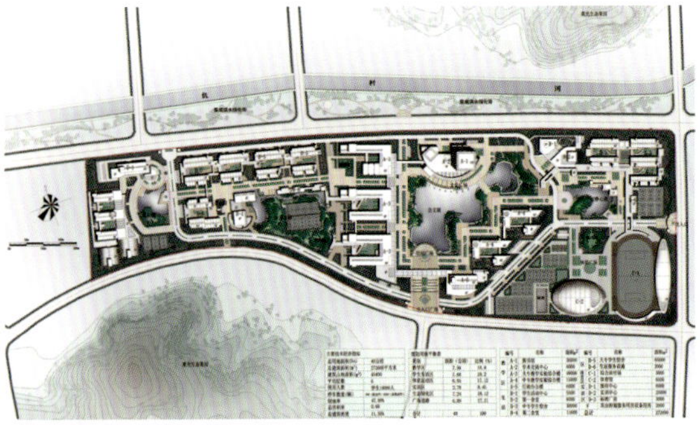

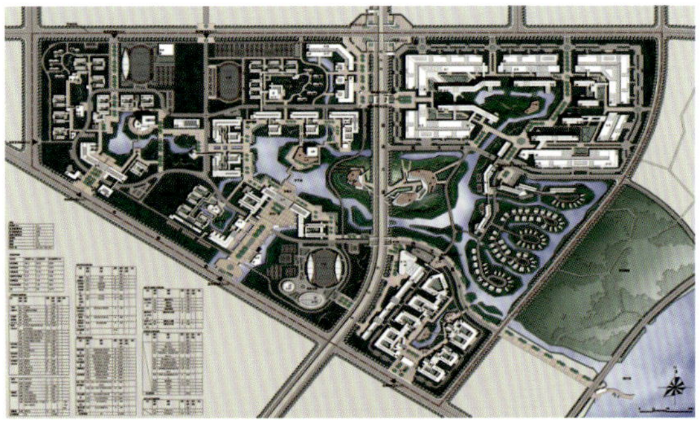

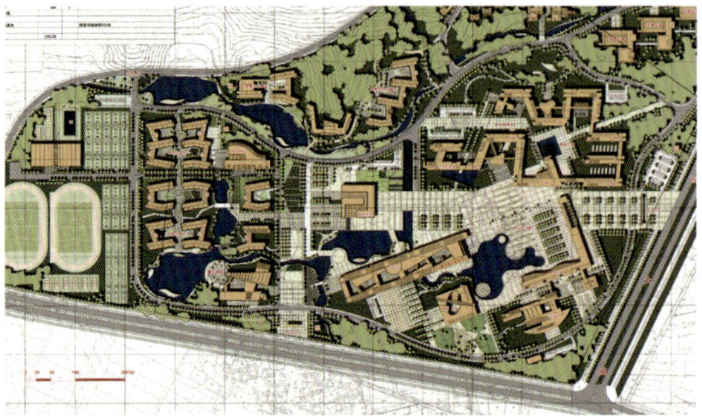

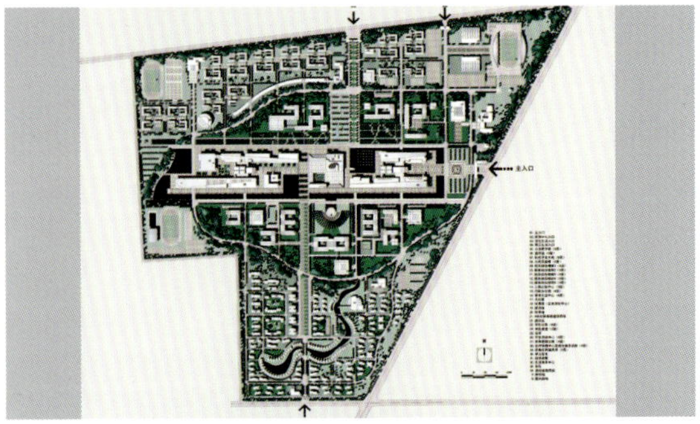

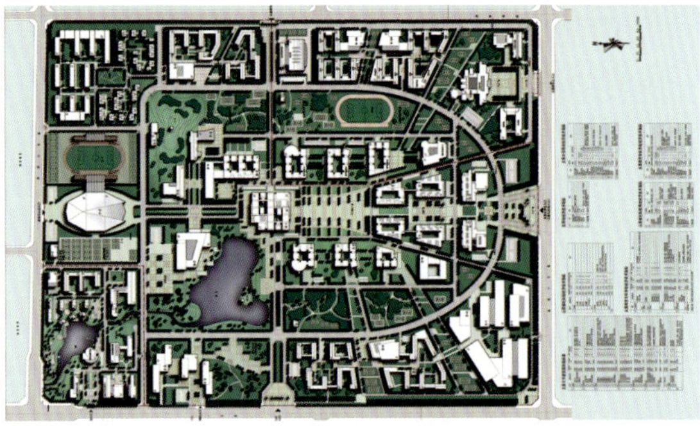

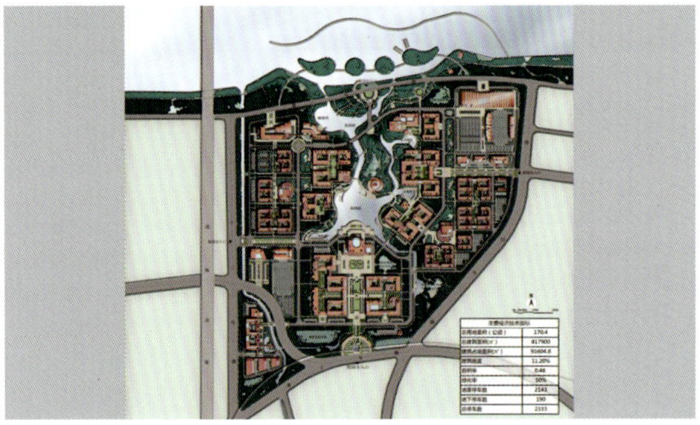

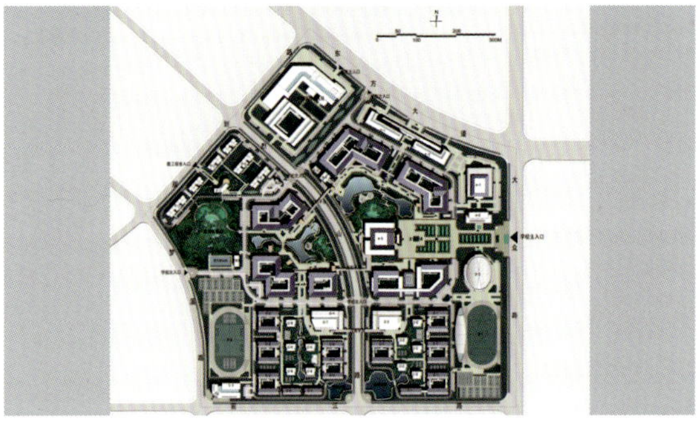

烟台汽车工程职业学院 Yantai Automobile Engineering professional College	天津国际医学城 Tianjin International Medical City	中国传媒大学南广学院 Communication University of China, Nanjing
西安电子科技大学 Xidian University	太原大学新校区 New Campus of Taiyuan University	湖南工业大学新校区 New Campus of Hunan University of Technology
北京航空航天大学 Beihang University	大连海洋大学新校园 New Campus of Dalian Ocean University	安徽中医学院新校区 New Campus of Anhui College of Chinese Medicine

南华大学新校区
New Campus of University of South China

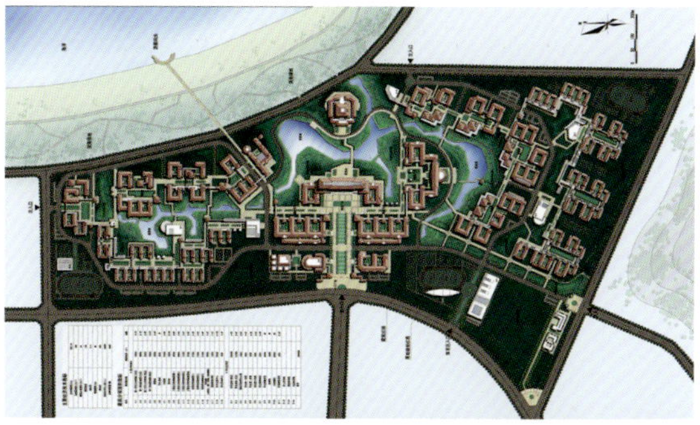

山东大学青岛校区
Qingdao Campus of Shandong University

浙江大学紫金港校区西区概念规划（2005 年）
Conceptual Planning for Zijingang Campus (West) of Zhejiang University (2005)

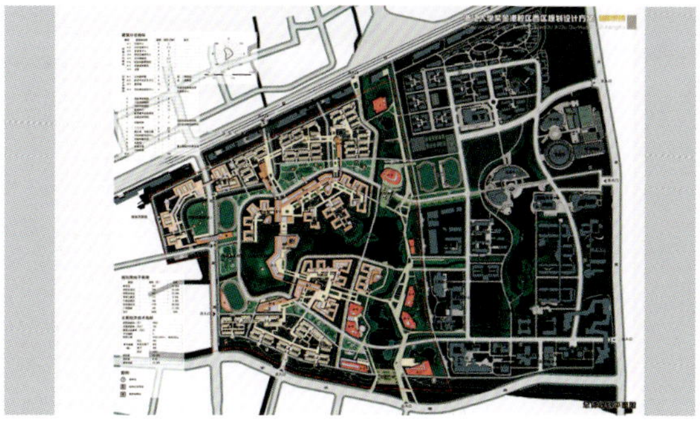

浙江大学紫金港校区西区概念规划（2009 年）
Conceptual Planning for Zijingang Campus (West) of Zhejiang University (2009)

莆田学院新校区修建性详细规划
Constructive Detailed Planning of the New Campus of Putian College

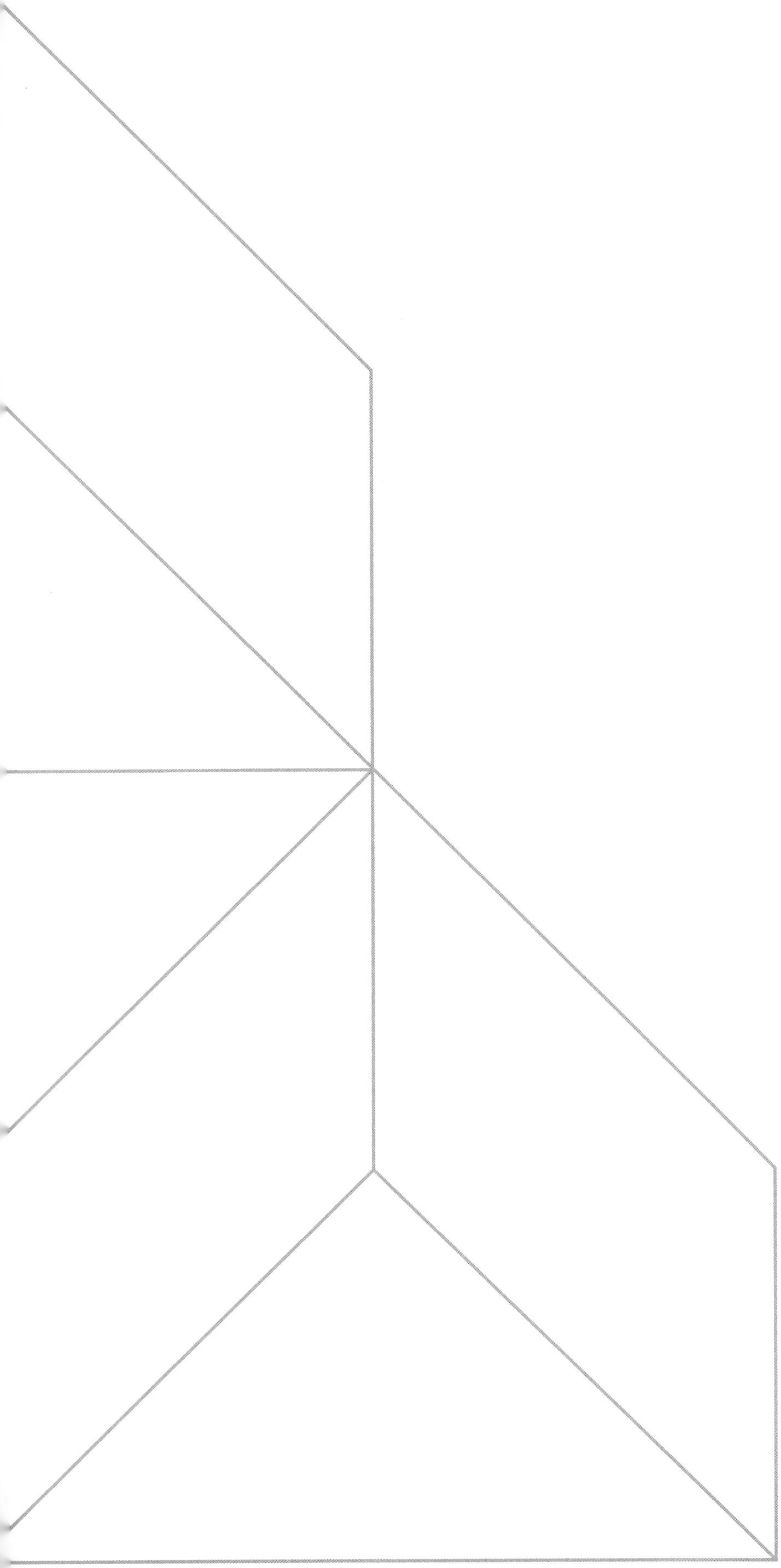

获奖作品一览
AWARD-WINNING WORKS

奖项	作品	日期
国家级		
国家级优秀设计项目金奖	华南理工大学逸夫人文馆	2006
国家级优秀设计项目银奖	华南师范大学南海学院	2004
国家级优秀设计项目银奖	浙江大学紫金港校区东教学组团	2004
国家级优秀设计项目银奖	福州大学图书馆	2009
国家级优秀设计项目铜奖	广州大学城广东药学院学院教学楼及管理楼	2006
国家级优秀设计项目铜奖	华南理工大学院系办公实验楼群	2006
中国建筑学会中华人民共和国成立 60 周年建筑创作大奖	华南理工大学逸夫人文馆	2009
中国建筑学会中华人民共和国成立 60 周年建筑创作大奖	重庆工学院花溪校区公共教学楼	2009
中国建筑学会中华人民共和国成立 60 周年建筑创作大奖	广州大学城广东药学院教学区	2009
中国建筑学会中华人民共和国成立 60 周年建筑创作大奖	福州大学图书馆	2009
中国建筑学会中华人民共和国成立 60 周年建筑创作大奖	浙江大学紫金港校区东教学组团	2009
中国建筑学会中华人民共和国成立 60 周年建筑创作大奖	华南师范大学南海学院	2009
中国建筑学会中华人民共和国成立 60 周年建筑创作大奖	2008 年奥运摔跤比赛馆（中国农业大学体育馆）	2009
中国建筑学会中华人民共和国成立 60 周年建筑创作大奖	广州大学城华南理工大学院系办公实验楼群	2009
国家优质工程银质奖	广州大学城华南理工大学院系办公实验楼	2006
国家优质工程银质奖	郑州大学核心教学区	2006
国家优质工程银质奖	郑州大学图书馆	2006
国家优质工程银质奖	中国农业大学体育馆工程	2008
国家优质工程银质奖	广州大学城建设项目华南理工大学体育馆工程	2008
国家工程建设质量奖审定委员会 全国工程建设项目优秀设计成果三等奖	中山大学科技综合楼二期工程	2013
国家工程建设质量奖审定委员会 全国工程建设项目优秀设计成果二等奖	福建工程学院新校区图书馆工程	2014

AWARDS	WORKS	YEAR
STATE-LEVEL		
Gold Award for National Excellent Design Project	Sir Run Run Shaw Building of Humanities, South China University of Technology	2006
Silver Award for National Excellent Design Project	Nanhai College of South China Normal University	2004
Silver Award for National Excellent Design Project	East Teaching Building Cluster, Zijingang Campus, Zhejiang University	2004
Silver Award for National Excellent Design Project	Library of Fuzhou University	2009
Bronze Award for National Excellent Design Project	Teaching Buildings and Management Buildings of Guangdong Pharmaceutical University, Guangzhou Higher Education Mega Center	2006
Bronze Award for National Excellent Design Project	Office and Laboratory Building Group, South China University of Technology	2006
ASC Grand Architectural Creation Award	Sir Run Run Shaw Building of Humanities, South China University of Technology	2009
ASC Grand Architectural Creation Award	Public Teaching Buildings of Huaxi Campus of Chongqing Institute of Technology	2009
ASC Grand Architectural Creation Award	Teaching Area of Guangdong Pharmaceutical University, Guangzhou Higher Education Mega Center	2009
ASC Grand Architectural Creation Award	Library of Fuzhou University	2009
ASC Grand Architectural Creation Award	East Teaching Building Cluster, Zijingang Campus, Zhejiang University	2009
ASC Grand Architectural Creation Award	Nanhai College of South China Normal University	2009
ASC Grand Architectural Creation Award	Wrestling Arena for Beijing 2008 Olympic Games (Gymnasium of China Agricultural University)	2009
ASC Grand Architectural Creation Award	Office and Laboratory Building Group, South China University of Technology	2009
Silver Award for National High-quality Project	Office and Laboratory Building, South China University of Technology	2006
Silver Award for National High-quality Project	Central Teaching Area of Zhengzhou University	2006
Silver Award for National High-quality Project	Library of Zhengzhou University	2006
Silver Award for National High-quality Project	Gymnasium Project of China Agricultural University	2008
Silver Award for National High-quality Project	Gymnasium of South China University of Technology, Guangzhou Higher Education Mega Center	2008
The Third Prize for Excellent Design of National Engineering Construction Project by National Engineering Construction Quality Award Evaluation Committee	Science and Technology Complex (Phase II), Sun Yat-sen University	2013
The Second Prize for Excellent Design of National Engineering Construction Project by National Engineering Construction Quality Award Evaluation Committee	Library of Fujian Institute of Technology	2014

注：因项目设计在实施过程中存在变动，获奖作品名称与前文项目设计名称存在差异，以实际作品名称为准。

国家级

奖项	作品	日期
中国施工企业管理协会国家优质工程奖	福建工程学院新校区图书馆工程	2014
第七届中国土木工程詹天佑奖	广州大学城建设项目	2007
第八届中国土木工程詹天佑奖	北京工业大学体育馆	2008
全国十大建设科技成就奖	广州大学城	2008
中国建筑学会建筑创作奖优秀奖	广州大学城广东药学院校区	2006
中国建筑学会建筑创作奖提名奖	华南理工大学逸夫科学馆	1996
中国建筑学会建筑创作奖佳作奖	华南理工大学逸夫人文馆	2004
中国建筑学会建筑创作奖佳作奖	华南师范大学南海学院	2004
中国建筑学会建筑创作奖佳作奖	广州大学城华南理工大学院系办公实验楼群	2006
中国建筑学会建筑创作奖佳作奖	郑州大学新校区核心教学区	2006
中国建筑学会建筑创作奖佳作奖	福州大学图书馆	2008
中国建筑学会建筑创作奖佳作奖	南京工程学院行政办公楼	2008
中国建筑学会建筑创作奖佳作奖	中国农业大学体育馆	2008
中国建筑学会中国建筑设计奖（建筑创作）金奖	钱学森图书馆	2013
中国建筑学会中国建筑设计奖（建筑暖通）金奖	钱学森图书馆	2013
中国建筑学会第三届中国威海国际建筑设计大赛铜奖	重庆工学院花溪校区	2006
中国建筑学会第三届中国威海国际建筑设计大赛优秀奖	南京工业大学江浦校区图书馆	2006
中国建筑学会蓝星杯第五届中国威海国际建筑设计大奖优秀奖	广州大学城广东药学院多功能体育馆	2009
中国建筑学会蓝星杯第五届中国威海国际建筑设计大奖优秀奖	2008 北京奥运会羽毛球馆	2009
中国建筑学会蓝星杯第五届中国威海国际建筑设计大奖优秀奖	2008 北京奥运会摔跤比赛馆	2009
中国建筑学会蓝星杯第五届中国威海国际建筑设计大奖优秀奖	无锡商业职业学院实验实训楼 B	2009

STATE-LEVEL

AWARDS	WORKS	YEAR
National High-quality Project Award by China Association of Construction Enterprise Management	Library of Fujian Institute of Technology	2014
The 7th Tien-yow Jeme Civil Engineering Prize	Guangzhou Higher Education Mega Center	2007
The 8th Tien-yow Jeme Civil Engineering Prize	Gymnasium of Beijing University of Technology	2008
National Top 10 Scientific Achievements Award	Guangzhou Higher Education Mega Center	2008
Excellence Award of ASC Architectural Creation Award	Guangdong Pharmaceutical University, Guangzhou Higher Education Mega Center	2006
Nominee of ASC Architectural Creation Award	Sir Run Run Shaw Science Building of South China University of Technology	1996
Honorable Mention of ASC Architectural Creation Award	Sir Run Run Shaw Building of Humanities, South China University of Technology	2004
Honorable Mention of ASC Architectural Creation Award	Nanhai College of South China Normal University	2004
Honorable Mention of ASC Architectural Creation Award	Office and Laboratory Building Group, South China University of Technology	2006
Honorable Mention of ASC Architectural Creation Award	Central Teaching Area of Zhongzhou University	2006
Honorable Mention of ASC Architectural Creation Award	Library of Fuzhou University	2008
Honorable Mention of ASC Architectural Creation Award	Administration Building of Nanjing Institute of Technology	2008
Honorable Mention of ASC Architectural Creation Award	Gymnasium of Beijing University of Technology	2008
Gold Award of ASC China Architectural Design Award (Architectural Creation)	Qian Xuesen Library	2013
Gold Award of ASC China Architectural Design Award (HVAC)	Qian Xuesen Library	2013
Bronze Award, The 3rd China Weihai International Architectural Design Award & Competition	Huaxi Campus of Chongqing Institute of Technology	2006
Excellence Award, The 3rd China Weihai International Architectural Design Award & Competition	Library of Jiangpu Campus, Nanjing Tech University	2006
Excellence Award, Blue Star Cup • The 5th China Weihai International Architectural Design Award & Competition	Multifunctional Gymnasium, Guangdong Pharmaceutical University, Guangzhou Higher Education Mega Center	2009
Excellence Award, Blue Star Cup • The 5th China Weihai International Architectural Design Award & Competition	Badminton Gymnasium for Beijing 2008 Olympic Games	2009
Excellence Award, Blue Star Cup • The 5th China Weihai International Architectural Design Award & Competition	Wrestling Arena for Beijing 2008 Olympic Games	2009
Excellence Award, Blue Star Cup • The 5th China Weihai International Architectural Design Award & Competition	Laboratory and Training Building B of Wuxi Vocational Institute of Commerce	2009

奖项	作品	日期
国家级		
中国建筑学会蓝星杯第五届中国威海国际建筑设计大奖优秀奖	临沂大学艺术中心建筑设计方案	2009
中国建筑学会蓝星杯第五届中国威海国际建筑设计大奖优秀奖	重庆师范大学大学城校区图文信息中心	2009
中国建筑学会蓝星杯第五届中国威海国际建筑设计大奖优秀奖	汶川县三江小学重建建筑方案设计	2009
中国建筑学会第七届中国威海国际建筑设计大赛优秀奖	重庆理工大学花溪校区图书馆项目	2013
中国建筑学会第七届中国威海国际建筑设计大赛优秀奖	泰州高教园区中心共享区方案项目	2013
中国建筑学会第七届中国威海国际建筑设计大赛优秀奖	融合新生——华南理工大学南校区民居改造方案项目	2013
中国建筑学会中华人民共和国成立 60 周年建筑创作大奖入围奖	中山医学院教学楼群	2009
中国建筑学会中华人民共和国成立 60 周年建筑创作大奖入围奖	北京工业大学体育馆	2009
中国建筑学会全国优秀结构设计三等奖	中国农业大学体育馆	2009
中国勘察设计协会建筑工程二等奖	南京工程学院图书信息中心	2009
中国勘察设计协会建筑工程二等奖	中国农业大学体育馆	2009
中国勘察设计协会建筑工程二等奖	北京工业大学体育馆	2009
中国勘察设计协会建筑工程二等奖	华南理工大学大学城校区前广场建筑群	2009
中国勘察设计协会建筑工程三等奖	广州大学城广东药学院多功能体育馆	2009
中国勘察设计协会建筑工程三等奖	广州体育学院后勤管理大楼	2009
中国勘察设计协会建筑工程三等奖	中国矿业大学科技博物馆	2009
中国勘察设计协会建筑工程公建二等奖	东莞职业技术学院图书馆	2013
中国勘察设计协会建筑工程公建三等奖	上海大学校本部东区组团	2013
中国室内装饰协会室内设计铜奖	南京工程学院图书信息中心设计	2011
中国城市规划协会规划设计表扬奖	烟台汽车工程职业学院新校区修建性详细规划	2009
国际残疾人奥林匹克委员会（IPC）与国际体育与休闲建筑协会（IAKS）杰出功勋奖	中国农业大学体育馆	2011

AWARDS	WORKS	YEAR
STATE-LEVEL		
Excellence Award, Blue Star Cup • The 5th China Weihai International Architectural Design Award & Competition	Architectural Design for Arts Center of Linyi University	2009
Excellence Award, Blue Star Cup • The 5th China Weihai International Architectural Design Award & Competition	Library and Information Center of Chongqing Normal University (Chongqing University Town)	2009
Excellence Award, Blue Star Cup • The 5th China Weihai International Architectural Design Award & Competition	Architectural Scheme Design for Reconstruction of Sanjiang Primary School in Wenchuan County	2009
Excellence Award, The 7th China Weihai International Architectural Design Award & Competition	Library of Huaxi Campus of Chongqing Institute of Technology	2013
Excellence Award, The 7th China Weihai International Architectural Design Award & Competition	Schematic Design for Central Shared Area of Taizhou Higher Education Park	2013
Excellence Award, The 7th China Weihai International Architectural Design Award & Competition	Integration and Renewal - Schematic Design for Residential Renovation of SCUT South Campus	2013
Finalist of ASC Grand Architectural Creation Award for the 60th Founding Anniversary of PRC	Teaching Complex of Zhongshan School of Medicine, Sun Yat-sen University	2009
Finalist of ASC Grand Architectural Creation Award for the 60th Founding Anniversary of PRC	Gymnasium of Beijing University of Technology	2009
The Third Prize of National Excellent Structural Design Award by ASC	Gymnasium of China Agricultural University	2009
The Second Prize for Construction Engineering of China Exploration and Design Trade Association	Library and Information Center of Nanjing Institute of Technology	2009
The Second Prize for Construction Engineering of China Exploration and Design Trade Association	Gymnasium of China Agricultural University	2009
The Second Prize for Construction Engineering of China Exploration and Design Trade Association	Gymnasium of Beijing University of Technology	2009
The Second Prize for Construction Engineering of China Exploration and Design Trade Association	Buildings at Front Square of South China University of Technology, Guangzhou Higher Education Mega Center	2009
The Third Prize for Construction Engineering of China Exploration and Design Trade Association	Multifunctional Gymnasium, Guangdong Pharmaceutical University, Guangzhou Higher Education Mega Center	2009
The Third Prize for Construction Engineering of China Exploration and Design Trade Association	BOH Management Building of Guangzhou Sport University	2009
The Third Prize for Construction Engineering of China Exploration and Design Trade Association	Science Museum of China University of Mining & Technology	2009
The Second Prize for Construction Engineering (Public Building) of China Exploration and Design Trade Association	Library of Dongguan Polytechnic	2013
The Third Prize for Construction Engineering (Public Building) of China Exploration and Design Trade Association	Building Cluster of East Campus of Shanghai University	2013
Bronze Award for Interior Design of China National Interior Decoration Association	Library and Information Center of Nanjing Institute of Technology	2011
Honorable Mention for Planning and Design of China Association of City Planning	Constructive Detailed Planning of New Campus of Yantai Automobile Engineering Professional College	2009
IPC/IAKS Outstanding Merit Award	Gymnasium of China Agricultural University	2011

奖项	作品	日期
省部级		
建设部优秀建筑工程设计一等奖	华南理工大学逸夫人文馆	2005
建设部优秀建筑工程设计二等奖	江门五邑大学教学主楼	1987
建设部优秀建筑工程设计二等奖	华南理工大学逸夫科学馆	1995
建设部优秀建筑工程设计二等奖	浙江大学紫金港校区东教学组团	2003
建设部优秀建筑工程设计二等奖	华南师范大学南海学院	2003
建设部优秀建筑工程设计二等奖	广州大学城广东药学院教学楼及管理楼	2005
建设部优秀建筑工程设计二等奖	广州大学城华南理工大学院系办公实验楼群	2005
建设部优秀建筑工程设计三等奖	郑州大学新校区首期工程	2003
建设部优秀建筑工程设计三等奖	东华大学松江校区图文信息中心	2005
建设部优秀建筑工程设计三等奖	四川大学新校区第二基础实验楼	2005
建设部优秀勘察设计三等奖	武汉水利电力大学主教学楼	2001
建设部优秀建筑规划设计三等奖	西安电子科技大学总体规划	2005
建设部优秀工程勘察设计银奖	福州大学新校区图书馆	2008
教育部优秀规划设计一等奖	澳门大学横琴新校区规划设计	2013
教育部优秀建筑设计三等奖	河海大学综合体育馆	2013
教育部优秀建筑设计二等奖	上海大学东区学院组团	2013
教育部优秀建筑设计一等奖	钱学森图书馆	2013
教育部优秀建筑设计三等奖	河海大学江宁校区商学楼	2013
教育部优秀智能化专业设计三等奖	上海交通大学钱学森图书馆	2013
教育部优秀建筑设计奖一等奖	华南理工大学逸夫科学馆	1995
教育部优秀建筑设计奖一等奖	郑州大学新校区首期工程理科系群	2003
教育部优秀建筑设计奖一等奖	浙江大学紫金港校区东教学组团	2003

AWARDS	WORKS	YEAR
PROVINCIAL-/MINISTERIAL-LEVEL		
The First Prize for Excellent Construction Engineering Design by the Ministry of Construction	Sir Run Run Shaw Building of Humanities, South China University of Technology	2005
The Second Prize for Excellent Construction Engineering Design by the Ministry of Construction	Main Teaching Building of Wuyi University, Jiangmen	1987
The Second Prize for Excellent Construction Engineering Design by the Ministry of Construction	Sir Run Run Shaw Science Building of South China University of Technology	1995
The Second Prize for Excellent Construction Engineering Design by the Ministry of Construction	East Teaching Building Cluster, Zijingang Campus, Zhejiang University	2003
The Second Prize for Excellent Construction Engineering Design by the Ministry of Construction	Nanhai College of South China Normal University	2003
The Second Prize for Excellent Construction Engineering Design by the Ministry of Construction	Teaching Buildings and Management Buildings, Guangdong Pharmaceutical University, Guangzhou Higher Education Mega Center	2005
The Second Prize for Excellent Construction Engineering Design by the Ministry of Construction	Office and Laboratory Building Group, South China University of Technology, Guangzhou Higher Education Mega Center	2005
The Third Prize for Excellent Construction Engineering Design by the Ministry of Construction	New Campus of Zhengzhou University (Phase I)	2003
The Third Prize for Excellent Construction Engineering Design by the Ministry of Construction	Library and Information Center of Songjiang Campus of Donghua University	2005
The Third Prize for Excellent Construction Engineering Design by the Ministry of Construction	No. 2 Basic Experiment Building of Sichuan University (New Campus)	2005
The Third Prize for Excellent Engineering Exploration and Design by the Ministry of Construction	Main Teaching Building of Wuhan University of Hydraulic and Electrical Engineering	2001
The Third Prize for Excellent Architectural Planning and Design by the Ministry of Construction	Master Planning of Xidian University	2005
Silver Award for Excellent Engineering Exploration and Design by the Ministry of Construction	Library of New Campus of Fuzhou University	2008
The First Prize of Excellent Planning and Design Award by the Ministry of Education	Planning and Design of Hengqin New Campus of Macau University	2003
The Third Prize of Excellent Architectural Design Award by the Ministry of Education	Gymnasium of Hohai University	2003
The Second Prize of Excellent Architectural Design Award by the Ministry of Education	Building Cluster of East Campus of Shanghai University	2003
The First Prize of Excellent Architectural Design Award by the Ministry of Education	Qian Xuesen Library	2003
The Third Prize of Excellent Architectural Design Award by the Ministry of Education	Business Building of Jiangning Campus of Hohai University	2003
The Third Prize for Excellent Intelligent Design by the Ministry of Education	Qian Xuesen Library of Shanghai Jiao Tong University	2003
The First Prize of Excellent Architectural Design Award by the Ministry of Education	Sir Run Run Shaw Science Building of South China University of Technology	1995
The First Prize of Excellent Architectural Design Award by the Ministry of Education	Engineering & Science Buildings of New Campus of Zhengzhou University (Phase I)	2003
The First Prize of Excellent Architectural Design Award by the Ministry of Education	East Teaching Building Cluster, Zijingang Campus, Zhejiang University	2003

奖项	作品	日期
省部级		
教育部优秀建筑设计奖一等奖	华南师范大学南海分院	2003
教育部优秀建筑设计奖二等奖	合肥学院图书馆	2011
教育部优秀建筑规划奖一等奖	南京工程学院江宁校区总体规划	2011
教育部优秀建筑规划奖一等奖	江南大学蠡湖校区总体规划	2003
教育部优秀建筑设计奖一等奖	华南理工大学逸夫人文馆	2005
教育部优秀建筑设计奖一等奖	四川大学新校区第二基础实验楼	2005
教育部优秀工程勘察奖一等奖	广州大学城广东药学院教学区首期工程	2005
教育部优秀规划设计奖一等奖	广州大学城广东药学院校区修建性详细规划	2005
教育部优秀规划设计奖一等奖	重庆工学院花溪校区总体规划	2005
教育部优秀建筑设计奖一等奖	福州大学新校区图书馆	2007
教育部优秀建筑设计奖一等奖	重庆工学院花溪校区公共教学楼	2007
教育部优秀建筑设计奖一等奖	2008 年奥运摔跤比赛馆（中国农业大学体育馆）	2009
教育部全国教育建筑优秀设计奖二等奖	江门五邑大学教学主楼	1987
教育部优秀建筑设计奖二等奖	东莞理工学院综合实验楼	2000
教育部优秀建筑设计奖二等奖	武汉水利电力大学教学楼	2001
教育部优秀建筑规划奖二等奖	郑州大学新校区总体规划	2003
教育部优秀建筑设计奖二等奖	东华大学松江校区图文信息中心	2005
教育部优秀建筑设计奖二等奖	郑州大学核心教学区教学楼群	2005
教育部优秀规划设计奖二等奖	广州大学城校区组团二华南理工大学新校区总体规划	2007
教育部优秀建筑设计奖二等奖	国防科技大学科技楼及图书馆	2007
教育部优秀建筑设计奖二等奖	南京工业大学江蒲校区图书馆	2007
教育部优秀建筑设计奖二等奖	南京工程学院图书信息中心	2009

AWARDS	WORKS	YEAR
PROVINCIAL-/MINISTERIAL-LEVEL		
The First Prize of Excellent Architectural Design Award by the Ministry of Education	Nanhai College of South China Normal University	2003
The Second Prize of Excellent Architectural Design Award by the Ministry of Education	Library of Hefei University	2011
The First Prize of Excellent Architecture and Planning Award by the Ministry of Education	Master Planning of Jiangning Campus of Nanjing Institute of Technology	2011
The First Prize of Excellent Architecture and Planning Award by the Ministry of Education	Master Planning of Lihu Campus of Jiangnan University	2003
The First Prize of Excellent Architectural Design Award by the Ministry of Education	Sir Run Run Shaw Building of Humanities, South China University of Technology	2005
The First Prize of Excellent Architectural Design Award by the Ministry of Education	No. 2 Basic Experiment Building of Sichuan University (New Campus)	2005
The First Prize of Excellent Engineering Exploration Award by the Ministry of Education	Teaching Area of Guangdong Pharmaceutical University, Guangzhou Higher Education Mega Center (Phase I)	2005
The First Prize of Excellent Planning and Design Award by the Ministry of Education	Constructive Detailed Planning of Guangdong Pharmaceutical University, Guangzhou Higher Education Mega Center	2005
The First Prize of Excellent Planning and Design Award by the Ministry of Education	Master Planning of Huaxi Campus of Chongqing Institute of Technology	2005
The First Prize of Excellent Architectural Design Award by the Ministry of Education	Library of New Campus of Fuzhou University	2007
The First Prize of Excellent Architectural Design Award by the Ministry of Education	Public Teaching Buildings of Huaxi Campus of Chongqing Institute of Technology	2007
The First Prize of Excellent Architectural Design Award by the Ministry of Education	Wrestling Arena for Beijing 2008 Olympic Games (Gymnasium of China Agricultural University)	2009
The Second Prize for National Excellent Architectural Design of Education Building by the Ministry of Education	Main Teaching Building of Wuyi University, Jiangmen	1987
The Second Prize of Excellent Architectural Design Award by the Ministry of Education	Laboratory Building of Dongguan University of Technology	2000
The Second Prize of Excellent Architectural Design Award by the Ministry of Education	Teaching Building of Wuhan University of Hydraulic and Electrical Engineering	2001
The Second Prize for Excellent Architecture and Planning by the Ministry of Education	Master Planning of New Campus, Zhengzhou University	2003
The Second Prize of Excellent Architectural Design Award by the Ministry of Education	Library and Information Center of Songjiang Campus of Donghua University	2005
The Second Prize of Excellent Architectural Design Award by the Ministry of Education	Teaching Building Cluster of Central Teaching Area of Zhengzhou University	2005
The Second Prize of Excellent Architectural Design Award by the Ministry of Education	Master Planning for New Campus of South China University of Technology, Guangzhou Higher Education Mega Center	2007
The Second Prize of Excellent Planning and Design Award by the Ministry of Education	Science and Technology Building and Library of National University of Defense Technology	2007
The Second Prize of Excellent Architectural Design Award by the Ministry of Education	Library of Jiangpu Campus of Nanjing Tech University	2007
The Second Prize of Excellent Architectural Design Award by the Ministry of Education	Library and Information Center of Nanjing Institute of Technology	2009

奖项	作品	日期
省部级		
教育部优秀规划设计奖二等奖	琼州学院三亚校区总体规划设计	2009
教育部优秀建筑设计奖三等奖	广州体育学院体育馆	1989
教育部优秀建筑设计奖三等奖	华南理工大学设计绘图大楼	1989
教育部优秀建筑设计奖三等奖	华南理工大学 2 号楼	1989
教育部优秀建筑设计奖三等奖	华南理工大学文体活动中心	1998
教育部优秀建筑设计奖三等奖	东莞市技工学校教学楼群	2000
教育部优秀建筑设计奖三等奖	广东工业大学主教学楼	2001
教育部优秀建筑设计奖三等奖	东莞蛤地小学教学楼	2001
教育部优秀建筑设计奖三等奖	南京邮电大学仙林校区教学楼组群	2005
教育部优秀建筑设计奖三等奖	华南理工大学 31、32 号教学楼	2005
教育部优秀建筑设计奖三等奖	广东医学院实验楼	2005
教育部优秀工程勘察奖三等奖	华南理工大学科技园总体规划首期工程	2005
教育部优秀规划设计奖三等奖	西安电子科技大学总体规划	2005
教育部优秀规划设计奖三等奖	广州大学城中心区城市设计及控制性详细规划	2005
教育部优秀规划设计奖三等奖	南京邮电大学仙林校区修建性详细规划	2005
教育部优秀规划设计奖三等奖	重庆大学虎溪校区修建性详细规划	2005
教育部优秀规划设计奖三等奖	长沙理工大学云塘校区	2007
教育部优秀规划设计奖三等奖	重庆工程职业技术学院江津新校区总体规划设计	2011
教育部优秀建筑设计奖三等奖	翡翠园小学	2007
教育部优秀建筑设计奖三等奖	河海大学江宁校区图书馆	2007
教育部优秀建筑设计奖三等奖	华南理工大学西区体育馆	2007
教育部优秀建筑设计奖三等奖	南京工程学院行政办公楼	2007

AWARDS	WORKS	YEAR
PROVINCIAL-/MINISTERIAL-LEVEL		
The Second Prize of Excellent Planning and Design Award by the Ministry of Education	Master Planning and Design for Sanya Campus, Qiongzhou University	2009
The Third Prize of Excellent Architectural Design Award by the Ministry of Education	Gymnasium of Guangzhou Sport University	1989
The Third Prize of Excellent Architectural Design Award by the Ministry of Education	Design and Drafting Building of South China University of Technology	1989
The Third Prize of Excellent Architectural Design Award by the Ministry of Education	No. 2 Building of South China University of Technology	1989
The Third Prize of Excellent Architectural Design Award by the Ministry of Education	Culture and Sports Activities Center of South China University of Technology	1998
The Third Prize of Excellent Architectural Design Award by the Ministry of Education	Teaching Building Cluster of Dongguan Technical School	2000
The Third Prize of Excellent Architectural Design Award by the Ministry of Education	Main Teaching Building of Guangdong University of Technology	2001
The Third Prize of Excellent Architectural Design Award by the Ministry of Education	Teaching Building of Hadi Primary School, Dongguan	2001
The Third Prize of Excellent Architectural Design Award by the Ministry of Education	Teaching Building Cluster of Xianlin Campus, Nanjing University of Posts and Telecommunications	2005
The Third Prize of Excellent Architectural Design Award by the Ministry of Education	No. 31 and No. 32 Buildings, South China University of Technology	2005
The Third Prize of Excellent Architectural Design Award by the Ministry of Education	Laboratory Building of Guangdong Medical University	2005
The Third Prize of Excellent Engineering Exploration Award by the Ministry of Education	Master Planning for Science and Technology Park of South China University of Technology (Phase I)	2005
The Third Prize of Excellent Planning and Design Award by the Ministry of Education	Master Planning of Xidian University	2005
The Third Prize of Excellent Planning and Design Award by the Ministry of Education	Urban Design and Regulatory Detailed Planning for Central Area of Guangzhou Higher Education Mega Center	2005
The Third Prize of Excellent Planning and Design Award by the Ministry of Education	Constructive Detailed Planning for Xianlin Campus, Nanjing University of Posts and Telecommunications	2005
The Third Prize of Excellent Planning and Design Award by the Ministry of Education	Constructive Detailed Planning for Huxi Campus of Chongqing University	2005
The Third Prize of Excellent Planning and Design Award by the Ministry of Education	Yuntang Campus, Changsha University of Science & Technology	2007
The Third Prize of Excellent Planning and Design Award by the Ministry of Education	Master Planning and Design for Jiangjin New Campus of Chongqing Vocational Institute of Engineering	2011
The Third Prize of Excellent Architectural Design Award by the Ministry of Education	Feicuiyuan Primary School	2007
The Third Prize of Excellent Architectural Design Award by the Ministry of Education	Library of Jiangning Campus of Hohai University	2007
The Third Prize of Excellent Architectural Design Award by the Ministry of Education	Gymnasium in West Area of South China University of Technology	2007
The Third Prize of Excellent Architectural Design Award by the Ministry of Education	Administration Building of Nanjing Institute of Technology	2007

奖项	作品	日期
省部级		
教育部优秀建筑设计奖三等奖	南京审计学院教学中心区	2007
教育部优秀规划设计奖三等奖	南京审计学院蒲口新校区总体规划	2007
教育部优秀工程勘察奖三等奖	肇庆学院图书馆勘察设计	2007
教育部优秀建筑设计奖三等奖	重庆大学虎溪校区教学实验楼群	2007
教育部优秀建筑设计奖三等奖	上海大学校本部东区扩建一期工程	2009
教育部优秀建筑设计奖三等奖	中国矿业大学南湖校区图文信息中心	2009
教育部优秀建筑设计奖三等奖	南京工程学院文理学院教学楼群	2009
教育部优秀建筑设计奖三等奖	广州大学城华南理工大学体育馆	2009
教育部优秀建筑设计奖三等奖	南京审计学院学生活动中心	2009
教育部优秀规划设计奖三等奖	太原大学新校区修建性详细规划	2009
教育部优秀规划设计奖三等奖	湖南工业大学校园规划设计	2009
教育部优秀建筑设计奖表扬奖	广州嘉禾中学教学楼	1991
教育部优秀建筑设计奖表扬奖	广东省税务学校教学综合楼	1993
教育部优秀建筑设计奖表扬奖	华南理工大学图书馆	1993
国家教育委员会优秀建筑设计奖一等奖	华南理工大学逸夫科学馆	1994
全国优秀教育建筑优秀建筑设计奖二等奖	东莞市技工学校教育楼群	1998
全国优秀教育建筑优秀建筑设计奖二等奖	东莞理工学院综合实验楼	1998
全国优秀教育建筑优秀建筑设计奖三等奖	华南理工大学交通大楼	1998
全国优秀教育建筑优秀建筑设计奖优秀奖	福州大学逸夫科教馆	1998
全国优秀教育建筑优秀建筑设计奖优秀奖	华南理工大学逸夫工程馆	1998
全国优秀教育建筑优秀建筑设计奖优秀奖	广东外语外贸大学教学楼与教学办公楼	1998

AWARDS	WORKS	YEAR
PROVINCIAL-/MINISTERIAL-LEVEL		
The Third Prize of Excellent Architectural Design Award by the Ministry of Education	Central Teaching Area of Nanjing Audit University	2007
The Third Prize of Excellent Architectural Design Award by the Ministry of Education	Master Planning for Pukou Campus of Nanjing Audit University	2007
The Third Prize of Excellent Engineering Exploration Award by the Ministry of Education	Exploration and Design for Library of Zhaoqing University	2007
The Third Prize of Excellent Architectural Design Award by the Ministry of Education	Teaching and Laboratory Building Group, Huxi Campus of Chongqing University	2007
The Third Prize of Excellent Architectural Design Award by the Ministry of Education	Expansion of East Campus of Shanghai University (Phase I)	2009
The Third Prize of Excellent Architectural Design Award by the Ministry of Education	Library and Information Center of South Lake Campus of China University of Mining & Technology	2009
The Third Prize of Excellent Architectural Design Award by the Ministry of Education	Teaching Building Cluster of School of Arts and Sciences of Nanjing Institute of Technology	2009
The Third Prize of Excellent Architectural Design Award by the Ministry of Education	Gymnasium of South China University of Technology, Guangzhou Higher Education Mega Center	2009
The Third Prize of Excellent Architectural Design Award by the Ministry of Education	Student Activities Center of Nanjing Audit University	2009
The Third Prize of Excellent Planning and Design Award by the Ministry of Education	Constructive Detailed Planning for New Campus of Taiyuan University	2009
The Third Prize of Excellent Planning and Design Award by the Ministry of Education	Campus Planning and Design for Hunan University of Technology	2009
Honorable Mention of Excellent Architectural Design Award by the Ministry of Education	Teaching Building of Guangzhou Jiahe Middle School	1991
Honorable Mention of Excellent Architectural Design Award by the Ministry of Education	Teaching Complex of Taxation School of Guangdong Province	1993
Honorable Mention of Excellent Architectural Design Award by the Ministry of Education	Library of South China University of Technology	1993
The First Prize of Excellent Architectural Design Award by the State Education Commission of the PRC	Sir Run Run Shaw Science Building of South China University of Technology	1994
The Second Prize of Excellent Architectural Design Award for National Excellent Education Building	Teaching Buildings of Dongguan Polytechnic	1998
The Second Prize of Excellent Architectural Design Award for National Excellent Education Building	Laboratory Building of Dongguan University of Technology	1998
The Third Prize of Excellent Architectural Design Award for National Excellent Education Building	Transportation Building of South China University of Technology	1998
Excellence Award of Excellent Architectural Design Award for National Excellent Education Building	Sir Run Run Shaw Science Building of Fuzhou University	1998
Excellence Award of Excellent Architectural Design Award of National Excellent Education Building	Sir Run Run Shaw Engineering Building of South China University of Technology	1998
Excellence Award of Excellent Architectural Design Award of National Excellent Education Building	Teaching and Office Building of Guangdong University of Foreign Studies	1998

奖项	作品	日期
省部级		
广东省优秀建筑设计奖一等奖	华南理工大学院系办公实验楼群	2004
广东省优秀建筑设计奖一等奖	广州大学城广东药学院教学楼与管理楼	2004
广东省优秀建筑设计奖二等奖	上海东华大学淞江校区综合实验楼、化学实验楼	2004
广东省优秀建筑设计奖二等奖	广州大学城华南理工大学新校区公共教学楼	2004
广东省优秀建筑设计奖三等奖	广州大学城广东药学院办公楼	2004
广东省优秀建筑设计奖三等奖	广东医学院东莞校区实验楼	2004
广东省优秀工程勘察奖一等奖	上海东华大学松江校区纺织化工学院楼	2007
广东省优秀工程勘察奖一等奖	北京工业大学体育馆（2008 年奥运会羽毛球馆）	2009
广东省优秀工程勘察奖一等奖	广州大学城广东药学院多功能体育馆	2009
广东省工程勘察设计行业协会一等奖	东莞职业技术学院图书馆	2013
广东省优秀工程勘察奖二等奖	华南理工大学大学城校区公共教学主楼	2007
广东省优秀工程勘察奖二等奖	广州大学城华南理工大学科技楼 B	2007
广东省优秀工程勘察奖二等奖	南京审计学院公共教学楼	2007
广东省优秀工程勘察奖二等奖	华南理工大学大学城校区广场前区建筑群（图书馆、学术报告厅）	2009
广东省优秀工程勘察奖二等奖	广州体育学院后勤管理大楼	2009
广东省优秀工程勘察奖二等奖	中国矿业大学科技博物馆	2009
广东省优秀工程勘察奖二等奖	广州体育学院后勤管理大楼	2009
广东省工程勘察设计行业协会二等奖	北京工业大学体育馆建筑环境与设备设计	2013
广东省优秀工程勘察奖三等奖	广州培英中学鹤洞校区图书馆	2007
广东省优秀工程勘察奖三等奖	华南理工大学 29 号楼	2009
广东省优秀工程勘察奖三等奖	广州大学城华南理工大学专家楼（大学城中心酒店）	2009

AWARDS	WORKS	YEAR
PROVINCIAL-/MINISTERIAL-LEVEL		
The First Prize of Excellent Architectural Design Award of Guangdong Province	Office and Laboratory Building Group, South China University of Technology	2004
The First Prize of Excellent Architectural Design Award of Guangdong Province	Teaching Building and Management Building of Guangdong Pharmaceutical University, Guangzhou Higher Education Mega Center	2004
The Second Prize of Excellent Architectural Design Award of Guangdong Province	Laboratory Building and Chemistry Laboratory Building of Songjiang Campus of Donghua University, Shanghai	2004
The Second Prize of Excellent Architectural Design Award of Guangdong Province	Public Teaching Buildings of New Campus of South China University of Technology, Guangzhou Higher Education Mega Center	2004
The Third Prize of Excellent Architectural Design Award of Guangdong Province	Office Building of Guangdong Pharmaceutical University, Guangzhou Higher Education Mega Center	2004
The Third Prize of Excellent Architectural Design Award of Guangdong Province	Laboratory Building of Dongguan Campus of Guangdong Pharmaceutical University	2004
The First Prize of Excellent Engineering Exploration Award of Guangdong Province	Building of School of Textile Chemical Engineering, Songjiang Campus of Donghua University	2007
The First Prize of Excellent Engineering Exploration Award of Guangdong Province	Gymnasium of Beijing University of Technology (Badminton Gymnasium for Beijing 2008 Olympic Games)	2009
The First Prize of Excellent Engineering Exploration Award of Guangdong Province	Multifunctional Gymnasium of Guangdong Pharmaceutical University, Guangzhou Higher Education Mega Center	2009
The First Prize of Guangdong Engineering Geotechnical Survey & Design Association	Library of Dongguan Polytechnic	2013
The Second Prize of Excellent Engineering Exploration Award of Guangdong Province	Main Public Teaching Buildings of South China University of Technology, Guangzhou Higher Education Mega Center	2007
The Second Prize of Excellent Engineering Exploration Award of Guangdong Province	Technology Building B of South China University of Technology, Guangzhou Higher Education Mega Center	2007
The Second Prize of Excellent Engineering Exploration Award of Guangdong Province	Public Teaching Buildings of Nanjing Audit University	2007
The Second Prize of Excellent Engineering Exploration Award of Guangdong Province	Buildings (Library and Lecture Hall) at Front Square of South China University of Technology, Guangzhou Higher Education Mega Center	2009
The Second Prize of Excellent Engineering Exploration Award of Guangdong Province	BOH Management Building of Guangzhou Sport University	2009
The Second Prize of Excellent Engineering Exploration Award of Guangdong Province	Science Museum of China University of Mining & Technology	2009
The Second Prize of Excellent Engineering Exploration Award of Guangdong Province	BOH Management Building of Guangzhou Sport University	2009
The Second Prize of Guangdong Engineering Geotechnical Survey & Design Association	Built Environment and MEP Design for Gymnasium of Beijing University of Technology	2013
The Third Prize of Excellent Engineering Exploration Award of Guangdong Province	Library of Hedong Campus of Guangzhou Peiying Middle School	2007
The Third Prize of Excellent Engineering Exploration Award of Guangdong Province	No. 29 Building of South China University of Technology	2009
The Third Prize of Excellent Engineering Exploration Award of Guangdong Province	Experts Guesthouse of South China University of Technology, Guangzhou Higher Education Mega Center (University Town Center SCU Hotel)	2009

奖项	作品	日期
省部级		
广东省工程勘察设计行业协会三等奖	中山大学科技综合楼二期	2013
广东省优秀工程勘察奖表扬奖	广州大学城华南理工大学校区首期工程	2004
广东省注册建筑师协会优秀建筑创作奖创作奖	浙江大学紫金港校区东教学组团	2003
广东省注册建筑师协会优秀建筑创作奖创作奖	华南师范大学南海学院	2003
广东省注册建筑师协会优秀建筑创作奖创作奖	华南理工大学逸夫人文馆	2005
广东省注册建筑师协会优秀建筑创作奖创作奖	广州大学城华南理工大学院系办公实验楼群	2005
广东省注册建筑师协会优秀建筑创作奖创作奖	南京工业大学江浦校区	2007
广东省注册建筑师协会优秀建筑创作奖提名奖	郑州大学新校区首期工程	2003
广东省注册建筑师协会优秀建筑创作奖提名奖	南京河海大学	2003
广东省注册建筑师协会优秀建筑创作奖提名奖	培英中学鹤洞校区图书馆	2005
广东省注册建筑师协会优秀建筑创作奖提名奖	北京工业大学体育馆	2005
广东省注册建筑师协会优秀建筑创作奖提名奖	郑州大学核心教学楼群	2005
广东省注册建筑师协会优秀建筑创作奖佳作奖	无锡商业职业学校实验实训大楼 B 组群	2007
广东省注册建筑师协会优秀建筑创作奖佳作奖	广州大学城华南理工大学二期体育馆	2007
广东省注册建筑师协会优秀建筑创作奖创作奖	南京工程学院图书信息中心	2009
广东省注册建筑师协会优秀建筑创作奖创作奖	汶川三江小学	2009
广东省注册建筑师协会优秀建筑创作奖创作奖	南开大学图书馆	2009
广东省注册建筑师协会优秀建筑创作奖佳作奖	华南理工大学大学城校区前广场建筑群（图书馆、学术报告厅）	2009
广东省注册建筑师协会优秀建筑创作奖佳作奖	南京工程学院文理学院教学楼群	2009
广东省注册建筑师协会优秀建筑创作奖佳作奖	广州市康复实验学校中标实施方案	2009
广东省注册建筑师协会优秀建筑创作奖创作奖	钱学森纪念馆	2011

AWARDS	WORKS	YEAR
PROVINCIAL-/MINISTERIAL-LEVEL		
The Third Prize of Guangdong Engineering Geotechnical Survey & Design Association	Science & Technology Complex of Sun Yat-sen University (Phase II)	2013
Honorable Mention of Excellent Engineering Exploration Award of Guangdong Province	South China University of Technology, Guangzhou Higher Education Mega Center (Phase I)	2004
Creation Award of Excellent Architectural Creation Award by Guangdong Chapter of Association of Chinese Registered Architects	East Teaching Building Cluster, Zijingang Campus, Zhejiang University	2003
Creation Award of Excellent Architectural Creation Award by Guangdong Chapter of Association of Chinese Registered Architects	Nanhai College of South China Normal University	2003
Creation Award of Excellent Architectural Creation Award by Guangdong Chapter of Association of Chinese Registered Architects	Sir Run Run Shaw Building of Humanities, South China University of Technology	2005
Creation Award of Excellent Architectural Creation Award by Guangdong Chapter of Association of Chinese Registered Architects	Office and Laboratory Building Group, South China University of Technology, Guangzhou Higher Education Mega Center	2005
Creation Award of Excellent Architectural Creation Award by Guangdong Chapter of Association of Chinese Registered Architects	Jiangpu Campus, Nanjing Tech University	2007
Finalist of Excellent Architectural Creation Award by Guangdong Chapter of Association of Chinese Registered Architects	New Campus of Zhengzhou University (Phase I)	2003
Finalist of Excellent Architectural Creation Award by Guangdong Chapter of Association of Chinese Registered Architects	Hohai University, Nanjing	2003
Finalist of Excellent Architectural Creation Award by Guangdong Chapter of Association of Chinese Registered Architects	Library of Hedong Campus of Guangzhou Peiying Middle School	2005
Finalist of Excellent Architectural Creation Award by Guangdong Chapter of Association of Chinese Registered Architects	Gymnasium of Beijing University of Technology	2005
Finalist of Excellent Architectural Creation Award by Guangdong Chapter of Association of Chinese Registered Architects	Central Teaching Building Cluster of Zhengzhou University	2005
Honorable Mention of Excellent Architectural Creation Award by Guangdong Chapter of Association of Chinese Registered Architects	Laboratory and Training Building B of Wuxi Vocational Institute of Commerce	2007
Honorable Mention of Excellent Architectural Creation Award by Guangdong Chapter of Association of Chinese Registered Architects	Gymnasium of South China University of Technology, Guangzhou Higher Education Mega Center (Phase II)	2007
Creation Award of Excellent Architectural Creation Award by Guangdong Chapter of Association of Chinese Registered Architects	Library and Information Center of Nanjing Institute of Technology	2009
Creation Award of Excellent Architectural Creation Award by Guangdong Chapter of Association of Chinese Registered Architects	Sanjiang Primary School of Wenchuan	2009
Creation Award of Excellent Architectural Creation Award by Guangdong Chapter of Association of Chinese Registered Architects	Library of Nankai University	2009
Honorable Mention of Excellent Architectural Creation Award by Guangdong Chapter of Association of Chinese Registered Architects	Buildings (Library and Lecture Hall) at Front Square of South China University of Technology, Guangzhou Higher Education Mega Center	2009
Honorable Mention of Excellent Architectural Creation Award by Guangdong Chapter of Association of Chinese Registered Architects	Teaching Building Cluster of School of Arts and Sciences of Nanjing Institute of Technology	2009
Honorable Mention of Excellent Architectural Creation Award by Guangdong Chapter of Association of Chinese Registered Architects	Implementation Design for Guangzhou Rehabilitation Experimental School	2009
Creation Award of Excellent Architectural Creation Award by Guangdong Chapter of Association of Chinese Registered Architects	Qian Xuesen Memorial Hall	2011

奖项	作品	日期
省部级		
广东省注册建筑师协会优秀建筑创作奖创作奖	上海大学东区二期学院楼群	2011
广东省注册建筑师协会优秀建筑创作奖优秀建筑创作奖	重庆理工大学花溪校区图书馆	2013
广东省注册建筑师协会优秀建筑创作奖优秀建筑佳作奖	中山大学科技楼二期	2013
广东省注册建筑师协会优秀建筑创作奖优秀建筑佳作奖	武汉理工大学南湖校区图书馆	2013
广东省城乡规划协会城乡规划设计二等奖	广州大学城组团二修建性详细规划项目	2005
广东省城乡规划协会城乡规划设计三等奖	江南大学新校区总体规划项目	2005
广东省城乡规划协会城乡规划设计三等奖	山西省高校新校区总体规划	2011
广东省城市规划协会优秀城乡规划设计三等奖	温州肯恩大学建设工程项目	2013
广东省城市规划协会优秀城乡规划设计表扬奖	广西银行学校相思湖新校区建设工程项目	2013
广东省住房和城乡建设厅岭南特色建筑设计金奖	华南理工大学建筑设计研究院工作室	2012
广东省住房和城乡建设厅岭南特色建筑设计银奖	华南理工大学逸夫人文馆	2012
广东省住房和城乡建设厅岭南特色建筑设计铜奖	华南师范大学南海学院	2012
广东省住房和城乡建设厅岭南特色建筑设计铜奖	广州大学城华南理工大学二期体育场馆	2012
广东省住房和城乡建设厅岭南特色建筑设计铜奖	东莞职业技术学院图书馆	2014
广东省土木建筑学会詹天佑故乡杯	华南理工大学二期工程	2009
广西壮族自治区建设厅 2007 年度广西优秀工程设计一等奖	南宁市委党校相思湖新区罗文新校园	2008
河南省勘察设计创新奖创新奖	郑州大学核心教学楼群	2005
机械部优秀工程设计奖二等奖	郑州大学核心教学楼群	2005
山东省住房和城乡建设厅山东省优秀城市规划设计奖一等奖	烟台汽车工程职业学院新校区修建性详细规划	2009

AWARDS	WORKS	YEAR
PROVINCIAL-/MINISTERIAL-LEVEL		
Creation Award of Excellent Architectural Creation Award by Guangdong Chapter of Association of Chinese Registered Architects	Building Cluster of East Campus of Shanghai University (Phase II)	2011
Creation Award of Excellent Architectural Creation Award by Guangdong Chapter of Association of Chinese Registered Architects	Library of Huaxi Campus of Chongqing Institute of Technology	2013
Honorable Mention of Excellent Architectural Creation Award by Guangdong Chapter of Association of Chinese Registered Architects	Science Complex (Phase II), Sun Yat-sen University	2013
Honorable Mention of Excellent Architectural Creation Award by Guangdong Chapter of Association of Chinese Registered Architects	Library of Nanhu Campus of Wuhan University of Technology	2013
The Second Prize for Urban and Rural Planning and Design by Guangdong Urban and Rural Planning Society	Constructive Detailed Planning for Cluster II, Guangzhou Higher Education Mega Center	2005
The Third Prize for Urban and Rural Planning and Design by Guangdong Urban and Rural Planning Society	Master Planning for New Campus of Jiangnan University	2005
The Third Prize for Urban and Rural Planning and Design by Guangdong Urban and Rural Planning Society	Master Planning for New Campus of Shanxi Higher Education Mega Center	2011
The Third Prize for Excellent Urban and Rural Planning and Design by Guangdong City Planning Association	Construction Project for Wenzhou-Kean University	2013
Honorable Mention for Excellent Urban and Rural Planning and Design by Guangdong City Planning Association	Construction Project for Xiangsihu New Campus of Guangxi Banking School	2013
Gold Award for Lingnan-style Architectural Design by Guangdong Province Housing & Urban-Rural Construction Department	Studio of Architectural Design & Research Institute of South China University of Technology	2012
Silver Award for Lingnan-style Architectural Design by Guangdong Province Housing & Urban-Rural Construction Department	Sir Run Run Shaw Building of Humanities, South China University of Technology	2012
Bronze Award for Lingnan-style Architectural Design by Guangdong Province Housing & Urban-Rural Construction Department	Nanhai College of South China Normal University	2012
Bronze Award for Lingnan-style Architectural Design by Guangdong Province Housing & Urban-Rural Construction Department	Gymnasium of South China University of Technology, Guangzhou Higher Education Mega Center (Phase II)	2012
Bronze Award for Lingnan-style Architectural Design by Guangdong Province Housing & Urban-Rural Construction Department	Library of Dongguan Polytechnic	2014
Tien-yow Jeme Hometown Cup Prize by The Civil Engineering and Architectural Society of Guangdong	South China University of Technology (Phase II)	2009
The First Prize for Excellent Engineering Design of Guangxi by Department of Construction of Guangxi Zhuang Autonomous Region (2007)	Luowen New Campus of CPC Nanning Municipal Party College	2008
Innovation Award of Exploration and Design Innovation Award of Henan Province	Central Teaching Building Cluster of Zhengzhou University	2005
The Second Prize of Excellent Engineering Design Award by the Ministry of Machinery Industry	Central Teaching Building Cluster of Zhengzhou University	2005
The First Prize of Excellent Urban Planning and Design Award of Shandong by Department of Housing and Urban-Rural Development of Shandong Province	Constructive Detailed Planning of New Campus of Yantai Automobile Engineering Professional College	2009